Riverside Edition

THE WRITINGS OF HENRY DAVID THOREAU

WITH BIBLIOGRAPHICAL INTRODUCTIONS AND FULL INDEXES

VOLUME X

Henry D. Thoreau.

MISCELLANIES

BY

HENRY DAVID THOREAU

WITH A BIOGRAPHICAL SKETCH

BY

RALPH WALDO EMERSON

AND A GENERAL INDEX
TO THE WRITINGS

BOSTON AND NEW YORK
HOUGHTON, MIFFLIN AND COMPANY
The Riverside Press, Cambridge

The Riverside Press, Cambridge, Mass., U. S. A.
Electrotyped and Printed by H. O. Houghton & Company.

CONTENTS

INTRODUCTORY NOTE

THE biographical sketch which introduces this volume was in its original form an address by Mr. Emerson at the funeral of Mr. Thoreau. He expanded it for use in *The Atlantic Monthly*, August, 1862, and it has until now done service in the volume *Excursions*, the first collection of Thoreau's papers which was published after his death.

The contents of *Excursions* in the present series represented the fugitive papers by Thoreau upon subjects with which he is most identified, aspects of nature, especially seen in longer or shorter journeys. The papers here grouped under the title *Miscellanies* are the product of the somewhat less known Thoreau, the student of human life, of literature and religion, though the reader may easily have discovered both sides of his nature in *A Week*, which blends observation and reflection, and is a transcript from a diary which records the march of the "daughters of Time," as

" To each they offer gifts after his will
  Bread, kingdoms, stars, and sky that holds them all."

The several papers are arranged substantially in the order of their first appearance. One only, heretofore printed among Thoreau's writings, is omitted, for *Prayers* as Mr. Edward W. Emerson shows,[1] was written by Mr. R. W. Emerson, and published by him in *The Dial*. The verses included in it were alone by Thoreau.

The earliest production of Thoreau which has found its way into print appears to be an essay, dated July, 1840, and headed *The Service; Qualities of the Recruit*. Mr. Sanborn, who read extracts from this essay before the Concord Summer School of Philosophy in 1882, states that it probably was the one offered to *The Dial* which Miss Margaret Fuller rejected, accompanying her rejection with criticism, as narrated by Mr. Sanborn in his *Thoreau*. These extracts are reprinted here from *Concord Lectures in Philosophy*, published by Moses King, Cambridge, Mass.

Paradise (to be) Regained was in the form of a review of a book by J. A. Etzler, and was published in *The Democratic Review*, New York, for November, 1843. It was written during Thoreau's short residence in Staten Island.

Herald of Freedom was printed in *The Dial*,

[1] *Emerson in Concord*, p. 133.

April, 1844, as a commendatory notice of the anti-slavery paper of that name conducted by the fearless Nathaniel P. Rogers.

Wendell Phillips before the Concord Lyceum was a letter addressed to Mr. Garrison, the editor of *The Liberator*, and published in that journal, March 28, 1845.

Thomas Carlyle and his Works was printed first in *Graham's Magazine*, March and April, 1847. It was written during Thoreau's stay at Walden. The history of his adventure in getting the article published is amusingly told in the letters written by his faithful friend Horace Greeley, who acted as his intermediary. The letters will be found in Mr. Sanborn's *Thoreau*, pp. 219–224.

Civil Disobedience, under the title *Resistance to Civil Government*, was printed in 1849 in the first number of *Æsthetic Papers*, edited by Miss Elizabeth Peabody.

Slavery in Massachusetts was an address, delivered at the Anti-slavery Convention at Framingham, Massachusetts, July 4, 1854, and was printed in *The Liberator* for July 21 of the same year.

A Plea for Captain John Brown was read before the citizens of Concord, Massachusetts, October 30, 1859. It was taken from his diary written during the eventful period of Brown's expedition. When Captain Brown lay in prison, Thoreau did not wait for a public meeting, but went about among his neighbors, summoning them to come together to hear what he had to say. *The Last Days of John Brown* was read for the author at North Elba, July 4, 1860, and was printed in *The Liberator* on the 27th of the same month. *After the Death of John Brown* contains the remarks made at Concord by Thoreau on the day of the execution. It is reprinted from a volume, *Echoes from Harper's Ferry*.

Life without Principle is a posthumous paper first published in *The Atlantic Monthly*, October, 1863.

The Dial published besides various original papers by Thoreau compilations made by him from ancient writings, translations, and poems. The compilations representing his taste and judgment only are not here preserved, but his translation of *The Prometheus Bound* and of some of the verses of Pindar, published originally in 1843 and 1844, are given. His translations from Anacreon are included in *A Week on the Concord and Merrimack Rivers*. In that volume also and in *Walden* are imbedded many of Thoreau's poems, and it has not been found expedient to reproduce them in a collection here, but to gather the few, already printed in *The Dial* and in Mr. Sanborn's *Thoreau*, which are not found in other volumes in this series.

The General Index covers the contents of the ten volumes, and has been prepared for this edition.

The portrait of Thoreau prefixed to this volume is from an ambrotype taken in 1861 at New Bedford. Mr. Ricketson, for whom the picture was made, writes: "His health was then failing, — he had a racking cough, — but his face, except a shade of sadness in the eyes, did not show it." He quotes from a letter of Miss Sophia Thoreau these words: "I discover a slight shade about the eyes, expressive of weariness; but a stranger might not observe it. I am very glad to possess a picture of so late a date. The crayon, drawn eight years ago next summer [*i. e.*, in 1854], we considered good; it betrays the poet. Mr. Channing, Mr. Emerson, Mr. Alcott, and many other friends who have looked at the ambrotype, express much satisfaction."

BIOGRAPHICAL SKETCH

BY R. W. EMERSON

HENRY DAVID THOREAU was the last male descendant of a French ancestor who came to this country from the Isle of Guernsey. His character exhibited occasional traits drawn from this blood in singular combination with a very strong Saxon genius.

He was born in Concord, Massachusetts, on the 12th of July, 1817. He was graduated at Harvard College in 1837, but without any literary distinction. An iconoclast in literature, he seldom thanked colleges for their service to him, holding them in small esteem, whilst yet his debt to them was important. After leaving the University, he joined his brother in teaching a private school, which he soon renounced. His father was a manufacturer of lead-pencils, and Henry applied himself for a time to this craft, believing he could make a better pencil than was then in use. After completing his experiments, he exhibited his work to chemists and artists in Boston, and having obtained their certificates to its excellence and to its equality with the

best London manufacture, he returned home
contented. His friends congratulated him that
he had now opened his way to fortune. But he
replied, that he should never make another pencil. "Why should I? I would not do again
what I have done once." He resumed his endless walks and miscellaneous studies, making
every day some new acquaintance with Nature,
though as yet never speaking of zoölogy or botany, since, though very studious of natural
facts, he was incurious of technical and textual
science.

At this time, a strong, healthy youth, fresh
from college, whilst all his companions were
choosing their profession, or eager to begin
some lucrative employment, it was inevitable
that his thoughts should be exercised on the
same question, and it required rare decision to
refuse all the accustomed paths, and keep his
solitary freedom at the cost of disappointing the
natural expectations of his family and friends:
all the more difficult that he had a perfect
probity, was exact in securing his own independence, and in holding every man to the like
duty. But Thoreau never faltered. He was a
born protestant. He declined to give up his
large ambition of knowledge and action for any
narrow craft or profession, aiming at a much
more comprehensive calling, the art of living

well. If he slighted and defied the opinions of others, it was only that he was more intent to reconcile his practice with his own belief. Never idle or self-indulgent, he preferred, when he wanted money, earning it by some piece of manual labor agreeable to him, as building a boat or a fence, planting, grafting, surveying, or other short work, to any long engagements. With his hardy habits and few wants, his skill in wood-craft, and his powerful arithmetic, he was very competent to live in any part of the world. It would cost him less time to supply his wants than another. He was therefore secure of his leisure.

A natural skill for mensuration, growing out of his mathematical knowledge, and his habit of ascertaining the measures and distances of objects which interested him, the size of trees, the depth and extent of ponds and rivers, the height of mountains, and the air-line distance of his favorite summits, — this, and his intimate knowledge of the territory about Concord, made him drift into the profession of land-surveyor. It had the advantage for him that it led him continually into new and secluded grounds, and helped his studies of Nature. His accuracy and skill in this work were readily appreciated, and he found all the employment he wanted.

He could easily solve the problems of the

surveyor, but he was daily beset with graver questions, which he manfully confronted. He interrogated every custom, and wished to settle all his practice on an ideal foundation. He was a protestant *à l'outrance*, and few lives contain so many renunciations. He was bred to no profession; he never married; he lived alone; he never went to church; he never voted; he refused to pay a tax to the State; he ate no flesh, he drank no wine, he never knew the use of tobacco; and, though a naturalist, he used neither trap nor gun. He chose, wisely, no doubt, for himself, to be the bachelor of thought and Nature. He had no talent for wealth, and knew how to be poor without the least hint of squalor or inelegance. Perhaps he fell into his way of living without forecasting it much, but approved it with later wisdom. "I am often reminded," he wrote in his journal, "that, if I had bestowed on me the wealth of Crœsus, my aims must be still the same, and my means essentially the same." He had no temptations to fight against, — no appetites, no passions, no taste for elegant trifles. A fine house, dress, the manners and talk of highly cultivated people were all thrown away on him. He much preferred a good Indian, and considered these refinements as impediments to conversation, wishing to meet his companion on the simplest terms. He declined invitations to dinner-parties, because there each was in every one's way, and he could not meet the individuals to any purpose. "They make their pride," he said, "in making their dinner cost much; I make my pride in making my dinner cost little." When asked at table what dish he preferred, he answered, "The nearest." He did not like the taste of wine, and never had a vice in his life. He said, "I have a faint recollection of pleasure derived from smoking dried lily-stems, before I was a man. I had commonly a supply of these. I have never smoked anything more noxious."

He chose to be rich by making his wants few, and supplying them himself. In his travels, he used the railroad only to get over so much country as was unimportant to the present purpose, walking hundreds of miles, avoiding taverns, buying a lodging in farmers' and fishermen's houses, as cheaper, and more agreeable to him, and because there he could better find the men and the information he wanted.

There was somewhat military in his nature not to be subdued, always manly and able, but rarely tender, as if he did not feel himself except in opposition. He wanted a fallacy to expose, a blunder to pillory, I may say required a little sense of victory, a roll of the drum, to

call his powers into full exercise. It cost him
nothing to say No; indeed, he found it much
easier than to say Yes. It seemed as if his first
instinct on hearing a proposition was to contro-
vert it, so impatient was he of the limitations
of our daily thought. This habit, of course, is
a little chilling to the social affections; and
though the companion would in the end acquit
him of any malice or untruth, yet it mars conversation. Hence, no equal, companion stood
in affectionate relations with one so pure and
guileless. "I love Henry," said one of his
friends, "but I cannot like him; and as for
taking his arm, I should as soon think of taking
the arm of an elm-tree."

Yet, hermit and stoic as he was, he was
really fond of sympathy, and threw himself
heartily and childlike into the company of
young people whom he loved, and whom he delighted to entertain, as he only could, with the
varied and endless anecdotes of his experiences
by field and river. And he was always ready
to lead a huckleberry party or a search for
chestnuts or grapes. Talking, one day, of a
public discourse, Henry remarked, that whatever succeeded with the audience was bad. I
said, "Who would not like to write something
which all can read, like 'Robinson Crusoe'?
and who does not see with regret that his page

is not solid with a right materialistic treatment, which delights everybody?" Henry objected, of course, and vaunted the better lectures which reached only a few persons. But, at supper, a young girl, understanding that he was to lecture at the Lyceum, sharply asked him, "whether his lecture would be a nice, interesting story, such as she wished to hear, or whether it was one of those old philosophical things that she did not care about." Henry turned to her, and bethought himself, and, I saw, was trying to believe that he had matter that might fit her and her brother, who were to sit up and go to the lecture, if it was a good one for them.

He was a speaker and actor of the truth, — born such, — and was ever running into dramatic situations from this cause. In any circumstance, it interested all bystanders to know what part Henry would take, and what he would say; and he did not disappoint expectation, but used an original judgment on each emergency. In 1845 he built himself a small framed house on the shores of Walden Pond, and lived there two years alone, a life of labor and study. This action was quite native and fit for him. No one who knew him would tax him with affectation. He was more unlike his neighbors in his thought than in his action. As soon as he had exhausted the advantages of that solitude, he abandoned it. In 1847, not approving some uses to which the public expenditure was applied, he refused to pay his town tax, and was put in jail. A friend paid the tax for him, and he was released. The like annoyance was threatened the next year. But, as his friends paid the tax, notwithstanding his protest, I believe he ceased to resist. No opposition or ridicule had any weight with him. He coldly and fully stated his opinion without affecting to believe that it was the opinion of the company. It was of no consequence, if every one present held the opposite opinion. On one occasion he went to the University Library to procure some books. The librarian refused to lend them. Mr. Thoreau repaired to the President, who stated to him the rules and usages, which permitted the loan of books to resident graduates, to clergymen who were alumni, and to some others resident within a circle of ten miles' radius from the College. Mr. Thoreau explained to the President that the railroad had destroyed the old scale of distances, — that the library was useless, yes, and President and College useless, on the terms of his rules, — that the one benefit he owed to the College was its library, — that, at this moment, not only his want of books was imperative, but he wanted a large number of books, and assured him that he, Thoreau, and not the librarian, was the proper custodian of these. In short, the President found the petitioner so formidable, and the rules getting to look so ridiculous, that he ended by giving him a privilege which in his hands proved unlimited thereafter.

No truer American existed than Thoreau. His preference of his country and condition was genuine, and his aversation from English and European manners and tastes almost reached contempt. He listened impatiently to news or *bon mots* gleaned from London circles; and though he tried to be civil, these anecdotes fatigued him. The men were all imitating each other, and on a small mould. Why can they not live as far apart as possible, and each be a man by himself? What he sought was the most energetic nature; and he wished to go to Oregon, not to London. "In every part of Great Britain," he wrote in his diary, "are discovered traces of the Romans, their funereal urns, their camps, their roads, their dwellings. But New England, at least, is not based on any Roman ruins. We have not to lay the foundations of our houses on the ashes of a former civilization."

But, idealist as he was, standing for abolition of slavery, abolition of tariffs, almost for abolition of government, it is needless to say he found himself not only unrepresented in actual politics, but almost equally opposed to every class of reformers. Yet he paid the tribute of his uniform respect to the Anti-Slavery Party. One man, whose personal acquaintance he had formed, he honored with exceptional regard. Before the first friendly word had been spoken for Captain John Brown, after the arrest, he sent notices to most houses in Concord, that he would speak in a public hall on the condition and character of John Brown, on Sunday evening, and invited all people to come. The Republican Committee, the Abolitionist Committee, sent him word that it was premature and not advisable. He replied, "I did not send to you for advice, but to announce that I am to speak." The hall was filled at an early hour by people of all parties, and his earnest eulogy of the hero was heard by all respectfully, by many with a sympathy that surprised themselves.

It was said of Plotinus that he was ashamed of his body, and 't is very likely he had good reason for it, — that his body was a bad servant, and he had not skill in dealing with the material world, as happens often to men of abstract intellect. But Mr. Thoreau was equipped with a most adapted and serviceable body. He was of short stature, firmly built,

of light complexion, with strong, serious blue
eyes, and a grave aspect, — his face covered in
the late years with a becoming beard. His
senses were acute, his frame well-knit and
hardy, his hands strong and skillful in the use
of tools. And there was a wonderful fitness of
body and mind. He could pace sixteen rods
more accurately than another man could measure them with rod and chain. He could find
his path in the woods at night, he said, better
by his feet than his eyes. He could estimate
the measure of a tree very well by his eyes; he
could estimate the weight of a calf or a pig, like
a dealer. From a box containing a bushel or
more of loose pencils, he could take up with his
hands fast enough just a dozen pencils at every
grasp. He was a good swimmer, runner,
skater, boatman, and would probably outwalk
most countrymen in a day's journey. And the
relation of body to mind was still finer than we
have indicated. He said he wanted every
stride his legs made. The length of his walk
uniformly made the length of his writing. If
shut up in the house, he did not write at all.

He had a strong common sense, like that
which Rose Flammock, the weaver's daughter,
in Scott's romance, commends in her father, as
resembling a yardstick which, whilst it measures
dowlas and diaper, can equally well measure

tapestry and cloth of gold. He had always a
new resource. When I was planting forest-
trees, and had procured half a peck of acorns,
he said that only a small portion of them would
be sound, and proceeded to examine them, and
select the sound ones. But finding this took
time, he said, "I think, if you put them all into
water, the good ones will sink;" which experi-
ment we tried with success. He could plan a
garden, or a house, or a barn; would have been
competent to lead a "Pacific Exploring Expedition;" could give judicious counsel in the gravest private or public affairs.

He lived for the day, not cumbered and mor-
tified by his memory. If he brought you yes-
terday a new proposition, he would bring you
to-day another not less revolutionary. A very
industrious man, and setting, like all highly
organized men, a high value on his time, he
seemed the only man of leisure in town, always
ready for any excursion that promised well, or
for conversation prolonged into late hours.
His trenchant sense was never stopped by his
rules of daily prudence, but was always up to
the new occasion. He liked and used the simplest food, yet, when some one urged a vegeta-
ble diet, Thoreau thought all diets a very small
matter, saying that "the man who shoots the
buffalo lives better than the man who boards

at the Graham House." He said, "You can sleep near the railroad, and never be disturbed: Nature knows very well what sounds are worth attending to, and has made up her mind not to hear the railroad-whistle. But things respect the devout mind, and a mental ecstasy was never interrupted." He noted what repeatedly befell him, that, after receiving from a distance a rare plant, he would presently find the same in his own haunts. And those pieces of luck which happen only to good players happened to him. One day, walking with a stranger, who inquired where Indian arrow-heads could be found, he replied, "Everywhere," and, stooping forward, picked one on the instant from the ground. At Mount Washington, in Tuckerman's Ravine, Thoreau had a bad fall, and sprained his foot. As he was in the act of getting up from his fall, he saw for the first time the leaves of the *Arnica mollis.*

His robust common sense, armed with stout hands, keen perceptions, and strong will, cannot yet account for the superiority which shone in his simple and hidden life. I must add the cardinal fact, that there was an excellent wisdom in him, proper to a rare class of men, which showed him the material world as a means and symbol. This discovery, which sometimes yields to poets a certain casual and interrupted light, serving for the ornament of their writing, was in him an unsleeping insight; and whatever faults or obstructions of temperament might cloud it, he was not disobedient to the heavenly vision. In his youth, he said, one day, "The other world is all my art: my pencils will draw no other; my jack-knife will cut nothing else; I do not use it as a means." This was the muse and genius that ruled his opinions, conversation, studies, work, and course of life. This made him a searching judge of men. At first glance he measured his companion, and, though insensible to some fine traits of culture, could very well report his weight and calibre. And this made the impression of genius which his conversation often gave.

He understood the matter in hand at a glance, and saw the limitations and poverty of those he talked with, so that nothing seemed concealed from such terrible eyes. I have repeatedly known young men of sensibility converted in a moment to the belief that this was the man they were in search of, the man of men, who could tell them all they should do. His own dealing with them was never affectionate, but superior, didactic, — scorning their petty ways, — very slowly conceding, or not conceding at all, the promise of his society at their houses, or even at his own. "Would he

not walk with them?" "He did not know.
There was nothing so important to him as his
walk; he had no walks to throw away on company." Visits were offered him from respect-
ful parties, but he declined them. Admiring
friends offered to carry him at their own cost to
the Yellow-Stone River, — to the West Indies,
— to South America. But though nothing
could be more grave or considered than his
refusals, they remind one in quite new relations
of that fop Brummel's reply to the gentleman
who offered him his carriage in a shower, "But
where will *you* ride, then?" — and what accus-
ing silences, and what searching and irresistible
speeches, battering down all defenses, his companions can remember!

Mr. Thoreau dedicated his genius with such
entire love to the fields, hills, and waters of his
native town, that he made them known and interesting to all reading Americans, and to people over the sea. The river on whose banks he
was born and died he knew from its springs to
its confluence with the Merrimack. He had
made summer and winter observations on it
for many years, and at every hour of the day
and the night. The result of the recent survey of the Water Commissioners appointed by
the State of Massachusetts he had reached, by
his private experiments, several years earlier.

Every fact which occurs in the bed, on the banks, or in the air over it; the fishes, and their spawning and nests, their manners, their food; the shad-flies which fill the air on a certain evening once a year, and which are snapped at by the fishes so ravenously that many of these die of repletion; the conical heaps of small stones on the river-shallows, one of which heaps will sometimes overfill a cart, — these heaps the huge nests of small fishes; the birds which frequent the stream, heron, duck, sheldrake, loon, osprey; the snake, musk-rat, otter, woodchuck, and fox, on the banks; the turtle, frog, hyla, and cricket, which make the banks vocal, — were all known to him, and, as it were, townsmen and fellow-creatures; so that he felt an absurdity or violence in any narrative of one of these by itself apart, and still more of its dimensions on an inch-rule, or in the exhibition of its skeleton, or the specimen of a squirrel or a bird in brandy. He liked to speak of the manners of the river, as itself a lawful creature, yet with exactness, and always to an observed fact. As he knew the river, so the ponds in this region.

One of the weapons he used, more important than microscope or alcohol-receiver to other investigators, was a whim which grew on him by indulgence, yet appeared in gravest statement, namely, of extolling his own town and neigh-borhood as the most favored centre for natural observation. He remarked that the Flora of Massachusetts embraced almost all the impor-tant plants of America, — most of the oaks, most of the willows, the best pines, the ash, the maple, the beech, the nuts. He returned Kane's "Arctic Voyage" to a friend of whom he had borrowed it, with the remark, that "most of the phenomena noted might be ob-served in Concord." He seemed a little envi-ous of the Pole, for the coincident sunrise and sunset, or five minutes' day after six months: a splendid fact, which Annursnuc had never afforded him. He found red snow in one of his walks, and told me that he expected to find yet the *Victoria regia* in Concord. He was the attorney of the indigenous plants, and owned to a preference of the weeds to the imported plants, as of the Indian to the civilized man, — and noticed, with pleasure, that the willow bean-poles of his neighbor had grown more than his beans. "See these weeds," he said, "which have been hoed at by a million farmers all spring and summer, and yet have prevailed, and just now come out triumphant over all lanes, pastures, fields, and gardens, such is their vigor. We have insulted them with low names, too, — as Pigweed, Wormwood, Chickweed, Shad-Blossom." He says, "They have brave names, too, — Ambrosia, Stellaria, Amelanchia, Amaranth, etc."

I think his fancy for referring everything to the meridian of Concord did not grow out of any ignorance or depreciation of other longitudes or latitudes, but was rather a playful expression of his conviction of the indifferency of all places, and that the best place for each is where he stands. He expressed it once in this wise: "I think nothing is to be hoped from you, if this bit of mould under your feet is not sweeter to you to eat than any other in this world, or in any world."

The other weapon with which he conquered all obstacles in science was patience. He knew how to sit immovable, a part of the rock he rested on, until the bird, the reptile, the fish, which had retired from him, should come back, and resume its habits, nay, moved by curiosity, should come to him and watch him.

It was a pleasure and a privilege to walk with him. He knew the country like a fox or a bird, and passed through it as freely by paths of his own. He knew every track in the snow or on the ground, and what creature had taken this path before him. One must submit abjectly to such a guide, and the reward was great. Under his arm he carried an old music-

book to press plants; in his pocket, his diary
and pencil, a spy-glass for birds, microscope,
jack-knife, and twine. He wore straw hat,
stout shoes, strong gray trousers to brave shrub-
oaks and smilax, and to climb a tree for a
hawk's or a squirrel's nest. He waded into
the pool for the water-plants, and his strong
legs were no insignificant part of his armor.
On the day I speak of he looked for the Meny-
anthes, detected it across the wide pool, and,
on examination of the florets, decided that it
had been in flower five days. He drew out of
his breast-pocket his diary, and read the names
of all the plants that should bloom on this day,
whereof he kept account as a banker when his
notes fall due. The Cypripedium not due till
to-morrow. He thought, that, if waked up
from a trance, in this swamp, he could tell by
the plants what time of the year it was within
two days. The redstart was flying about, and
presently the pine grosbeaks, whose brilliant
scarlet makes the rash gazer wipe his eye, and
whose fine clear note Thoreau compared to that
of a tanager which has got rid of its hoarseness.
Presently he heard a note which he called that
of the night-warbler, a bird he had never identified, had been in search of twelve years, which
always, when he saw it, was in the act of diving down into a tree or bush, and which it was

vain to seek; the only bird that sings indifferently by night and by day. I told him he must beware of finding and booking it, lest life should have nothing more to show him. He said, "What you seek in vain for, half your life, one day you come full upon all the family at dinner. You seek it like a dream, and as soon as you find it you become its prey."

His interest in the flower or the bird lay very deep in his mind, was connected with Nature, — and the meaning of Nature was never attempted to be defined by him. He would not offer a memoir of his observations to the Natural History Society. "Why should I? To detach the description from its connections in my mind would make it no longer true or valuable to me; and they do not wish what belongs to it." His power of observation seemed to indicate additional senses. He saw as with microscope, heard as with ear-trumpet, and his memory was a photographic register of all he saw and heard. And yet none knew better than he that it is not the fact that imports, but the impression or effect of the fact on your mind. Every fact lay in glory in his mind, a type of the order and beauty of the whole.

His determination on Natural History was organic. He confessed that he sometimes felt like a hound or a panther, and, if born among

Indians, would have been a fell hunter. But, restrained by his Massachusetts culture, he played out the game in this mild form of botany and ichthyology. His intimacy with animals suggested what Thomas Fuller records of Butler the apiologist, that "either he had told the bees things or the bees had told him." Snakes coiled round his leg, the fishes swam into his hand, and he took them out of the water; he pulled the woodchuck out of its hole by the tail, and took the foxes under his protection from the hunters. Our naturalist had perfect magnanimity; he had no secrets: he would carry you to the heron's haunt, or even to his most prized botanical swamp, — possibly knowing that you could never find it again, yet willing to take his risks.

No college ever offered him a diploma, or a professor's chair; no academy made him its corresponding secretary, its discoverer, or even its member. Perhaps these learned bodies feared the satire of his presence. Yet so much knowledge of Nature's secret and genius few others possessed, none in a more large and religious synthesis. For not a particle of respect had he to the opinions of any man or body of men, but homage solely to the truth itself; and as he discovered everywhere among doctors some leaning of courtesy, it discredited them.

He grew to be revered and admired by his townsmen, who had at first known him only as an oddity. The farmers who employed him as a surveyor soon discovered his rare accuracy and skill, his knowledge of their lands, of trees, of birds, of Indian remains, and the like, which enabled him to tell every farmer more than he knew before of his own farm; so that he began to feel as if Mr. Thoreau had better rights in his land than he. They felt, too, the superiority of character which addressed all men with a native authority.

Indian relics abound in Concord, — arrowheads, stone chisels, pestles, and fragments of pottery; and on the river-bank, large heaps of clam-shells and ashes mark spots which the savages frequented. These, and every circumstance touching the Indian, were important in his eyes. His visits to Maine were chiefly for love of the Indian. He had the satisfaction of seeing the manufacture of the bark-canoe, as well as of trying his hand in its management on the rapids. He was inquisitive about the making of the stone arrow-head, and in his last days charged a youth setting out for the Rocky Mountains to find an Indian who could tell him that: "It was well worth a visit to California to learn it." Occasionally, a small party of Penobscot Indians would visit Concord, and pitch their tents for a few weeks in summer on the river-bank. He failed not to make acquaintance with the best of them; though he well knew that asking questions of Indians is like catechising beavers and rabbits. In his last visit to Maine he had great satisfaction from Joseph Polis, an intelligent Indian of Oldtown, who was his guide for some weeks.

He was equally interested in every natural fact. The depth of his perception found likeness of law throughout Nature, and I know not any genius who so swiftly inferred universal law from the single fact. He was no pedant of a department. His eye was open to beauty, and his ear to music. He found these, not in rare conditions, but wheresoever he went. He thought the best of music was in single strains; and he found poetic suggestion in the humming of the telegraph-wire.

His poetry might be bad or good; he no doubt wanted a lyric facility and technical skill; but he had the source of poetry in his spiritual perception. He was a good reader and critic, and his judgment on poetry was to the ground of it. He could not be deceived as to the presence or absence of the poetic element in any composition, and his thirst for this made him negligent and perhaps scornful of superficial graces. He would pass by many delicate rhythms, but he would have detected every live stanza or line in a volume, and knew very well where to find an equal poetic charm in prose. He was so enamored of the spiritual beauty that he held all actual written poems in very light esteem in the comparison. He admired Æschylus and Pindar; but, when some one was commending them, he said that "Æschylus and the Greeks, in describing Apollo and Orpheus, had given no song, or no good one. They ought not to have moved trees, but to have chanted to the gods such a hymn as would have sung all their old ideas out of their heads, and new ones in." His own verses are often rude and defective. The gold does not yet run pure, is drossy and crude. The thyme and marjoram are not yet honey. But if he want lyric fineness and technical merits, if he have not the poetic temperament, he never lacks the causal thought, showing that his genius was better than his talent. He knew the worth of the Imagination for the uplifting and consolation of human life, and liked to throw every thought into a symbol. The fact you tell is of no value, but only the impression. For this reason his presence was poetic, always piqued the curiosity to know more deeply the secrets of his mind. He had many reserves, an unwillingness to exhibit to profane eyes what was still sacred in his own, and knew well how to throw a poetic veil over his experience. All readers of "Walden" will remember his mythical record of his disappointments : —

"I long ago lost a hound, a bay horse, and a turtle-dove, and am still on their trail. Many are the travelers I have spoken concerning them, describing their tracks, and what calls they answered to. I have met one or two who had heard the hound, and the tramp of the horse, and even seen the dove disappear behind a cloud; and they seemed as anxious to recover them as if they had lost them themselves." [1]

His riddles were worth the reading, and I confide, that, if at any time I do not understand the expression, it is yet just. Such was the wealth of his truth that it was not worth his while to use words in vain. His poem entitled "Sympathy" reveals the tenderness under that triple steel of stoicism, and the intellectual subtilty it could animate. His classic poem on "Smoke" suggests Simonides, but is better than any poem of Simonides. His biography is in his verses. His habitual thought makes all his poetry a hymn to the Cause of causes, the Spirit which vivifies and controls his own.

> "I hearing get, who had but ears,
> And sight, who had but eyes before;

[1] *Walden*, p. 29.

I moments live, who lived but years,
And truth discern, who knew but learning's lore."

And still more in these religious lines: —

" Now chiefly is my natal hour,
And only now my prime of life;
I will not doubt the love untold,
Which not my worth or want hath bought,
Which wooed me young, and wooes me old,
And to this evening hath me brought."

Whilst he used in his writings a certain pet-
ulance of remark in reference to churches or
churchmen, he was a person of a rare, tender,
and absolute religion, a person incapable of any
profanation, by act or by thought. Of course,
the same isolation which belonged to his original thinking and living detached him from the
social religious forms. This is neither to be
censured nor regretted. Aristotle long ago explained it, when he said, "One who surpasses
his fellow-citizens in virtue is no longer a part
of the city. Their law is not for him, since he
is a law to himself."

Thoreau was sincerity itself, and might for-
tify the convictions of prophets in the ethical
laws by his holy living. It was an affirmative
experience which refused to be set aside. A
truth-speaker he, capable of the most deep and
strict conversation; a physician to the wounds
of any soul; a friend, knowing not only the

secret of friendship, but almost worshiped by those few persons who resorted to him as their confessor and prophet, and knew the deep value of his mind and great heart. He thought that without religion or devotion of some kind nothing great was ever accomplished; and he thought that the bigoted sectarian had better bear this in mind.

His virtues, of course, sometimes ran into extremes. It was easy to trace to the inexorable demand on all for exact truth that austerity which made this willing hermit more solitary even than he wished. Himself of a perfect probity, he required not less of others. He had a disgust at crime, and no worldly success could cover it. He detected paltering as readily in dignified and prosperous persons as in beggars, and with equal scorn. Such dangerous frankness was in his dealing that his admirers called him "that terrible Thoreau," as if he spoke when silent, and was still present when he had departed. I think the severity of his ideal interfered to deprive him of a healthy sufficiency of human society.

The habit of a realist to find things the reverse of their appearance inclined him to put every statement in a paradox. A certain habit of antagonism defaced his earlier writings, — a trick of rhetoric not quite outgrown in his later, of substituting for the obvious word and thought its diametrical opposite. He praised wild mountains and winter forests for their domestic air, in snow and ice he would find sultriness, and commended the wilderness for resembling Rome and Paris. "It was so dry, that you might call it wet."

The tendency to magnify the moment, to read all the laws of Nature in the one object or one combination under your eye, is of course comic to those who do not share the philosopher's perception of identity. To him there was no such thing as size. The pond was a small ocean; the Atlantic, a large Walden Pond. He referred every minute fact to cosmical laws. Though he meant to be just, he seemed haunted by a certain chronic assumption that the science of the day pretended completeness, and he had just found out that the *savans* had neglected to discriminate a particular botanical variety, had failed to describe the seeds or count the sepals. "That is to say," we replied, "the blockheads were not born in Concord ; but who said they were? It was their unspeakable misfortune to be born in London, or Paris, or Rome; but, poor fellows, they did what they could, considering that they never saw Bateman's Pond, or Nine - Acre Corner, or Becky-Stow's Swamp. Besides, what were you sent into the world for, but to add this observation.?"

Had his genius been only contemplative, he had been fitted to his life, but with his energy and practical ability he seemed born for great enterprise and for command; and I so much regret the loss of his rare powers of action, that I cannot help counting it a fault in him that he had no ambition. Wanting this, instead of engineering for all America, he was the captain of a huckleberry party. Pounding beans is good to the end of pounding empires one of these days; but if, at the end of years, it is still only beans!

But these foibles, real or apparent, were fast vanishing in the incessant growth of a spirit so robust and wise, and which effaced its defeats with new triumphs. His study of Nature was a perpetual ornament to him, ánd inspired his friends with curiosity to see the world through his eyes, and to hear his adventures. They possessed every kind of interest.

He had many elegances of his own, whilst he scoffed at conventional elegance. Thus, he could not bear to hear the sound of his own steps, the grit of gravel; and therefore never willingly walked in the road, but in the grass, on mountains and in woods. His senses were acute, and he remarked that by night every

dwelling-house gives out bad air, like a slaugh-
ter-house. He liked the pure fragrance of
melilot. He honored certain plants with special regard, and, over all, the pond-lily, — then,
the gentian, and the *Mikania scandens*, and
"life-everlasting," and a bass-tree which he
visited every year when it bloomed, in the middle of July. He thought the scent a more
oracular inquisition than the sight, — more
oracular and trustworthy. The scent, of
course, reveals what is concealed from the other
senses. By it he detected earthiness. He delighted in echoes, and said they were almost the
only kind of kindred voices that he heard. He
loved Nature so well, was so happy in her solitude, that he became very jealous of cities, and
the sad work which their refinements and arti-
fices made with man and his dwelling. The
axe was always destroying his forest.

"Thank God," he said, "they cannot cut
down the clouds!" "All kinds of figures are
drawn on the blue ground with this fibrous
white paint."

I subjoin a few sentences taken from his
unpublished manuscripts, not only as records of
his thought and feeling, but for their power of
description and literary excellence.

"Some circumstantial evidence is very strong,
as when you find a trout in the milk."

"The chub is a soft fish, and tastes like boiled brown paper salted."

"The youth gets together his materials to build a bridge to the moon, or, perchance, a palace or temple on the earth, and at length the middle-aged man concludes to build a wood-shed with them."

"The locust z-ing."

"Devil's-needles zigzagging along the Nut-Meadow brook."

"Sugar is not so sweet to the palate as sound to the healthy ear."

"I put on some hemlock-boughs, and the rich salt crackling of their leaves was like mustard to the ear, the crackling of uncountable regiments. Dead trees love the fire."

"The bluebird carries the sky on his back."

"The tanager flies through the green foliage as if it would ignite the leaves."

"If I wish for a horse-hair for my compass sight, I must go to the stable; but the hair-bird, with her sharp eyes, goes to the road."

"Immortal water, alive ever to the super-ficies."

"Fire is the most tolerable third party."

"Nature made ferns for pure leaves, to show what she could do in that line."

"No tree has so fair a bole and so handsome an instep as the beech."

"How did these beautiful rainbow-tints get into the shell of the fresh-water clam, buried in the mud at the bottom of our dark river?"

"Hard are the times when the infant's shoes are second-foot."

"We are strictly confined to our men to whom we give liberty."

"Nothing is so much to be feared as fear. Atheism may comparatively be popular with God himself."

"Of what significance the things you can forget? A little thought is sexton to all the world."

"How can we expect a harvest of thought who have not had a seed-time of character?"

"Only he can be trusted with gifts who can present a face of bronze to expectations."

"I ask to be melted. You can only ask of the metals that they be tender to the fire that melts them. To naught else can they be tender."

There is a flower known to botanists, one of the same genus with our summer plant called "life - everlasting," a *Gnaphalium* like that which grows on the most inaccessible cliffs of the Tyrolese mountains, where the chamois dare hardly venture, and which the hunter, tempted by its beauty, and by his love (for it is im-

mensely valued by the Swiss maidens), climbs
the cliffs to gather, and is sometimes found
dead at the foot, with the flower in his hand.
It is called by botanists the *Gnaphalium leon-
topodium*, but by the Swiss *Edelweiss*, which
signifies *Noble Purity*. Thoreau seemed to me
living in the hope to gather this plant, which
belonged to him of right. The scale on which
his studies proceeded was so large as to require
longevity, and we were the less prepared for his
sudden disappearance. The country knows not
yet, or in the least part, how great a son it has
lost. It seems an injury that he should leave
in the midst his broken task, which none else
can finish, — a kind of indignity to so noble a
soul, that it should depart out of Nature before
yet he has been really shown to his peers for
what he is. But he, at least, is content. His
soul was made for the noblest society; he had
in a short life exhausted the capabilities of this
world; wherever there is knowledge, wherever
there is virtue, wherever there is beauty, he
will find a home.

MISCELLANIES

THE SERVICE: QUALITIES OF THE RECRUIT

THE brave man is the elder son of creation who has stepped buoyantly into his inheritance, while the coward, who is the younger, waiteth patiently for his decease. He rides as wide of this earth's gravity as a star, and by yielding incessantly to all impulses of the soul is drawn upward and becomes a fixed star. His bravery consists not so much in resolute action as healthy and assured rest. Its palmy state is a staying at home, compelling alliance in all directions. So stands his life to heaven as some fair sunlit tree against the western horizon, and by sunrise is planted on some eastern hill to glisten in the first rays of the dawn. The brave man braves nothing, nor knows he of his bravery. . . . He does not present the gleaming edge to ward off harm, for that will oftenest attract the lightning, but rather is the all-pervading ether, which the lightning does not strike, but purifies. It is the profanity of his companion, as a flash across the face of his sky, which lights up and reveals its serene depth.

A pyramid some artisan may measure with his line, but if he give you the dimensions of the Parthenon in feet and inches, the figures will not embrace it like a cord, but dangle from its entablature like an elastic drapery.

The golden mean in ethics, as in physics, is the centre of the system and that about which all revolve, and though to a distant and plodding planet it be an uttermost extreme, yet one day, when that planet's year is completed, it will be found to be central.

The coward wants resolution, which the brave man can do without. He recognizes no faith above a creed, thinking this straw by which he is moored does him good service, because his sheet anchor does not drag.

The divinity in man is the true vestal fire of the temple which is never permitted to go out, but burns as steadily and with as pure a flame on the obscure provincial altar as in Numa's temple at Rome. In the meanest are all the materials of manhood, only they are not rightly disposed.

We say justly that the weak person is flat, for like all flat substances, he does not stand in the direction of his strength, that is, on his edge, but affords a convenient surface to put upon. He slides all the way through life. Most things are strong in one direction, a straw longitudinally, a board in the direction of its edge, but the brave man is a perfect sphere, which cannot fall on its flat side and is equally strong every way. The coward is wretchedly spheroidal at best, too much educated or drawn out on one side and depressed on the other, or may be likened to a hollow sphere, whose disposition of matter is least where the greatest bulk is intended. We shall not attain to be spherical by lying on one or the other side for an eternity, but only by resigning ourselves implicitly to the law of gravity in us shall we find our axis coincident with the celestial axis, and by revolving incessantly through all circles acquire a perfect sphericity.

It is not enough that our life is an easy one. We must live on the stretch, retiring to our rest like soldiers on the eve of a battle, looking forward with ardor to the strenuous sortie of the morrow.

PARADISE (TO BE) REGAINED[1]

WE learn that Mr. Etzler is a native of
Germany, and originally published his book
in Pennsylvania, ten or twelve years ago; and
now a second English edition, from the original American one, is demanded by his readers
across the water, owing, we suppose, to the recent spread of Fourier's doctrines.   It is one
of the signs of the times.   We confess that we
have risen from reading this book with enlarged
ideas, and grander conceptions of our duties in
this world.   It did expand us a little.   It is
worth attending to, if only that it entertains
large questions.   Consider what Mr. Etzler
proposes: —

"Fellow-men!   I promise to show the means
of creating a paradise within ten years, where
everything desirable for human life may be had
by every man in superabundance, without labor,
and without pay; where the whole face of nature shall be changed into the most beautiful

[1] The Paradise within the Reach of all Men, without Labor,
by Powers of Nature and Machinery.   An Address to all intelligent Men.   In Two Parts.   By J. A. Etzler.   Part First.
Second English Edition.   London.   1842.   Pp. 55.

forms, and man may live in the most magnificent palaces, in all imaginable refinements of luxury, and in the most delightful gardens; where he may accomplish, without labor, in one year, more than hitherto could be done in thousands of years; may level mountains, sink valleys, create lakes, drain lakes and swamps, and intersect the land everywhere with beautiful canals, and roads for transporting heavy loads of many thousand tons, and for traveling one thousand miles in twenty-four hours; may cover the ocean with floating islands movable in any desired direction with immense power and celerity, in perfect security, and with all comforts and luxuries, bearing gardens and palaces, with thousands of families, and provided with rivulets of sweet water; may explore the interior of the globe, and travel from pole to pole in a fortnight; provide himself with means, unheard of yet, for increasing his knowledge of the world, and so his intelligence; lead a life of continual happiness, of enjoyments yet unknown; free himself from almost all the evils that afflict mankind, except death, and even put death far beyond the common period of human life, and finally render it less afflicting. Mankind may thus live in and enjoy a new world, far superior to the present, and raise themselves far higher in the scale of being."

It would seem from this and various indications beside, that there is a transcendentalism in mechanics as well as in ethics. While the whole field of the one reformer lies beyond the boundaries of space, the other is pushing his schemes for the elevation of the race to its utmost limits. While one scours the heavens, the other sweeps the earth. One says he will reform himself, and then nature and circumstances will be right. Let us not obstruct ourselves, for that is the greatest friction. It is of little importance though a cloud obstruct the view of the astronomer compared with his own blindness. The other will reform nature and circumstances, and then man will be right. Talk no more vaguely, says he, of reforming the world, — I will reform the globe itself. What matters it whether I remove this humor out of my flesh, or this pestilent humor from the fleshy part of the globe? Nay, is not the latter the more generous course? At present the globe goes with a shattered constitution in its orbit. Has it not asthma, and ague, and fever, and dropsy, and flatulence, and pleurisy, and is it not afflicted with vermin? Has it not its healthful laws counteracted, and its vital energy which will yet redeem it? No doubt the simple powers of nature, properly directed by man, would make it healthy and a paradise; as the

laws of man's own constitution but wait to be
obeyed, to restore him to health and happiness.
Our panaceas cure but few ails, our general
hospitals are private and exclusive. We must
set up another Hygeia than is now worshiped.
Do not the quacks even direct small doses for
children, larger for adults, and larger still for
oxen and horses? Let us remember that we
are to prescribe for the globe itself.

This fair homestead has fallen to us, and how
little have we done to improve it, how little
have we cleared and hedged and ditched! We
are too inclined to go hence to a "better land,"
without lifting a finger, as our farmers are moving to the Ohio soil; but would it not be more
heroic and faithful to till and redeem this New
England soil of the world? The still youthful
energies of the globe have only to be directed
in their proper channel. Every gazette brings
accounts of the untutored freaks of the wind,
— shipwrecks and hurricanes which the mariner
and planter accept as special or general provi-
dences; but they touch our consciences, they
remind us of our sins. Another deluge would
disgrace mankind. We confess we never had
much respect for that antediluvian race. A
thoroughbred business man cannot enter heartily upon the business of life without first looking into his accounts. How many things are

now at loose ends.   Who knows which way the wind will blow to-morrow?   Let us not succumb to nature.   We will marshal the clouds and restrain tempests; we will bottle up pestilent exhalations; we will probe for earthquakes, grub them up, and give vent to the dangerous gas; we will disembowel the volcano, and extract its poison, take its seed out.   We will wash water, and warm fire, and cool ice, and underprop the earth.   We will teach birds to fly, and fishes to swim, and ruminants to chew the cud.   It is time we had looked into these things.

And it becomes the moralist, too, to inquire what man might do to improve and beautify the system; what to make the stars shine more brightly, the sun more cheery and joyous, the moon more placid and content.   Could he not heighten the tints of flowers and the melody of birds?   Does he perform his duty to the inferior races?   Should he not be a god to them?   What is the part of magnanimity to the whale and the beaver?   Should we not fear to exchange places with them for a day, lest by their behavior they should shame us?   Might we not treat with magnanimity the shark and the tiger, not descend to meet them on their own level, with spears of shark's teeth and bucklers of tiger's skin?   We slander the hyena; man is the fiercest and cruellest animal. Ah! he is of little faith; even the erring comets and meteors would thank him, and return his kindness in their kind.

How meanly and grossly do we deal with nature! Could we not have a less gross labor? What else do these fine inventions suggest, — magnetism, the daguerreotype, electricity? Can we not do more than cut and trim the forest, — can we not assist in its interior economy, in the circulation of the sap? Now we work superficially and violently. We do not suspect how much might be done to improve our relation to animated nature even; what kindness and refined courtesy there might be.

There are certain pursuits which, if not wholly poetic and true, do at least suggest a nobler and finer relation to nature than we know. The keeping of bees, for instance, is a very slight interference. It is like directing the sunbeams. All nations, from the remotest antiquity, have thus fingered nature. There are Hymettus and Hybla, and how many bee-renowned spots beside? There is nothing gross in the idea of these little herds, — their hum like the faintest low of kine in the meads. A pleasant reviewer has lately reminded us that in some places they are led out to pasture where the flowers are most abundant. "Columella tells us," says he, "that the inhabitants of Arabia sent their hives into Attica to benefit by the later-blowing flowers." Annually are the hives, in immense pyramids, carried up the Nile in boats, and suffered to float slowly down the stream by night, resting by day, as the flowers put forth along the banks; and they determine the richness of any locality, and so the profitableness of delay, by the sinking of the boat in the water. We are told, by the same reviewer, of a man in Germany, whose bees yielded more honey than those of his neighbors, with no apparent advantage; but at length he informed them, that he had turned his hives one degree more to the east, and so his bees, having two hours the start in the morning, got the first sip of honey. True, there is treachery and selfishness behind all this, but these things suggest to the poetic mind what might be done.

Many examples there are of a grosser interference, yet not without their apology. We saw last summer, on the side of a mountain, a dog employed to churn for a farmer's family, traveling upon a horizontal wheel, and though he had sore eyes, an alarming cough, and withal a demure aspect, yet their bread did get buttered for all that. Undoubtedly, in the most brilliant successes, the first rank is always sacrificed. Much useless traveling of horses, *in*

extenso, has of late years been improved for
man's behoof, only two forces being taken advantage of, — the gravity of the horse, which is
the centripetal, and his centrifugal inclination
to go ahead. Only these two elements in the
calculation. And is not the creature's whole
economy better economized thus? Are not all
finite beings better pleased with motions rela-
tive than absolute? And what is the great
globe itself but such a wheel, — a larger treadmill, — so that our horse's freest steps over
prairies are oftentimes balked and rendered of
no avail by the earth's motion on its axis? But
here he is the central agent and motive-power;
and, for variety of scenery, being provided with
a window in front, do not the ever-varying
activity and fluctuating energy of the creature
himself work the effect of the most varied scenery on a country road? It must be confessed
that horses at present work too exclusively for
men, rarely men for horses; and the brute degenerates in man's society.

It will be seen that we contemplate a time
when man's will shall be law to the physical
world, and he shall no longer be deterred by
such abstractions as time and space, height and
depth, weight and hardness, but shall indeed be
the lord of creation. "Well," says the faith-

less reader, "'life is short, but art is long;'
where is the power that will effect all these
changes?" This it is the very object of Mr.
Etzler's volume to show. At present, he would
merely remind us that there are innumerable
and immeasurable powers already existing in
nature, unimproved on a large scale, or for generous and universal ends, amply sufficient for
these purposes. He would only indicate their
existence, as a surveyor makes known the existence of a water-power on any stream; but for
their application he refers us to a sequel to
this book, called the "Mechanical System." A
few of the most obvious and familiar of these
powers are the Wind, the Tide, the Waves, the
Sunshine. Let us consider their value.

First, there is the power of the Wind, constantly exerted over the globe. It appears
from observation of a sailing-vessel, and from
scientific tables, that the average power of the
wind is equal to that of one horse for every one
hundred square feet. We do not attach much
value to this statement of the comparative
power of the wind and horse, for no common
ground is mentioned on which they can be
compared. Undoubtedly, each is incomparably
excellent in its way, and every general comparison made for such practical purposes as are
contemplated, which gives a preference to the

one, must be made with some unfairness to the other. The scientific tables are, for the most part, true only in a tabular sense. We suspect that a loaded wagon, with a light sail, ten feet square, would not have been blown so far by the end of the year, under equal circumstances, as a common racer or dray horse would have drawn it. And how many crazy structures on our globe's surface, of the same dimensions, would wait for dry-rot if the traces of one horse were hitched to them, even to their windward side? Plainly this is not the principle of comparison. But even the steady and constant force of the horse may be rated as equal to his weight at least. Yet we should prefer to let the zephyrs and gales bear, with all their weight, upon our fences, than that Dobbin, with feet braced, should lean ominously against them for a season.

Nevertheless, here is an almost incalculable power at our disposal, yet how trifling the use we make of it. It only serves to turn a few mills, blow a few vessels across the ocean, and a few trivial ends besides. What a poor compliment do we pay to our indefatigable and energetic servant!

Men having discovered the power of falling water, which, after all, is comparatively slight, how eagerly do they seek out and improve these

privileges? Let a difference of but a few feet
in level be discovered on some stream near a
populous town, some slight occasion for gravity
to act, and the whole economy of the neighborhood is changed at once. Men do indeed speculate about and with this power as if it were
the only privilege. But meanwhile this aerial
stream is falling from far greater heights with
more constant flow, never shrunk by drought,
offering mill-sites wherever the wind blows; a
Niagara in the air, with no Canada side; —
only the application is hard.

There are the powers, too, of the Tide and
Waves, constantly ebbing and flowing, lapsing
and relapsing, but they serve man in but few
ways. They turn a few tide-mills, and perform
a few other insignificant and accidental services
only. We all perceive the effect of the tide;
how imperceptibly it creeps up into our harbors
and rivers, and raises the heaviest navies as
easily as the lightest chip. Everything that
floats must yield to it. But man, slow to take
nature's constant hint of assistance, makes
slight and irregular use of this power, in careen-
ing ships and getting them afloat when aground.

This power may be applied in various ways.
A large body, of the heaviest materials that
will float, may first be raised by it, and being
attached to the end of a balance reaching from

the land, or from a stationary support fastened to the bottom, when the tide falls the whole weight will be brought to bear upon the end of the balance. Also, when the tide rises, it may be made to exert a nearly equal force in the opposite direction. It can be employed wherever a *point d'appui* can be obtained.

Verily, the land would wear a busy aspect at the spring and neap tide, and these island ships, these *terræ infirmæ*, which realize the fables of antiquity, affect our imagination. We have often thought that the fittest locality for a human dwelling was on the edge of the land, that there the constant lesson and impression of the sea might sink deep into the life and character of the landsman, and perhaps impart a marine tint to his imagination. It is a noble word, that *mariner*, — one who is conversant with the sea. There should be more of what it signifies in each of us. It is a worthy country to belong to, — we look to see him not disgrace it. Perhaps we should be equally mariners and terreners, and even our Green Mountains need some of that sea-green to be mixed with them.

The computation of the power of the Waves is less satisfactory. While only the average power of the wind and the average height of the tide were taken before, now the extreme height of the waves is used, for they are made to rise ten feet above the level of the sea, to which, adding ten more for depression, we have twenty feet, or the extreme height of a wave. Indeed, the power of the waves, which is produced by the wind blowing obliquely and at disadvantage upon the water, is made to be, not only three thousand times greater than that of the tide, but one hundred times greater than that of the wind itself, meeting its object at right angles. Moreover, this power is measured by the area of the vessel, and not by its length mainly, and it seems to be forgotten that the motion of the waves is chiefly undulatory, and exerts a power only within the limits of a vibration, else the very continents, with their extensive coasts, would soon be set adrift.

Finally, there is the power to be derived from Sunshine, by the principle on which Archimedes contrived his burning-mirrors, a multiplication of mirrors reflecting the rays of the sun upon the same spot, till the requisite degree of heat is obtained. The principal application of this power will be to the boiling of water and production of steam. So much for these few and more obvious powers, already used to a trifling extent. But there are innumerable others in nature, not described nor discovered. These, however, will do for the present. This would be to make the sun and the moon equally our

satellites. For, as the moon is the cause of
the tides, and the sun the cause of the wind,
which, in turn, is the cause of the waves, all the
work of this planet would be performed by these
far influences.

"We may store up water in some eminent
pond, and take out of this store, at any time, as
much water through the outlet as we want to
employ, by which means the original power
may react for many days after it has ceased.
. . . Such reservoirs of moderate elevation or
size need not be made artificially, but will be
found made by nature very frequently, requiring but little aid for their completion. They
require no regularity of form. Any valley,
with lower grounds in its vicinity, would answer
the purpose. Small crevices may be filled up.
Such places may be eligible for the beginning
of enterprises of this kind."

The greater the height, of course, the less
water required. But suppose a level and dry
country; then hill and valley, and "eminent
pond," are to be constructed by main force; or,
if the springs are unusually low, then dirt and
stones may be used, and the disadvantage aris-
ing from friction will be counterbalanced by
their greater gravity. Nor shall a single rood
of dry land be sunk in such artificial ponds as
may be wanted, but their surfaces "may be cov-

ered with rafts decked with fertile earth, and
all kinds of vegetables which may grow there as
well as anywhere else."

And, finally, by the use of thick envelopes
retaining the heat, and other contrivances, "the
power of steam caused by sunshine may react
at will, and thus be rendered perpetual, no matter how often or how long the sunshine may be
interrupted."

Here is power enough, one would think, to
accomplish somewhat. These are the Powers
below. O ye millwrights, ye engineers, ye
operatives and speculators of every class, never
again complain of a want of power: it is the
grossest form of infidelity. The question is,
not how we shall execute, but what. Let us
not use in a niggardly manner what is thus generously offered.

Consider what revolutions are to be effected
in agriculture. First, in the new country a
machine is to move along, taking out trees and
stones to any required depth, and piling them
up in convenient heaps; then the same machine,
"with a little alteration," is to plane the ground
perfectly, till there shall be no hills nor valleys,
making the requisite canals, ditches, and roads
as it goes along. The same machine, "with
some other little alterations," is then to sift
the ground thoroughly, supply fertile soil from

other places if wanted, and plant it; and finally
the same machine, "with a little addition," is
to reap and gather in the crop, thresh and grind
it, or press it to oil, or prepare it any way for
final use. For the description of these machines we are referred to "Etzler's Mechanical
System," pages 11 to 27. We should be
pleased to see that "Mechanical System." We
have great faith in it. But we cannot stop for
applications now.

Who knows but by accumulating the power
until the end of the present century, using
meanwhile only the smallest allowance, reserv-
ing all that blows, all that shines, all that ebbs
and flows, all that dashes, we may have got
such a reserved accumulated power as to run
the earth off its track into a new orbit, some
summer, and so change the tedious vicissitude
of the seasons? Or, perchance, coming generations will not abide the dissolution of the
globe, but, availing themselves of future inventions in aerial locomotion, and the navigation of space, the entire race may migrate from
the earth, to settle some vacant and more western planet, it may be still healthy, perchance
unearthy, not composed of dirt and stones,
whose primary strata only are strewn, and
where no weeds are sown. It took but little
art, a simple application of natural laws, a

canoe, a paddle, and a sail of matting, to people the isles of the Pacific, and a little more
will people the shining isles of space. Do we
not see in the firmament the lights carried along
the shore by night, as Columbus did? Let us
not despair nor mutiny.

"The dwellings also ought to be very different from what is known, if the full benefit of
our means is to be enjoyed. They are to be of
a structure for which we have no name yet.
They are to be neither palaces, nor temples, nor
cities, but a combination of all, superior to
whatever is known.

"Earth may be baked into bricks, or even
vitrified stone by heat, — we may bake large
masses of any size and form, into stone and
vitrified substance of the greatest durability,
lasting even thousands of years, out of clayey
earth, or of stones ground to dust, by the application of burning-mirrors. This is to be done
in the open air without other preparation than
gathering the substance, grinding and mixing it
with water and cement, moulding or casting it,
and bringing the focus of the burning mirrors
of proper size upon the same."

The character of the architecture is to be
quite different from what it ever has been hitherto; large solid masses are to be baked or cast
in one piece, ready shaped in any form that

may be desired. The building may, therefore, consist of columns two hundred feet high and upwards, of proportionate thickness, and of one entire piece of vitrified substance; huge pieces are to be moulded so as to join and hook on to each other firmly, by proper joints and folds, and not to yield in any way without breaking.

"Foundries, of any description, are to be heated by burning-mirrors, and will require no labor, except the making of the first moulds and the superintendence for gathering the metal and taking the finished articles away."

Alas! in the present state of science, we must take the finished articles away; but think not that man will always be the victim of circumstances.

The countryman who visited the city, and found the streets cluttered with bricks and lumber, reported that it was not yet finished; and one who considers the endless repairs and reforming of our houses might well wonder when they will be done. But why may not the dwellings of men on this earth be built, once for all, of some durable material, some Roman or Etruscan masonry, which will stand, so that time shall only adorn and beautify them? Why may we not finish the outward world for posterity, and leave them leisure to attend to the inner? Surely, all the gross necessities and economies might be cared for in a few years. All might be built and baked and stored up, during this, the term-time of the world, against the vacant eternity, and the globe go provisioned and furnished, like our public vessels, for its voyage through space, as through some Pacific Ocean, while we would "tie up the rudder and sleep before the wind," as those who sail from Lima to Manilla.

But, to go back a few years in imagination, think not that life in these crystal palaces is to bear any analogy to life in our present humble cottages. Far from it. Clothed, once for all, in some "flexible stuff," more durable than George Fox's suit of leather, composed of "fibres of vegetables," "glutinated" together by some "cohesive substances," and made into sheets, like paper, of any size or form, man will put far from him corroding care and the whole host of ills.

"The twenty-five halls in the inside of the square are to be each two hundred feet square and high; the forty corridors, each one hundred feet long and twenty wide; the eighty galleries, each from 1,000 to 1,250 feet long; about 7,000 private rooms, the whole surrounded and intersected by the grandest and most splendid colonnades imaginable; floors, ceilings, columns, with their various beautiful and fanciful intervals, all shining, and reflecting to infinity all objects and persons, with splendid lustre of all beautiful colors, and fanciful shapes and pictures.

"All galleries, outside and within the halls, are to be provided with many thousand commodious and most elegant vehicles, in which persons may move up and down like birds, in perfect security, and without exertion. . . . Any member may procure himself all the common articles of his daily wants, by a short turn of some crank, without leaving his apartment.

"One or two persons are sufficient to direct the kitchen business. They have nothing else to do but to superintend the cookery, and to watch the time of the victuals being done, and then to remove them, with the table and vessels, into the dining-hall, or to the respective private apartments, by a slight motion of the hand at some crank. . . . *Any very extraordinary desire of any person may be satisfied by going to the place where the thing is to be had; and anything that requires a particular preparation in cooking or baking may be done by the person who desires it.*"

This is one of those instances in which the individual genius is found to consent, as indeed it always does, at last, with the universal. This last sentence has a certain sad and sober truth, which reminds us of the scripture of all nations. All expression of truth does at length take this deep ethical form.   Here is hint of a place the most eligible of any in space, and of a servitor, in comparison with whom all other helps dwindle into insignificance.   We hope to hear more of him anon, for even a Crystal Palace would be deficient without his invaluable services.

And as for the environs of the establishment: —

"There will be afforded the most enrapturing views to be fancied, out of the private apartments, from the galleries, from the roof, from its turrets and cupolas, — gardens, as far as the eye can see, full of fruits and flowers, arranged in the most beautiful order, with walks, colonnades, aqueducts, canals, ponds, plains, amphitheatres, terraces, fountains, sculptural works, pavilions, gondolas, places for public amusement, etc., to delight the eye and fancy, the taste and smell. . . . The walks and roads are to be paved with hard vitrified large plates, so as to be always clean from all dirt in any weather or season. . . .

"The walks may be covered with porticoes adorned with magnificent columns, statues, and sculptural works; all of vitrified substance, and lasting forever.   At night the roof and the inside and outside of the whole square are illuminated by gas-light, which, in the mazes of many-colored crystal-like colonnades and vaultings, is reflected with a brilliancy that gives to the whole a lustre of precious stones, as far as the eye can see. Such are the future abodes of men. . . . Such is the life reserved to true intelligence, but withheld from ignorance, prejudice, and stupid adherence to custom."

Thus is Paradise to be Regained, and that old and stern decree at length reversed. Man shall no more earn his living by the sweat of his brow. All labor shall be reduced to "a short turn of some crank," and "taking the finished articles away." But there is a crank, — oh, how hard to be turned! Could there not be a crank upon a crank, — an infinitely small crank? — we would fain inquire. No, — alas! not. But there is a certain divine energy in every man, but sparingly employed as yet, which may be called the crank within, — the crank after all, — the prime mover in all machinery, — quite indispensable to all work. Would that we might get our hands on its handle! In fact, no work can be shirked. It may be postponed indefinitely, but not infinitely. Nor can any really important work be made easier by coöperation or machinery. Not one particle of labor now threatening any man can be routed without being performed. It cannot be hunted out of the vicinity like jackals and hyenas. It will not run. You may begin by sawing the little sticks, or you may saw the great sticks first, but sooner or later you must saw them both.

We will not be imposed upon by this vast application of forces. We believe that most things will have to be accomplished still by the application called Industry. We are rather pleased after all to consider the small private, but both constant and accumulated force, which stands behind every spade in the field. This it is that makes the valleys shine, and the deserts really bloom. Sometimes, we confess, we are so degenerate as to reflect with pleasure on the days when men were yoked liked cattle, and drew a crooked stick for a plough. After all, the great interests and methods were the same.

It is a rather serious objection to Mr. Etzler's schemes, that they require time, men, and money, three very superfluous and inconvenient things for an honest and well-disposed man to deal with. "The whole world," he tells us, "might therefore be really changed into a paradise, within less than ten years, commencing from the first year of an association for the purpose of constructing and applying the machinery." We are sensible of a startling incongruity when time and money are mentioned in this connection. The ten years which are proposed would be a tedious while to wait, if every man were at his post and did his duty, but quite too short a period, if we are to take time for it. But this fault is by no means peculiar to Mr. Etzler's schemes. There is far too much hurry and bustle, and too little patience and privacy, in all our methods, as if something were to be accomplished in centuries. The true reformer does not want time, nor money, nor coöperation, nor advice. What is time but the stuff delay is made of? And depend upon it, our virtue will not live on the interest of our money. He expects no income, but outgoes; so soon as we begin to count the cost, the cost begins. And as for advice, the information floating in the atmosphere of society is as evanescent and unserviceable to him as gossamer for clubs of Hercules. There is absolutely no common sense; it is common nonsense. If we are to risk a cent or a drop of our blood, who then shall advise us? For ourselves, we are too young for experience. Who is old enough? We are older by faith than by experience. In the unbending of the arm to do the deed there is experience worth all the maxims in the world.

"It will now be plainly seen that the execution of the proposals is not proper for individuals.   Whether it be proper for government at this time, before the subject has become popular, is a question to be decided; all that is to be done is to step forth, after mature reflection, to confess loudly one's conviction, and to constitute societies.   Man is powerful but in union with many.   Nothing great, for the improvement of his own condition, or that of his fellowmen, can ever be effected by individual enterprise."

Alas! this is the crying sin of the age, this want of faith in the prevalence of a man.   Nothing can be effected but by one man.   He who wants help wants everything.   True, this is the condition of our weakness, but it can never be the means of our recovery.   We must first succeed alone, that we may enjoy our success together.   We trust that the social movements which we witness indicate an aspiration not to be thus cheaply satisfied.   In this matter of reforming the world, we have little faith in corporations; not thus was it first formed.

But our author is wise enough to say, that the raw materials for the accomplishment of his purposes are "iron, copper, wood, earth chiefly, and a union of men whose eyes and understanding are not shut up by preconceptions."   Ay, this last may be what we want mainly, — a company of "odd fellows" indeed.

"Small shares of twenty dollars will be sufficient," — in all, from "200,000 to 300,000,"
— "to create the first establishment for a whole
community of from 3,000 to 4,000 individuals,"
— at the end of five years we shall have a principal of 200 millions of dollars, and so paradise
will be wholly regained at the end of the tenth
year. But, alas! the ten years have already
elapsed, and there are no signs of Eden yet,
for want of the requisite funds to begin the enterprise in a hopeful manner. Yet it seems a
safe investment. Perchance they could be hired
at a low rate, the property being mortgaged for
security, and, if necessary, it could be given up
in any stage of the enterprise, without loss,
with the fixtures.

But we see two main difficulties in the way:
first, the successful application of the powers
by machinery (we have not yet seen the "Mechanical System"), and, secondly, which is infinitely harder, the application of man to the
work by faith. This it is, we fear, which will
prolong the ten years to ten thousand at least.
It will take a power more than "80,000 times
greater than all the men on earth could effect
with their nerves" to persuade men to use that
which is already offered them. Even a greater
than this physical power must be brought to
bear upon that moral power. Faith, indeed,

is all the reform that is needed; it is itself a reform. Doubtless, we are as slow to conceive of Paradise as of Heaven, of a perfect natural as of a perfect spiritual world. We see how past ages have loitered and erred. "Is perhaps our generation free from irrationality and error? Have we perhaps reached now the summit of human wisdom, and need no more to look out for mental or physical improvement?" Undoubtedly, we are never so visionary as to be prepared for what the next hour may bring forth.

Μέλλει τὸ θεῖον δ' ἔστι τοιοῦτον φύσει.

The Divine is about to be, and such is its nature. In our wisest moments we are secreting a matter, which, like the lime of the shellfish, incrusts us quite over, and well for us if, like it, we cast our shells from time to time, though they be pearl and of fairest tint. Let us consider under what disadvantages Science has hitherto labored before we pronounce thus confidently on her progress.

Mr. Etzler is not one of the enlightened practical men, the pioneers of the actual, who move with the slow, deliberate tread of science, conserving the world; who execute the dreams of the last century, though they have no dreams of their own; yet he deals in the very raw but

still solid material of all inventions. He has
more of the practical than usually belongs to
so bold a schemer, so resolute a dreamer. Yet
his success is in theory, and not in practice, and
he feeds our faith rather than contents our understanding. His book wants order, serenity,
dignity, everything, — but it does not fail to
impart what only man can impart to man of
much importance, his own faith. It is true his
dreams are not thrilling nor bright enough, and
he leaves off to dream where he who dreams
just before the dawn begins. His castles in
the air fall to the ground, because they are not
built lofty enough; they should be secured to
heaven's roof. After all, the theories and
speculations of men concern us more than their
puny accomplishment. It is with a certain
coldness and languor that we loiter about the
actual and so-called practical. How little do
the most wonderful inventions of modern times
detain us. They insult nature. Every machine, or particular application, seems a slight
outrage against universal laws. How many fine
inventions are there which do not clutter the
ground? We think that those only succeed
which minister to our sensible and animal
wants, which bake or brew, wash or warm, or
the like. But are those of no account which
are patented by fancy and imagination, and suc-

ceed so admirably in our dreams that they give the tone still to our waking thoughts? Already nature is serving all those uses which science slowly derives on a much higher and grander scale to him that will be served by her. When the sunshine falls on the path of the poet, he enjoys all those pure benefits and pleasures which the arts slowly and partially realize from age to age. The winds which fan his cheek waft him the sum of that profit and happiness which their lagging inventions supply.

The chief fault of this book is, that it aims to secure the greatest degree of gross comfort and pleasure merely. It paints a Mahometan's heaven, and stops short with singular abruptness when we think it is drawing near to the precincts of the Christian's, — and we trust we have not made here a distinction without a difference. Undoubtedly if we were to reform this outward life truly and thoroughly, we should find no duty of the inner omitted. It would be employment for our whole nature; and what we should do thereafter would be as vain a question as to ask the bird what it will do when its nest is built and its brood reared. But a moral reform must take place first, and then the necessity of the other will be superseded, and we shall sail and plough by its force alone. There is a speedier way than the "Mechanical

System " can show to fill up marshes, to drown
the roar of the waves, to tame hyenas, secure
agreeable environs, diversify the land, and re-
fresh it with "rivulets of sweet water," and
that is by the power of rectitude and true behavior. It is only for a little while, only occasionally, methinks, that we want a garden.
Surely a good man need not be at the labor to
level a hill for the sake of a prospect, or raise
fruits and flowers, and construct floating islands,
for the sake of a paradise. He enjoys better
prospects than lie behind any hill. Where an
angel travels it will be paradise all the way, but
where Satan travels it will be burning marl and
cinders. What says Veeshnoo Sarma? "He
whose mind is at ease is possessed of all riches.
Is it not the same to one whose foot is inclosed
in a shoe, as if the whole surface of the earth
were covered with leather?"

He who is conversant with the supernal powers will not worship these inferior deities of the
wind, waves, tide, and sunshine. But we would
not disparage the importance of such calculations
as we have described. They are truths in physics, because they are true in ethics. The moral
powers no one would presume to calculate. Suppose we could compare the moral with the physical, and say how many horse-power the force
of love, for instance, blowing on every square

foot of a man's soul, would equal. No doubt
we are well aware of this force; figures would
not increase our respect for it; the sunshine is
equal to but one ray of its heat. The light of
the sun is but the shadow of love. "The souls
of men loving and fearing God," says Raleigh,
"receive influence from that divine light itself,
whereof the sun's clarity, and that of the stars,
is by Plato called but a shadow. *Lumen est
umbra Dei, Deus est Lumen Luminis.* Light
is the shadow of God's brightness, who is the
light of light," and, we may add, the heat of
heat. Love is the wind, the tide, the waves,
the sunshine. Its power is incalculable; it is
many horse-power. It never ceases, it never
slacks; it can move the globe without a resting-
place; it can warm without fire; it can feed
without meat; it can clothe without garments;
it can shelter without roof; it can make a paradise within which will dispense with a paradise
without. But though the wisest men in all ages
have labored to publish this force, and every
human heart is, sooner or later, more or less,
made to feel it, yet how little is actually applied
to social ends. True, it is the motive-power of
all successful social machinery; but, as in physics, we have made the elements do only a little
drudgery for us, steam to take the place of a
few horses, wind of a few oars, water of a few

cranks and hand-mills; as the mechanical forces
have not yet been generously and largely applied
to make the physical world answer to the ideal,
so the power of love has been but meanly and
sparingly applied, as yet. It has patented
only such machines as the almshouse, the hospital, and the Bible Society, while its infinite
wind is still blowing, and blowing down these
very structures too, from time to time. Still
less are we accumulating its power, and prepar-
ing to act with greater energy at a future time.
Shall we not contribute our shares to this enterprise, then?

HERALD OF FREEDOM [1]

WE had occasionally, for several years, met
with a number of this spirited journal, edited,
as abolitionists need not to be informed, by
Nathaniel P. Rogers, once a counselor at law in
Plymouth, still farther up the Merrimack, but
now, in his riper years, come down the hills
thus far, to be the Herald of Freedom to these
parts. We had been refreshed not a little by
the cheap cordial of his editorials, flowing like
his own mountain-torrents, now clear and spar-
kling, now foaming and gritty, and always spiced
with the essence of the fir and the Norway pine;
but never dark nor muddy, nor threatening with
smothered murmurs, like the rivers of the plain.
The effect of one of his effusions reminds us of
what the hydropathists say about the electricity
in fresh spring-water, compared with that which
has stood over night, to suit weak nerves. We
do not know of another notable and public instance of such pure, youthful, and hearty indignation at all wrong. The Church itself must

[1] Herald of Freedom. Published weekly by the New
Hampshire Anti-Slavery Society, Concord, N. H., vol. x.
No. 4.

love it, if it have any heart, though he is said
to have dealt rudely with its sanctity. His
clean attachment to the right, however, sanctions the severest rebuke we have read.

Mr. Rogers seems to us to have occupied an
honorable and manly position in these days,
and in this country, making the press a living
and breathing organ to reach the hearts of men,
and not merely "fine paper and good type,"
with its civil pilot sitting aft, and magnan-
imously waiting for the news to arrive, — the
vehicle of the earliest news, but the *latest intelligence*, — recording the indubitable and last
results, the marriages and deaths, alone. This
editor was wide awake, and standing on the
beak of his ship; not as a scientific explorer
under government, but a Yankee sealer rather,
who makes those unexplored continents his
harbors in which to refit for more adventurous
cruises. He was a fund of news and freshness
in himself, — had the gift of speech, and the
knack of writing; and if anything important
took place in the Granite State, we might be
sure that we should hear of it in good season.
No other paper that we know kept pace so well
with one forward wave of the restless public
thought and sentiment of New England, and asserted so faithfully and ingenuously the largest
liberty in all things. There was beside more

unpledged poetry in his prose than in the
verses of many an accepted rhymer; and we
were occasionally advertised by a mellow hunter's note from his trumpet, that, unlike most
reformers, his feet were still where they should
be, on the turf, and that he looked out from a
serener natural life into the turbid arena of
politics. Nor was slavery always a sombre
theme with him, but invested with the colors of
his wit and fancy, and an evil to be abolished
by other means than sorrow and bitterness of
complaint. He will fight this fight with what
cheer may be.

But to speak of his composition. It is a
genuine Yankee style, without fiction, — real
guessing and calculating to some purpose, and
reminds us occasionally, as does all free, brave,
and original writing, of its great master in these
days, Thomas Carlyle. It has a life above
grammar, and a meaning which need not be
parsed to be understood. But like those same
mountain-torrents, there is rather too much
slope to his channel, and the rainbow sprays and
evaporations go double-quick time to heaven,
while the body of his water falls headlong to
the plain. We would have more pause and
deliberation, occasionally, if only to bring his
tide to a head, — more frequent expansions of
the stream, — still, bottomless, mountain tarns,

perchance inland seas, and at length the deep
ocean itself.

Some extracts will show in what sense he was
a poet as well as a reformer. He thus raises
the anti-slavery "war-whoop" in New Hampshire, when an important convention is to be
held, sending the summons, —

"To none but the whole-hearted, fully-com-
mitted, cross-the-Rubicon spirits. . . . From
rich 'old Cheshire,' from Rockingham, with her
horizon setting down away to the salt sea . . .
from where the sun sets behind Kearsarge, even
to where he rises gloriously over *Moses Norris's*
own town of *Pittsfield*, — and from Amoskeag
to Ragged Mountains, — Coos — Upper Coos,
home of the everlasting hills, — send out your
bold advocates of human rights, wherever they
lay, scattered by lonely lake, or Indian stream,
or 'Grant,' or 'Location,' from the trout-
haunted brooks of the Amoriscoggin, and where
the adventurous streamlet takes up its mountain
march for the St. Lawrence.

"Scattered and insulated men, wherever the
light of philanthropy and liberty has beamed in
upon your solitary spirits, come down to us like
your streams and clouds and our own Grafton,
all about among your dear hills, and your moun-
tain-flanked valleys — whether you *home* along
the swift Ammonoosuck, the cold Pemigewas-
sett, or the ox-bowed Connecticut. . . .

"We are slow, brethren, dishonorably slow, in a cause like ours. Our feet should be as 'hinds' feet.' 'Liberty lies bleeding.' The leaden-colored wing of slavery obscures the land with its baleful shadow. Let us come together, and inquire at the hand of the Lord what is to be done."

And again; on occasion of a New England Convention in the Second-Advent Tabernacle, in Boston, he desires to try one more blast, as it were, "on Fabyan's White Mountain horn:"—

"Ho, then, people of the Bay State, — men, women, and children; children, women, and men, scattered friends of the *friendless*, wheresoever ye inhabit, — if habitations ye have, as such friends have not *always*, — along the sea-beat border of Old Essex and the Puritan Landing, and up beyond sight of the sea-cloud, among the inland hills, where the sun rises and sets upon the dry land, in that vale of the Connecticut, too fair for human content and too fertile for virtuous industry, — where deepens the haughtiest of earth's streams, on its seaward way, proud with the pride of old Massachusetts. Are there any friends of the friendless negro haunting such a valley as this? In God's name, I fear there are none, or few; for the very scene looks apathy and oblivion to the genius of humanity. I blow you the summons, though. Come, if any of you are there.

"And gallant little Rhode Island; *transcendent* abolitionists of the tiny Commonwealth. I need not call you. You are *called* the year round, and, instead of sleeping in your tents, stand harnessed, and with trumpets in your hands, — every one!

"Connecticut! yonder, the home of the Burleighs, the Monroes, and the Hudsons, and the native land of old George Benson! are you ready? 'All ready!'

"Maine here, off east, looking from my mountain post like an everglade. Where is your Sam. Fessenden, who stood storm-proof 'gainst New Organization in '38. Has he too much name as a jurist and orator, to be found at a New England Convention in '43? God forbid! Come one and all of you from 'Down East' to Boston, on the 30th, and let the sails of your coasters whiten all the sea-road. Alas! there are scarce enough of you to man a fishing boat. Come up mighty in your fewness."

Such timely, pure, and unpremeditated expressions of a public sentiment, such publicity of genuine indignation and humanity, as abound everywhere in this journal, are the most generous gifts which a man can make.

WENDELL PHILLIPS BEFORE THE CONCORD LYCEUM

CONCORD, MASS., *March* 12, 1845.

MR. EDITOR: —

We have now, for the third winter, had our spirits refreshed, and our faith in the destiny of the Commonwealth strengthened, by the presence and the eloquence of Wendell Phillips; and we wish to tender to him our thanks and our sympathy. The admission of this gentleman into the Lyceum has been strenuously opposed by a respectable portion of our fellow-citizens, who themselves, we trust, — whose descendants, at least, we know, — will be as faithful conservers of the true order, whenever that shall be the order of the day, — and in each instance the people have voted that they *would hear him*, by coming themselves and bringing their friends to the lecture-room, and being very silent that they *might* hear. We saw some men and women, who had long ago *come out*, *going in* once more through the free and hospitable portals of the Lyceum; and many of our neighbors confessed that they had had a "sound season" this once.

It was the speaker's aim to show what the State, and above all the Church, had to do, and now, alas! have done, with Texas and slavery, and how much, on the other hand, the individual should have to do with Church and State. These were fair themes, and not mistimed, and his words were addressed to "fit audience, *and not* few."

We must give Mr. Phillips the credit of being a clean, erect, and what was once called a consistent man. He at least is not responsible for slavery, nor for American Independence; for the hypocrisy and superstition of the Church, nor the timidity and selfishness of the State; nor for the indifference and willing ignorance of any. He stands so distinctly, so firmly, and so effectively alone, and one honest man is so much more than a host, that we cannot but feel that he does himself injustice when he reminds us of "the American Society, which he represents." It is rare that we have the pleasure of listening to so clear and orthodox a speaker, who obviously has so few cracks or flaws in his moral nature, — who, having words at his command in a remarkable degree, has much more than words, if these should fail, in his unquestionable earnestness and integrity, — and, aside from their admiration at his rhetoric, secures the genuine respect of his audience. He unconsciously tells his biography as he proceeds, and we see him early and earnestly deliberating on these subjects, and wisely and bravely, without counsel or consent of any, occupying a ground at first from which the varying tides of public opinion cannot drive him.

No one could mistake the genuine modesty and truth with which he affirmed, when speaking of the framers of the Constitution, "I am wiser than they," who with him has improved these sixty years' experience of its working; or the uncompromising consistency and frankness of the prayer which concluded, not like the Thanksgiving proclamations, with — "God save the Commonwealth of Massachusetts," but — God dash it into a thousand pieces, till there shall not remain a fragment on which a man can stand, and dare not tell his name, — referring to the case of Frederick ———; to our disgrace we know not what to call him, unless Scotland will lend us the spoils of one of her Douglasses, out of history or fiction, for a season, till we be hospitable and brave enough to hear his proper name, — a fugitive slave in one more sense than we; who has proved himself the possessor of a *fair* intellect, and has won a colorless reputation in these parts; and who, we trust, will be as superior to degradation from the sympathies of Freedom, as from the antipa-

thies of Slavery. When, said Mr. Phillips, he
communicated to a New Bedford audience, the
other day, his purpose of writing his life, and
telling his name, and the name of his master,
and the place he ran from, the murmur ran
round the room, and was anxiously whispered
by the sons of the Pilgrims, "He had better
not!" and it was echoed under the shadow of
Concord monument, "He had better not!"

We would fain express our appreciation of
the freedom and steady wisdom, so rare in the
reformer, with which he declared that he was
not born to abolish slavery, but to do right.
We have heard a few, a very few, good political speakers, who afforded us the pleasure of
great intellectual power and acuteness, of sol-
dier-like steadiness, and of a graceful and natural oratory; but in this man the audience might
detect a sort of moral principle and integrity,
which was more stable than their firmness, more
discriminating than his own intellect, and more
graceful than his rhetoric, which was not working for temporary or trivial ends. It is so rare
and encouraging to listen to an orator who is
content with another alliance than with the
popular party, or even with the sympathizing
school of the martyrs, who can afford sometimes
to be his own auditor if the mob stay away, and
hears himself without reproof, that we feel ourselves in danger of slandering all mankind by

affirming that here is one who is at the same time an eloquent speaker and a righteous man.

Perhaps, on the whole, the most interesting fact elicited by these addresses, is the readiness of the people at large, of whatever sect or party, to entertain, with good will and hospitality, the most revolutionary and heretical opinions, when frankly and adequately, and in some sort cheerfully, expressed. Such clear and candid declaration of opinion served like an electuary to whet and clarify the intellect of all parties, and furnished each one with an additional argument for that right he asserted.

We consider Mr. Phillips one of the most conspicuous and efficient champions of a true Church and State now in the field, and would· say to him, and such as are like him, "God speed you." If you know of any champion in the ranks of his opponents, who has the valor and courtesy even of Paynim chivalry, if not the Christian graces and refinement of this knight, you will do us a service by directing him to these fields forthwith, where the lists are now open, and he shall be hospitably entertained. For as yet the Red-cross knight has shown us only the gallant device upon his shield, and his admirable command of his steed, prancing and curveting in the empty lists; but we wait to see who, in the actual breaking of lances, will come tumbling upon the plain.

THOMAS CARLYLE AND HIS WORKS

THOMAS CARLYLE is a Scotchman, born about fifty years ago, "at Ecclefechan, Annandale," according to one authority. "His parents 'good farmer people,' his father an elder in the Secession church there, and a man of strong native sense, whose words were said to 'nail a subject to the wall.'" We also hear of his "excellent mother," still alive, and of "her fine old covenanting accents, concerting with his transcendental tones." He seems to have gone to school at Annan, on the shore of the Solway Frith, and there, as he himself writes, "heard of famed professors, of high matters classical, mathematical, a whole Wonderland of Knowledge," from Edward Irving, then a young man "fresh from Edinburgh, with college prizes, . . . come to see our schoolmaster, who had also been his." From this place, they say, you can look over into Wordsworth's country. Here first he may have become acquainted with Nature, with woods, such as are there, and rivers and brooks, some of whose names we have heard, and the last lapses of Atlantic billows.

He got some of his education, too, more or less
liberal, out of the University of Edinburgh,
where, according to the same authority, he had
to "support himself," partly by "private tui-
tion, translations for the booksellers, etc.," and
afterward, as we are glad to hear, "taught an
academy in Dysart, at the same time that Irving
was teaching in Kirkaldy," the usual middle
passage of a literary life. He was destined for
the Church, but not by the powers that rule
man's life; made his literary *début* in Fraser's
Magazine, long ago; read here and there in
English and French, with more or less profit,
we may suppose, such of us at least as are not
particularly informed, and at length found some
words which spoke to his condition in the German language, and set himself earnestly to un-
ravel that mystery, — with what success many
readers know.

After his marriage he "resided partly at
Comely Bank, Edinburgh; and for a year or
two at Craigenputtock, a wild and solitary farm-
house in the upper part of Dumfriesshire," at
which last place, amid barren heather hills,
he was visited by our countryman, Emerson.
With Emerson he still corresponds. He was
early intimate with Edward Irving, and continued to be his friend until the latter's death.
Concerning this "freest, brotherliest, bravest

human soul," and Carlyle's relation to him,
those whom it concerns will do well to consult
a notice of his death in Fraser's Magazine for
1835, reprinted in the Miscellanies. He also
corresponded with Goethe. Latterly, we hear,
the poet Sterling was his only intimate acquaintance in England.

He has spent the last quarter of his life in
London, writing books; has the fame, as all
readers know, of having made England acquainted with Germany, in late years, and done
much else that is novel and remarkable in literature. He especially is the literary man of
those parts. You may imagine him living in
altogether a retired and simple way, with small
family, in a quiet part of London, called Chelsea, a little out of the din of commerce, in
"Cheyne Row," there, not far from the "Chelsea
Hospital." "A little past this, and an old ivy-
clad church, with its buried generations lying
around it," writes one traveler, "you come to
an antique street running at right angles with
the Thames, and, a few steps from the river,
you find Carlyle's name on the door." "A
Scotch lass ushers you into the second story
front chamber, which is the spacious workshop
of the world maker." Here he sits a long time
together, with many books and papers about
him; many new books, we have been told, on

the upper shelves, uncut, with the "author's respects" in them; in late months, with many manuscripts in an old English hand, and innumerable pamphlets, from the public libraries, relating to the Cromwellian period; now, perhaps, looking out into the street on brick and pavement, for a change, and now upon some rod of grass ground in the rear; or, perchance, he steps over to the British Museum, and makes that his studio for the time. This is the fore part of the day; that is the way with literary men commonly; and then in the afternoon, we presume, he takes a short run of a mile or so through the suburbs out into the country; we think he would run that way, though so short a trip might not take him to very sylvan or rustic places. In the mean while, people are calling to *see* him, from various quarters, few very worthy of being *seen* by him; "distinguished travelers from America," not a few; to all and sundry of whom he gives freely of his yet unwritten rich and flashing soliloquy, in exchange for whatever they may have to offer; speaking his English, as they say, with a "broad Scotch accent," talking, to their astonishment and to ours, very much as he writes, a sort of Carlylese, his discourse "coming to its climaxes, ever and anon, in long, deep, chest-shaking bursts of laughter."

He goes to Scotland sometimes, to visit his native heath-clad hills, having some interest still in the earth there; such names as Craigenputtock and Ecclefechan, which we have already quoted, stand for habitable places there to him; or he rides to the seacoast of England in his vacations, upon his horse Yankee, bought by the sale of his books here, as we have been told.

How, after all, he gets his living; what proportion of his daily bread he earns by day-labor or job-work with his pen, what he inherits, what steals, — questions whose answers are so significant, and not to be omitted in his biography, — we, alas! are unable to answer here. It may be worth the while to state that he is not a Reformer in our sense of the term, — eats, drinks, and sleeps, thinks and believes, professes and practices, not according to the New England standard, nor to the Old English wholly. Nevertheless, we are told that he is a sort of lion in certain quarters there, "an amicable centre for men of the most opposite opinions," and "listened to as an oracle," "smoking his perpetual pipe."

A rather tall, gaunt figure, with intent face, dark hair and complexion, and the air of a student; not altogether well in body, from sitting too long in his workhouse, — he, born in the border country and descended from moss-troop-

ers, it may be. We have seen several pictures
of him here; one, a full-length portrait, with
hat and overall, if it did not tell us much, told
the fewest lies; another, we remember, was well
said to have "too combed a look;" one other
also we have seen in which we discern some features of the man we are thinking of; but the
only ones worth remembering, after all, are
those which he has unconsciously drawn of himself.

When we remember how these volumes came
over to us, with their encouragement and provocation from month to month, and what com-
motion they created in many private breasts,
we wonder that the country did not ring, from
shore to shore, from the Atlantic to the Pacific,
with its greeting; and the Boones and Crockets
of the West make haste to hail him, whose wide
humanity embraces them too. Of all that the
packets have brought over to us, has there been
any richer cargo than this? What else has
been English news for so long a season? What
else, of late years, has been England to us, —
to us who read books, we mean? Unless we
remembered it as the scene where the age of
Wordsworth was spending itself, and a few
younger muses were trying their wings, and
from time to time as the residence of Landor,
Carlyle alone, since the death of Coleridge, has

kept the promise of England. It is the best apology for all the bustle and the sin of commerce, that it has made us acquainted with the thoughts of this man. Commerce would not concern us much if it were not for such results as this. New England owes him a debt which she will be slow to recognize. His earlier essays reached us at a time when Coleridge's were the only recent words which had made any notable impression so far, and they found a field unoccupied by him, before yet any words of moment had been uttered in our midst. He had this advantage, too, in a teacher, that he stood near to his pupils; and he has no doubt afforded reasonable encouragement and sympathy to many an independent but solitary thinker.

It is remarkable, but on the whole, perhaps, not to be lamented, that the world is so unkind to a new book. Any distinguished traveler who comes to our shores is likely to get more dinners and speeches of welcome than he can well dispose of, but the best books, if noticed at all, meet with coldness and suspicion, or, what is worse, gratuitous, off-hand criticism. It is plain that the reviewers, both here and abroad, do not know how to dispose of this man. They approach him too easily, as if he were one of the men of letters about town, who grace

Mr. Somebody's administration, merely; but
he already belongs to literature, and depends
neither on the favor of reviewers, nor the honesty of booksellers, nor the pleasure of readers
for his success. He has more to impart than
to receive from his generation. He is another
such a strong and finished workman in his craft
as Samuel Johnson was, and, like him, makes
the literary class respectable. Since few are
yet out of their apprenticeship, or, even if they
learn to be able writers, are at the same time
able and valuable thinkers. The aged and crit-
ical eye, especially, is incapacitated to appreciate the works of this author. To such their
meaning is impalpable and evanescent, and they
seem to abound only in obstinate mannerisms,
Germanisms, and whimsical ravings of all kinds,
with now and then an unaccountably true and
sensible remark. On the strength of this last,
Carlyle is admitted to have what is called genius. We hardly know an old man to whom
these volumes are not hopelessly sealed. The
language, they say, is foolishness and a stum-
bling-block to them; but to many a clear-headed
boy they are plainest English, and dispatched
with such hasty relish as his bread and milk.
The fathers wonder how it is that the children
take to this diet so readily, and digest it with
so little difficulty. They shake their heads with

mistrust at their free and easy delight, and remark that "Mr. Carlyle is a very learned man;"
for they, too, not to be out of fashion, have got
grammar and dictionary, if the truth were
known, and with the best faith cudgeled their
brains to get a little way into the jungle, and
they could not but confess, as often as they
found the clue, that it was as intricate as Black-
stone to follow, if you read it honestly. But
merely reading, even with the best intentions,
is not enough: you must almost have written
these books yourself. Only he who has had the
good fortune to read them in the nick of time,
in the most perceptive and recipient season of
life, can give any adequate account of them.

Many have tasted of this well with an odd
suspicion, as if it were some fountain Arethuse
which had flowed under the sea from Germany,
as if the materials of his books had lain in some
garret there, in danger of being appropriated
for waste-paper. Over what German ocean,
from what Hercynian forest, he has been imported, piecemeal, into England, or whether he
has now all arrived, we are not informed. This
article is not invoiced in Hamburg nor in London. Perhaps it was contraband. However,
we suspect that this sort of goods cannot be imported in this way. No matter how skillful the
stevedore, all things being got into sailing trim,

wait for a Sunday, and aft wind, and then
weigh anchor, and run up the main-sheet, —
straightway what of transcendent and perma-
nent value is there resists the aft wind, and will
doggedly stay behind that Sunday, — it does
not travel Sundays; while biscuit and pork
make headway, and sailors cry heave-yo! It
must part company, if it open a seam. It is
not quite safe to send out a venture in this kind,
unless yourself go supercargo. Where a man
goes, there he is; but the slightest virtue is immovable, — it is real estate, not personal; who
would keep it, must consent to be bought and
sold with it.

However, we need not dwell on this charge
of a German extraction, it being generally
admitted, by this time, that Carlyle is English,
and an inhabitant of London. He has the English for his mother-tongue, though with a Scotch
accent, or never so many accents, and thoughts
also, which are the legitimate growth of native
soil, to utter therewith. His style is eminently
colloquial, and no wonder it is strange to meet
with in a book. It is not literary or classical;
it has not the music of poetry, nor the pomp of
philosophy, but the rhythms and cadences of
conversation endlessly repeated. It resounds
with emphatic, natural, lively, stirring tones,
muttering, rattling, exploding, like shells and

shot, and with like execution. So far as it is a merit in composition, that the written answer to the spoken word, and the spoken word to a fresh and pertinent thought in the mind, as well as to the half thoughts, the tumultuary misgivings and expectancies, this author is, perhaps, not to be matched in literature.

He is no mystic, either, more than Newton or Arkwright or Davy, and tolerates none. Not one obscure line, or half line, did he ever write. His meaning lies plain as the daylight, and he who runs may read; indeed, only he who runs *can* read, and keep up with the meaning. It has the distinctness of picture to his mind, and he tells us only what he sees printed in largest English type upon the face of things. He utters substantial English thoughts in plainest English dialects; for it must be confessed, he speaks more than one of these. All the shires of England, and all the shires of Europe, are laid under contribution to his genius; for to be English does not mean to be exclusive and narrow, and adapt one's self to the apprehension of his nearest neighbor only. And yet no writer is more thoroughly Saxon. In the translation of those fragments of Saxon poetry, we have met with the same rhythm that occurs so often in his poem on the French Revolution. And if you would know where many of those

obnoxious Carlyleisms and Germanisms came
from, read the best of Milton's prose, read those
speeches of Cromwell which he has brought to
light, or go and listen once more to your
mother's tongue. So much for his German
extraction.

Indeed, for fluency and skill in the use of
the English tongue, he is a master unrivaled.
His felicity and power of expression surpass
even his special merits as historian and critic.
Therein his experience has not failed him, but
furnished him with such a store of winged, ay
and legged words, as only a London life, perchance, could give account of. We had not
understood the wealth of the language before.
Nature is ransacked, and all the resorts and
purlieus of humanity are taxed, to furnish the
fittest symbol for his thought. He does not go
to the dictionary, the word-book, but to the
word-manufactory itself, and has made endless
work for the lexicographers. Yes, he has that
same English for his mother-tongue that you
have, but with him it is no dumb, muttering,
mumbling faculty, concealing the thoughts, but
a keen, unwearied, resistless weapon. He has
such command of it as neither you nor I have;
and it would be well for any who have a lost
horse to advertise, or a town-meeting warrant,
or a sermon, or a letter to write, to study this

universal letter-writer, for he knows more than
the grammar or the dictionary.

The style is worth attending to, as one of the
most important features of the man which we at
this distance can discern. It is for once quite
equal to the matter. It can carry all its load,
and never breaks down nor staggers. His
books are solid and workmanlike, as all that
England does; and they are graceful and readable also. They tell of huge labor done, well
done, and all the rubbish swept away, like the
bright cutlery which glitters in shop windows,
while the coke and ashes, the turnings, filings,
dust, and borings lie far away at Birmingham,
unheard of. He is a masterly clerk, scribe,
reporter, writer. He can reduce to writing
most things, — gestures, winks, nods, significant
looks, patois, brogue, accent, pantomime, and
how much that had passed for silence before
does he represent by written words. The countryman who puzzled the city lawyer, requiring
him to write, among other things, his call to
his horses, would hardly have puzzled him; he
would have found a word for it, all right and
classical, that would have started his team for
him. Consider the ceaseless tide of speech forever flowing in countless cellars, garrets, *par-
lors;* that of the French, says Carlyle, "only
ebbs toward the short hours of night," and what

a drop in the bucket is the printed word. Feeling, thought, speech, writing, and, we might add, poetry, inspiration, — for so the circle is completed; how they gradually dwindle at length, passing through successive colanders, into your history and classics, from the roar of the ocean, the murmur of the forest, to the squeak of a mouse; so much only parsed and spelt out, and punctuated, at last. The few who can talk like a book, they only get reported commonly. But this writer reports a new "Lieferung."

One wonders how so much, after all, was expressed in the old way, so much here depends upon the emphasis, tone, pronunciation, style, and spirit of the reading. No writer uses so profusely all the aids to intelligibility which the printer's art affords. You wonder how others had contrived to write so many pages without emphatic or italicized words, they are so expressive, so natural, so indispensable here, as if none had ever used the demonstrative pronouns demonstratively before. In another's sentences the thought, though it may be immortal, is as it were embalmed, and does not *strike* you, but here it is so freshly living, even the body of it not having passed through the ordeal of death, that it stirs in the very extremities, and the smallest particles and pronouns are all alive with it. It is not simple dictionary *it*, yours or mine, but IT. The words did not come at the command of grammar, but of a tyrannous, inexorable meaning; not like standing soldiers, by vote of Parliament, but any able-bodied countryman pressed into the service, for "Sire, it is not a revolt, it is a revolution."

We have never heard him speak, but we should say that Carlyle was a rare talker. He has broken the ice, and streams freely forth like a spring torrent. He does not trace back the stream of his thought, silently adventurous, up to its fountain-head, but is borne away with it, as it rushes through his brain like a torrent to overwhelm and fertilize. He holds a talk with you. His audience is such a tumultuous mob of thirty thousand as assembled at the University of Paris, before printing was invented. Philosophy, on the other hand, does not talk, but write, or, when it comes personally before an audience, lecture or read; and therefore it must be read to-morrow, or a thousand years hence. But the talker must naturally be attended to at once; he does not talk on without an audience; the winds do not long bear the sound of his voice. Think of Carlyle reading his French Revolution to any audience. One might say it was never written, but spoken; and thereafter reported and printed, that those not within sound of his voice might know something about it. Some men read to you something which they have written in a dead *language*, of course, but it may be in a living *letter*, in a Syriac, or Roman, or Runic character. Men must *speak* English who can *write* Sanskrit; they must speak a modern language who write, perchance, an ancient and universal one. We do not live in those days when the learned used a learned language. There is no writing of Latin with Carlyle; but as Chaucer, with all reverence to Homer, and Virgil, and Messieurs the Normans, sung his poetry in the homely Saxon tongue, — and Locke has at least the merit of having done philosophy into English, — so Carlyle has done a different philosophy still further into English, and thrown open the doors of literature and criticism to the populace.

Such a style, — so diversified and variegated! It is like the face of a country; it is like a New England landscape, with farm-houses and villages, and cultivated spots, and belts of forests and blueberry-swamps round about, with the fragrance of shad-blossoms and violets on certain winds. And as for the reading of it, it is novel enough to the reader who has used only the diligence, and old line mail-coach. It is like traveling, sometimes on foot, sometimes in a gig tandem; sometimes in a full coach, over highways, mended and unmended, for which you will prosecute the town; on level roads, through French departments, by Simplon roads over the Alps, and now and then he hauls up for a relay, and yokes in an unbroken colt of a Pegasus for a leader, driving off by cart-paths, and across lots, by corduroy roads and gridiron bridges; and where the bridges are gone, not even a string-piece left, and the reader has to set his breast and swim. You have got an expert driver this time, who has driven ten thousand miles, and was never known to upset; can drive six in hand on the edge of a precipice, and touch the leaders anywhere with his snapper.

With wonderful art he grinds into paint for his picture all his moods and experiences, so that all his forces may be brought to the encounter. Apparently writing without a particular design or responsibility, setting down his soliloquies from time to time, taking advantage of all his humors, when at length the hour comes to declare himself, he puts down in plain English, without quotation marks, what he, Thomas Carlyle, is ready to defend in the face of the world, and fathers the rest, often quite as defensible, only more modest, or plain spoken, or insinuating, upon "Sauerteig," or

some other gentleman long employed on the
subject.   Rolling his subject how many ways
in his mind, he meets it now face to face, wres-
tling with it at arm's length, and striving to get
it down, or throw it over his head; and if that
will not do, or whether it will do or not, tries
the back-stitch and side-hug with it, and downs
it again, scalps it, draws and quarters it, hangs
it in chains, and leaves it to the winds and dogs.
With his brows knit, his mind made up, his
will resolved and resistless, he advances, crashing his way through the host of weak, half-
formed, *dilettante* opinions, honest and dis-
honest ways of thinking, with their standards
raised, sentimentalities and conjectures, and
tramples them all into dust.   See how he prevails; you don't even hear the groans of the
wounded and dying.   Certainly it is not so well
worth the while to look through any man's eyes
at history, for the time, as through his; and
his way of looking at things is fastest getting
adopted by his generation.

It is not in man to determine what his style
shall be.   He might as well determine what his
thoughts shall be.   We would not have had
him write always as in the chapter on Burns,
and the Life of Schiller, and elsewhere.   No;
his thoughts were ever irregular and impetuous.
Perhaps as he grows older and writes more

he acquires a truer expression; it is in some respects manlier, freer, struggling up to a level with its fountain-head. We think it is the richest prose style we know of.

Who cares what a man's style is, so it is intelligible, — as intelligible as his thought. Literally and really, the style is no more than the *stylus*, the pen he writes with; and it is not worth scraping and polishing, and gilding, unless it will write his thoughts the better for it. It is something for use, and not to look at. The question for us is, not whether Pope had a fine style, wrote with a peacock's feather, but whether he uttered useful thoughts. Translate a book a dozen times from one language to another, and what becomes of its style? Most books would be worn out and disappear in this ordeal. The pen which wrote it is soon destroyed, but the poem survives. We believe that Carlyle has, after all, more readers, and is better known to-day for this very originality of style, and that posterity will have reason to thank him for emancipating the language, in some measure, from the fetters which a merely conservative, aimless, and pedantic literary class had imposed upon it, and setting an example of greater freedom and naturalness. No man's thoughts are new, but the style of their expression is the never-failing novelty which cheers and refreshes men. If we were to answer the question, whether the mass of men, as we know them, talk as the standard authors and reviewers write, or rather as this man writes, we should say that he alone begins to write their language at all, and that the former is, for the most part, the mere effigies of a language, not the best method of concealing one's thoughts even, but frequently a method of doing without thoughts at all.

In his graphic description of Richter's style, Carlyle describes his own pretty nearly; and no doubt he first got his own tongue loosened at that fountain, and was inspired by it to equal freedom and originality. "The language," as he says of Richter, "groans with indescribable metaphors and allusions to all things, human and divine, flowing onward, not like a river, but like an inundation; circling in complex eddies, chafing and gurgling, now this way, now that;" but in Carlyle, "the proper current" never "sinks out of sight amid the boundless uproar." Again: "His very language is Titanian, — deep, strong, tumultuous, shining with a thousand hues, fused from a thousand elements, and winding in labyrinthic mazes."

In short, if it is desirable that a man be eloquent, that he talk much, and address himself to his own age mainly, then this is not a bad style of doing it. But if it is desired rather that he pioneer into unexplored regions of thought, and speak to silent centuries to come, then, indeed, we could wish that he had cultivated the style of Goethe more, that of Richter less; not that Goethe's is the kind of utterance most to be prized by mankind, but it will serve for a model of the best that can be successfully cultivated.

But for style, and fine writing, and Augustan ages, that is but a poor style, and vulgar writing, and a degenerate age, which allows us to remember these things. This man has something to communicate. Carlyle's are not, in the common sense, works of art in their origin and aim; and yet, perhaps, no living English writer evinces an equal literary talent. They are such works of art only as the plough and corn-mill and steam-engine, — not as pictures and statues. Others speak with greater emphasis to scholars, as such, but none so earnestly and effectually to all who can read. Others give their advice, he gives his sympathy also. It is no small praise that he does not take upon himself the airs, has none of the whims, none of the pride, the nice vulgarities, the starched, impoverished isolation, and cold glitter of the spoiled children of genius. He does not need to husband his pearl, but excels by a greater humanity and sincerity.

He is singularly serious and untrivial. We are everywhere impressed by the rugged, unwearied, and rich sincerity of the man. We are sure that he never sacrificed one jot of his honest thought to art or whim, but to utter himself in the most direct and effectual way, — that is the endeavor. These are merits which will wear well. When time has worn deeper into the substance of these books, this grain will appear. No such sermons have come to us here out of England, in late years, as those of this preacher, — sermons to kings, and sermons to peasants, and sermons to all intermediate classes. It is in vain that John Bull, or any of his cousins, turns a deaf ear, and pretends not to hear them: nature will not soon be weary of repeating them. There are words less obviously true, more for the ages to hear, perhaps, but none so impossible for this age not to hear. What a cutting cimeter was that "Past and Present," going through heaps of silken stuffs, and glibly through the necks of men, too, without their knowing it, leaving no trace. He has the earnestness of a prophet. In an age of pedantry and dilettantism, he has no grain of these in his composition. There is nowhere else, surely, in recent readable English, or other books, such direct and effectual teaching, reproving, encouraging, stimulating, earnestly, vehemently, almost like Mahomet, like Luther; not looking behind him to see how his *Opera Omnia* will look, but forward to other work to be done. His writings are a gospel to the young of this generation; they will hear his manly, brotherly speech with responsive joy, and press forward to older or newer gospels.

We should omit a main attraction in these books, if we said nothing of their humor. Of this indispensable pledge of sanity, without some leaven of which the abstruse thinker may justly be suspected of mysticism, fanaticism, or insanity, there is a superabundance in Carlyle. Especially the transcendental philosophy needs the leaven of humor to render it light and digestible. In his later and longer works it is an unfailing accompaniment, reverberating through pages and chapters, long sustained without effort. The very punctuation, the italics, the quotation marks, the blank spaces and dashes, and the capitals, each and all are pressed into its service.

Carlyle's humor is vigorous and Titanic, and has more sense in it than the sober philosophy of many another. It is not to be disposed of by laughter and smiles merely; it gets to be too serious for that: only they may laugh who are not hit by it. For those who love a merry jest,

this is a strange kind of fun, — rather too practical joking, if they understand it. The pleasant humor which the public loves is but the
innocent pranks of the ballroom, harmless flow
of animal spirits, the light plushy pressure of
dandy pumps, in comparison. But when an
elephant takes to treading on your corns, why
then you are lucky if you sit high, or wear cow-
hide. His humor is always subordinate to a
serious purpose, though often the real charm
for the reader is not so much in the essential
progress and final upshot of the chapter as in
this indirect side-light illustration of every hue.
He sketches first, with strong, practical English
pencil, the essential features in outline, black
on white, more faithfully than Dryasdust would
have done, telling us wisely whom and what
to mark, to save time, and then with brush of
camel's hair, or sometimes with more expedi-
tious swab, he lays on the bright and fast colors
of his humor everywhere. One piece of solid
work, be it known, we have determined to do,
about which let there be no jesting, but all
things else under the heavens, to the right and
left of that, are for the time fair game. To us
this humor is not wearisome, as almost every
other is. Rabelais, for instance, is intolerable;
one chapter is better than a volume, — it may
be sport to him, but it is death to us. A mere

humorist, indeed, is a most unhappy man; and his readers are most unhappy also.

Humor is not so distinct a quality as, for the purposes of criticism, it is commonly regarded, but allied to every, even the divinest faculty. The familiar and cheerful conversation about every hearthside, if it be analyzed, will be found to be sweetened by this principle. There is not only a never-failing, pleasant, and earnest humor kept up there, embracing the domestic affairs, the dinner, and the scolding, but there is also a constant run upon the neighbors. and upon Church and State, and to cherish and maintain this, in a great measure, the fire is kept burning, and the dinner provided. There will be neighbors, parties to a very genuine, even romantic friendship, whose whole audible salutation and intercourse, abstaining from the usual cordial expressions, grasping of hands, or affectionate farewells, consists in the mutual play and interchange of a genial and healthy humor, which excepts nothing, not even themselves, in its lawless range. The child plays continually, if you will let it, and all its life is a sort of practical humor of a very pure kind, often of so fine and ethereal a nature, that its parents, its uncles and cousins, can in no wise participate in it, but must stand aloof in silent admiration, and reverence even. The more quiet the more profound it is. Even Nature is observed to have her playful moods or aspects, of which man seems sometimes to be the sport.

But, after all, we could sometimes dispense with the humor, though unquestionably incorporated in the blood, if it were replaced by this author's gravity. We should not apply to himself, without qualification, his remarks on the humor of Richter. With more repose in his inmost being, his humor would become more thoroughly genial and placid. Humor is apt to imply but a half satisfaction at best. In his pleasantest and most genial hour, man smiles but as the globe smiles, and the works of nature. The fruits *dry* ripe, and much as we relish some of them in their green and pulpy state, we lay up for our winter store, not out of these, but the rustling autumnal harvests. Though we never weary of this vivacious wit, while we are perusing its work, yet when we remember it from afar, we sometimes feel balked and disappointed, missing the security, the simplicity, and frankness, even the occasional magnanimity of acknowledged dullness and bungling. This never-failing success and brilliant talent become a reproach.

Besides, humor does not wear well. It is commonly enough said, that a joke will not bear repeating. The deepest humor will not keep.

Humors do not circulate but stagnate, or circulate partially. In the oldest literature, in the Hebrew, the Hindoo, the Persian, the Chinese, it is rarely humor, even the most divine, which still survives, but the most sober and private, painful or joyous thoughts, maxims of duty, to which the life of all men may be referred. After time has sifted the literature of a people, there is left only their SCRIPTURE, for that is WRITING, *par excellence*. This is as true of the poets, as of the philosophers and moralists by profession; for what subsides in any of these is the moral only, to reappear as dry land at some remote epoch.

We confess that Carlyle's humor is rich, deep, and variegated, in direct communication with the backbone and risible muscles of the globe, — and there is nothing like it; but much as we relish this jovial, this rapid and delugeous way of conveying one's views and impressions, when we would not converse but meditate, we pray for a man's diamond edition of his thought, without the colored illuminations in the margin, — the fishes and dragons and unicorns, the red or the blue ink, but its initial letter in distinct skeleton type, and the whole so clipped and condensed down to the very essence of it, that time will have little to do. We know not but we shall immigrate soon, and would fain take with us all the treasures of the East; and all kinds of *dry*, portable soups, in small tin canisters, which contain whole herds of English beeves boiled down, will be acceptable.

The difference between this flashing, fitful writing and pure philosophy is the difference between flame and light. The flame, indeed, yields light; but when we are so near as to observe the flame, we are apt to be incommoded by the heat and smoke. But the sun, that old Platonist, is set so far off in the heavens, that only a genial summer-heat and ineffable daylight can reach us. But many a time, we confess, in wintry weather, we have been glad to forsake the sunlight, and warm us by these Promethean flames. Carlyle must undoubtedly plead guilty to the charge of mannerism. He not only has his vein, but his peculiar manner of working it. He has a style which can be imitated, and sometimes is an imitator of himself.

Certainly, no critic has anywhere said what is more to the purpose, than this which Carlyle's own writings furnish, which we quote, as well for its intrinsic merit as for its pertinence here. "It is true," says he, thinking of Richter, "the beaten paths of literature lead the safeliest to the goal; and the talent pleases us most which submits to shine with new gracefulness through old forms. Nor is the noblest and most pecu-

liar mind too noble or peculiar for working by
prescribed laws; Sophocles, Shakespeare, Cer-
vantes, and, in Richter's own age, Goethe, how
little did they innovate on the given forms of
composition, how much in the spirit they
breathed into them! All this is true; and
Richter must lose of our esteem in proportion."
And again, in the chapter on Goethe, "We
read Goethe for years before we come to see
wherein the distinguishing peculiarity of his
understanding, of his disposition, even of his
way of writing, consists! It seems quite a simple style, [that of his?] remarkable chiefly for
its calmness, its perspicuity, in short, its com-
monness; and yet it is the most uncommon of
all styles." And this, too, translated for us by
the same pen from Schiller, which we will apply
not merely to the outward form of his works,
but to their inner form and substance. He is
speaking of the artist. "Let some beneficent
divinity snatch him, when a suckling, from the
breast of his mother, and nurse him with the
milk of a better time, that he may ripen to his
full stature beneath a distant Grecian sky.
And having grown to manhood, let him return,
a foreign shape, into his century; not, however, to delight it by his presence, but, dread-
ful, like the son of Agamemnon, to purify it.
The matter of his works he will take from the

present, but their form he will derive from a nobler time; nay, from beyond all time, from the absolute unchanging unity of his own nature."

But enough of this. Our complaint is already out of all proportion to our discontent.

Carlyle's works, it is true, have not the stereotyped success which we call classic. They are a rich but inexpensive entertainment, at which we are not concerned lest the host has strained or impoverished himself to feed his guests. It is not the most lasting word, nor the loftiest wisdom, but rather the word which comes last. For his genius it was reserved to give expression to the thoughts which were throbbing in a million breasts. He has plucked the ripest fruit in the public garden; but this fruit already least concerned the tree that bore it, which was rather perfecting the bud at the foot of the leaf-stalk. His works are not to be studied, but read with a swift satisfaction. Their flavor and gust is like what poets tell of the froth of wine, which can only be tasted once and hastily. On a review we can never find the pages we had read. Yet they are in some degree true natural products in this respect. All things are but once, and never repeated. These works were designed for such complete success that they serve but for a single occasion.

But he is willfully and pertinaciously unjust, even scurrilous, impolite, ungentlemanly; calls us "Imbeciles," "Dilettants," "Philistines," implying sometimes what would not sound well expressed. If he would adopt the newspaper style, and take back these hard names — But where is the reader who does not derive some benefit from these epithets, applying them to himself?

He is, in fact, the best tempered, and not the least impartial of reviewers. He goes out of his way to do justice to profligates and quacks. There is somewhat even Christian, in the rarest and most peculiar sense, in his universal brotherliness, his simple, child-like endurance, and earnest, honest endeavor, with sympathy for the like. Carlyle, to adopt his own classification, is himself the hero as literary man. There is no more notable workingman in England, in Manchester or Birmingham, or the mines round about. We know not how many hours a day he toils, nor for what wages, exactly: we only know the results for us.

Notwithstanding the very genuine, admirable, and loyal tributes to Burns, Schiller, Goethe, and others, Carlyle is not a critic of poetry. In the book of heroes, Shakespeare, the hero as poet, comes off rather slimly. His sympathy, as we said, is with the men of endeavor; not using the life got, but still bravely getting their life. "In fact," as he says of Cromwell, "everywhere we have to notice the decisive practical *eye* of this man, how he drives toward the practical and practicable; has a genuine insight into what *is* fact." You must have very stout legs to get noticed at all by him. He is thoroughly English in his love of practical men, and dislike for cant, and ardent enthusiastic heads that are not supported by any legs. He would kindly knock them down that they may regain some vigor by touching their mother earth. We have often wondered how he ever found out Burns, and must still refer a good share of his delight in him to neighborhood and early association. The Lycidas and Comus, appearing in Blackwood's Magazine, would probably go unread by him, nor lead him to expect a Paradise Lost. The condition-of-England question is a practical one. The condition of England demands a hero, not a poet. Other things demand a poet; the poet answers other demands. Carlyle in London, with this question pressing on him so urgently, sees no occasion for minstrels and rhapsodists there. Kings may have their bards when there are any kings. Homer would *certainly* go a-begging there. He lives in Chelsea, not on the plains of Hindostan, nor on the prairies of the West, where settlers are scarce, and a man must at least go *whistling* to himself.

What he says of poetry is rapidly uttered, and suggestive of a thought, rather than the deliberate development of any. He answers your question, What is poetry? by writing a special poem, as that Norse one, for instance, in the Book of Heroes, altogether wild and original; — answers your question, What is light? by kindling a blaze which dazzles you, and pales sun and moon, and not as a peasant might, by opening a shutter.

Carlyle is not a *seer*, but a brave looker-on and *reviewer;* not the most free and catholic observer of men and events, for they are likely to find him preoccupied, but unexpectedly free and catholic when they fall within the focus of his lens. He does not live in the present hour, and read men and books as they occur for his theme, but having chosen this, he directs his studies to this end. If we look again at his page, we are apt to retract somewhat that we have said. Often a genuine poetic feeling dawns through it, like the texture of the earth seen through the dead grass and leaves in the spring. The History of the French Revolution is a poem, at length translated into prose, — an Iliad, indeed, as he himself has it, — "The destructive wrath of Sansculotism, this is what

we speak, having unhappily no voice for singing."

One improvement we could suggest in this
last, as indeed in most epics, — that he should
let in the sun oftener upon his picture. It does
not often enough appear, but it is all revolution, the old way of human life turned simply
bottom upward, so that when at length we
are inadvertently reminded of the "Brest Ship-
ping," a St. Domingo colony, and that anybody
thinks of owning plantations, and simply turning
up the soil there, and that now at length, after
some years of this revolution, there is a falling off in the importation of sugar, we feel a
queer surprise. Had they not sweetened their
water with revolution then? It would be well if
there were several chapters headed "Work for
the Month," — Revolution-work inclusive, of
course, — "Altitude of the Sun," "State of the
Crops and Markets," "Meteorological Observations," "Attractive Industry," "Day Labor,"
etc., just to remind the reader that the French
peasantry did something beside go without
breeches, burn châteaus, get ready knotted
cords, and embrace and throttle one another by
turns. These things are sometimes hinted at,
but they deserve a notice more in proportion to
their importance. We want not only a back-
ground to the picture, but a ground under the

feet also. We remark, too, occasionally, an
unphilosophical habit, common enough elsewhere, in Alison's History of Modern Europe,
for instance, of saying, undoubtedly with effect,
that if a straw had not fallen this way or that,
why then — but, of course, it is as easy in philosophy to make kingdoms rise and fall as
straws.

The poet is blithe and cheery ever, and as
well as nature. Carlyle has not the simple
Homeric health of Wordsworth, nor the deliberate philosophic turn of Coleridge, nor the
scholastic taste of Landor, but, though sick and
under restraint, the constitutional vigor of one
of his old Norse heroes, struggling in a lurid
light, with Jötuns still, striving to throw the
old woman, and "she was Time," — striving to
lift the big cat, and that was "the Great World-
Serpent, which, tail in mouth, girds and keeps
up the whole created world." The smith,
though so brawny and tough, I should not call
the healthiest man. There is too much shop-
work, too great extremes of heat and cold, and
incessant ten-pound-ten and thrashing of the
anvil, in his life. But the haymaker's is a true
sunny perspiration, produced by the extreme of
summer heat only, and conversant with the
blast of the zephyr, not of the forge-bellows.
We know very well the nature of this man's

sadness, but we do not know the nature of his gladness.

The poet will maintain serenity in spite of all disappointments. He is expected to preserve an unconcerned and healthy outlook over the world, while he lives. *Philosophia practica est eruditionis meta*, — Philosophy practiced is the goal of learning; and for that other, *Oratoris est celare artem*, we might read, *Herois est celare pugnam*, — the hero will conceal his struggles. Poetry is the only life got, the only work done, the only pure product and free labor of man, performed only when he has put all the world under his feet, and conquered the last of his foes.

Carlyle speaks of Nature with a certain unconscious pathos for the most part. She is to him a receded but ever memorable splendor, casting still a reflected light over all his scenery. As we read his books here in New England, where there are potatoes enough, and every man can get his living peacefully and sportively as the birds and bees, and need think no more of that, it seems to us as if by the world he often meant London, at the head of the tide upon the Thames, the sorest place on the face of the earth, the very citadel of conservatism.

In his writings, we should say that he, as conspicuously as any, though with little enough expressed or even conscious sympathy, represents the Reformer class, and all the better for not being the acknowledged leader of any. In him the universal plaint is most settled, unappeasable, and serious. Until a thousand named and nameless grievances are righted, there will be no repose for him in the lap of nature, or the seclusion of science and literature. By foreseeing it, he hastens the crisis in the affairs of England, and is as good as many years added to her history.

To do himself justice, and set some of his readers right, he should give us some transcendent hero at length, to rule his demigods and Titans; develop, perhaps, his reserved and dumb reverence for Christ, not speaking to a London or Church of England audience merely. Let *not* "sacred silence meditate that sacred matter" forever, but let us have sacred speech and sacred scripture thereon.

Every man will include in his list of worthies those whom he himself best represents. Carlyle, and our countryman Emerson, whose place and influence must erelong obtain a more distinct recognition, are, to a certain extent, the complement of each other. The age could not do with one of them, it cannot do with both. To make a broad and rude distinction, to suit our present purpose, the former, as critic, deals with the men of action, — Mahomet, Luther, Cromwell; the latter with the thinkers, — Plato, Shakespeare, Goethe; for, though both have written upon Goethe, they do not meet in him. The one has more sympathy with the heroes, or practical reformers, the other with the observers, or philosophers. Put their worthies together, and you will have a pretty fair representation of mankind; yet with one or more memorable exceptions. To say nothing of Christ, who yet awaits a just appreciation from literature, the peacefully practical hero, whom Columbus may represent, is obviously slighted; but above and after all, the Man of the Age, come to be called workingman, it is obvious that none yet speaks to his condition, for the speaker is not yet in his condition.

Like speaks to like only; labor to labor, philosophy to philosophy, criticism to criticism, poetry to poetry. Literature speaks how much still to the past, how little to the future, how much to the East, how little to the West, —

> In the East fames are won,
> In the West deeds are done.

One merit in Carlyle, let the subject be what it may, is the freedom of prospect he allows, the entire absence of cant and dogma. He removes many cart-loads of rubbish, and leaves open a broad highway. His writings are all

unfenced on the side of the future and the possible.   Though he does but inadvertently direct
our eyes to the open heavens, nevertheless he
lets us wander broadly underneath, and shows
them to us reflected in innumerable pools and
lakes.

These volumes contain not the highest, but
a very practicable wisdom, which startles and
provokes, rather than informs us.   Carlyle does
not oblige us to think; we have thought enough
for him already, but he compels us to act.   We
accompany him rapidly through an endless gallery of pictures, and glorious reminiscences of
experiences unimproved.   " If they hear not
Moses and the prophets, neither will they be
persuaded, though one rose from the dead."
There is no calm philosophy of life here, such as
you might put at the end of the Almanac, to
hang over the farmer's hearth, how men shall
live in these winter, in these summer days.   No
philosophy, properly speaking, of love, or
friendship, or religion, or politics, or education,
or nature, or spirit; perhaps a nearer approach
to a philosophy of kingship, and of the place of
the literary man, than of anything else.   A
rare preacher, with prayer, and psalm, and sermon, and benediction, but no contemplation of
man's life from the serene oriental ground, nor

yet from the stirring occidental. No thanksgiving sermon for the holydays, or the Easter vacations, when all men submit to float on the full currents of life. When we see with what spirits, though with little heroism enough, woodchoppers, drovers, and apprentices take and spend life, playing all day long, sunning themselves, shading themselves, eating, drinking, sleeping, we think that the philosophy of their life written would be such a level natural history as the Gardener's Calendar and the works of the early botanists, inconceivably slow to come to practical conclusions.

There is no philosophy here for philosophers, only as every man is said to have his philosophy. No system but such as is the man himself; and, indeed, he stands compactly enough; no progress beyond the first assertion and challenge, as it were, with trumpet blast. One thing is certain, — that we had best be doing something in good earnest henceforth forever; that's an indispensable philosophy. The before impossible precept, "*know thyself*," he translates into the partially possible one, "*know what thou canst work at.*" Sartor Resartus is, perhaps, the sunniest and most philosophical, as it is the most autobiographical of his works, in which he drew most largely on the experience of his youth. But we miss everywhere a calm depth, like a lake, even stagnant, and must submit to rapidity and whirl, as on skates, with all kinds of skillful and antic motions, sculling, sliding, cutting punch-bowls and rings, forward and backward. The talent is very nearly equal to the genius. Sometimes it would be preferable to wade slowly through a Serbonian bog, and feel the juices of the meadow.

Beside some philosophers of larger vision, Carlyle stands like an honest, half-despairing boy, grasping at some details only of their world systems. Philosophy, certainly, is some account of truths, the fragments and very insignificant parts of which man will practice in this workshop; truths infinite and in harmony with infinity, in respect to which the very objects and ends of the so-called practical philosopher will be mere propositions, like the rest. It would be no reproach to a philosopher, that he knew the future better than the past, or even than the present. It is better worth knowing. He will prophesy, tell what is to be, or, in other words, what alone is, under appearances, laying little stress on the boiling of the pot, or, the condition-of-England question. He has no more to do with the condition of England than with her national debt, which a vigorous generation would not inherit. The philosopher's conception of things will, above all, be truer than other men's, and his philosophy will subordinate all the circumstances of life. To live like a philosopher is to live, not foolishly, like other men, but wisely and according to universal laws. If Carlyle does not take two steps in philosophy, are there any who take three? Philosophy having crept clinging to the rocks, so far, puts out its feelers many ways in vain. It would be hard to surprise him by the relation of any important human experience, but in some nook or corner of his works you will find that this, too, was sometimes dreamed of in his philosophy.

To sum up our most serious objections in a few words, we should say that Carlyle indicates a depth, — and we mean not impliedly, but distinctly, — which he neglects to fathom. We want to know more about that which he wants to know as well. If any luminous star or undissolvable nebula is visible from his station which is not visible from ours, the interests of science require that the fact be communicated to us. The universe expects every man to do his duty in his parallel of latitude. We want to hear more of his inmost life; his hymn and prayer more; his elegy and eulogy less; that he should speak more from his character, and less from his talent; communicate centrally with his readers, and not by a side; that he should say what he believes, without suspecting that men disbelieve it, out of his never-misunderstood nature. His genius can cover all the land with gorgeous palaces, but the reader does not abide in them, but pitches his tent rather in the desert and on the mountain-peak.

When we look about for something to quote, as the fairest specimen of the man, we confess that we labor under an unusual difficulty; for his philosophy is so little of the proverbial or sentential kind, and opens so gradually, rising insensibly from the reviewer's level, and developing its thought completely and in detail, that we look in vain for the brilliant passages, for point and antithesis, and must end by quoting his works entire. What in a writer of less breadth would have been the proposition which would have bounded his discourse, his column of victory, his Pillar of Hercules, and *ne plus ultra*, is in Carlyle frequently the same thought unfolded; no Pillar of Hercules, but a considerable prospect, north and south, along the Atlantic coast. There are other pillars of Hercules, like beacons and light-houses, still further in the horizon, toward Atlantis, set up by a few ancient and modern travelers; but, so far as this traveler goes, he clears and colonizes, and all the surplus population of London is bound thither at once. What we would quote is, in fact, his vivacity, and not any particular wisdom or sense, which last is ever synonymous with sentence (*sententia*), as in his contemporaries Coleridge, Landor, and Wordsworth. We have not attempted to discriminate between his works, but have rather regarded them all as one work, as is the man himself. We have not examined so much as remembered them. To do otherwise would have required a more indifferent, and perhaps even less just review than the present.

All his works might well enough be embraced under the title of one of them, a good specimen brick, "On Heroes, Hero-Worship, and the Heroic in History." Of this department he is the Chief Professor in the World's University, and even leaves Plutarch behind. Such intimate and living, such loyal and generous sympathy with the heroes of history, not one in one age only, but forty in forty ages, such an unparalleled reviewing and greeting of all past worth, with exceptions, to be sure, — but exceptions were the rule before, — it was, indeed, to make this the age of review writing, as if now one period of the human story were completing itself, and getting its accounts settled. This soldier has told the stories with new emphasis, and will be a memorable hander-down of fame to posterity. And with what wise discrimination he has selected his men, with reference both to his own genius and to theirs, — Mahomet, Dante, Cromwell, Voltaire, Johnson, Burns, Goethe, Richter, Schiller, Mirabeau, — could any of these have been spared? These we wanted to hear about. We have not as commonly the cold and refined judgment of the scholar and critic merely, but something more human and affecting. These eulogies have the glow and warmth of friendship. There is sympathy, not with mere fames, and formless, incredible things, but with kindred men, — not transiently, but life-long he has walked with them.

No doubt, some of Carlyle's worthies, should they ever return to earth, would find themselves unpleasantly put upon their good behavior, to sustain their characters; but if he can return a man's life more perfect to our hands than it was left at his death, following out the design of its author, we shall have no great cause to complain. We do not want a daguerreotype likeness. All biography is the life of Adam, — a much-experienced man, — and time withdraws something partial from the story of every individual, that the historian may supply something general. If these virtues were not in this man, perhaps they are in his biographer, — no fatal mistake. Really, in any other sense, we never do, nor desire to, come at the historical man, — unless we rob his grave, that is the nearest approach. Why did he die, then? *He* is with his bones, surely.

No doubt Carlyle has a propensity to *exaggerate* the heroic in history, that is, he creates you an ideal hero rather than another thing: he has most of that material. This we allow in all its senses, and in one narrower sense it is not so convenient. Yet what were history if he did not exaggerate it? How comes it that history never has to wait for facts, but for a man to write it? The ages may go on forgetting the facts never so long, he can remember two for every one forgotten. The musty records of history, like the catacombs, contain the perishable remains, but only in the breast of genius are embalmed the souls of heroes. There is very little of what is called criticism here; it is love and reverence, rather, which deal with qualities not relatively, but absolutely great; for whatever is admirable in a man is something infinite, to which we cannot set bounds. These sentiments allow the mortal to die, the immortal and divine to survive. There is something antique, even, in his style of treating his subject, reminding us that Heroes and Demi-gods, Fates and Furies, still exist; the common man is nothing to him, but after death the hero is apotheosized and has a place in heaven, as in the religion of the Greeks.

Exaggeration! was ever any virtue attributed to a man without exaggeration? was ever any vice, without infinite exaggeration? Do we not exaggerate ourselves to ourselves, or do we recognize ourselves for the actual men we are? Are we not all great men? Yet what are we actually to speak of? We live by exaggeration. What else is it to anticipate more than we enjoy? The lightning is an exaggeration of the light. Exaggerated history is poetry, and truth referred to a new standard. To a small man every greater is an exaggeration. He who cannot exaggerate is not qualified to utter truth. No truth, we think, was ever expressed but with this sort of emphasis, so that for the time there seemed to be no other. Moreover, you must speak loud to those who are hard of hearing, and so you acquire a habit of shouting to those who are not. By an immense exaggeration we appreciate our Greek poetry and philosophy, and Egyptian ruins; our Shakespeares and Miltons, our Liberty and Christianity. We give importance to this hour over all other hours. We do not live by justice, but by grace. As the sort of justice which concerns us in our daily intercourse is not that administered by the judge, so the historical justice which we prize is not arrived at by nicely balancing the evidence. In order to appreciate any, even the humblest man, you must first, by some good fortune, have acquired a sentiment of admiration, even of reverence, for him, and there never were such exaggerators as these.

To try him by the German rule of referring an author to his own standard, we will quote the following from Carlyle's remarks on history, and leave the reader to consider how far his practice has been consistent with his theory. "Truly, if History is Philosophy teaching by Experience, the writer fitted to compose history is hitherto an unknown man. The Experience itself would require All-knowledge to record it, were the All-wisdom, needful for such Philosophy as would interpret it, to be had for asking. Better were it that mere earthly Historians should lower such pretensions, more suitable for Omniscience than for human science; and aiming only at some picture of the things acted, which picture itself will at best be a poor approximation, leave the inscrutable purport of them an acknowledged secret; or, at most, in reverent faith, far different from that teaching of Philosophy, pause over the mysterious vestiges of Him whose path is in the great deep of Time, whom History indeed reveals, but only all History, and in Eternity, will clearly reveal."

Carlyle is a critic who lives in London to tell this generation who have been the great men of our race. We have read that on some exposed place in the city of Geneva, they have fixed a brazen indicator for the use of travelers, with the names of the mountain summits in the horizon marked upon it, "so that by taking sight across the index you can distinguish them at once. You will not mistake Mont Blanc, if you see him, but until you get accustomed to the panorama, you may easily mistake one of his court for the king." It stands there a piece of mute brass, that seems nevertheless to know in what vicinity it is: and there perchance it will stand, when the nation that placed it there has passed away, still in sympathy with the mountains, forever discriminating in the desert.

So, we may say, stands this man, pointing as long as he lives, in obedience to some spiritual magnetism, to the summits in the historical horizon, for the guidance of his fellows.

Truly, our greatest blessings are very cheap. To have our sunlight without paying for it, without any duty levied, — to have our poet there in England, to furnish us entertainment, and, what is better, provocation, from year to year, all our lives long, to make the world seem richer for us, the age more respectable, and life

better worth the living, — all without expense
of acknowledgment even, but silently accepted
out of the east like morning light as a matter
of course.

CIVIL DISOBEDIENCE

I HEARTILY accept the motto, — "That government is best which governs least;" and I should like to see it acted up to more rapidly and systematically. Carried out, it finally amounts to this, which also I believe, — "That government is best which governs not at all;" and when men are prepared for it, that will be the kind of government which they will have. Government is at best but an expedient; but most governments are usually, and all governments are sometimes, inexpedient. The objections which have been brought against a standing army, and they are many and weighty, and deserve to prevail, may also at last be brought against a standing government. The standing army is only an arm of the standing government. The government itself, which is only the mode which the people have chosen to execute their will, is equally liable to be abused and perverted before the people can act through it. Witness the present Mexican war, the work of comparatively a few individuals using the standing government as their tool; for, in the outset, the people would not have consented to this measure.

This American government, — what is it but a tradition, though a recent one, endeavoring to transmit itself unimpaired to posterity, but each instant losing some of its integrity? It has not the vitality and force of a single living man; for a single man can bend it to his will. It is a sort of wooden gun to the people themselves. But it is not the less necessary for this; for the people must have some complicated machinery or other, and hear its din, to satisfy that idea of government which they have. Governments show thus how successfully men can be imposed on, even impose on themselves, for their own advantage. It is excellent, we must all allow. Yet this government never of itself furthered any enterprise, but by the alacrity with which it got out of its way. *It* does not keep the country free. *It* does not settle the West. *It* does not educate. The character inherent in the American people has done all that has been accomplished; and it would have done somewhat more, if the government had not sometimes got in its way. For government is an expedient by which men would fain succeed in letting one another alone; and, as has been said, when it is most expedient, the governed are most let alone by it. Trade and commerce, if they were not made of India-rubber, would never manage to bounce over the obstacles which legislators are continually putting in their way; and, if one were to judge these men wholly by the effects of their actions and not partly by their intentions, they would deserve to be classed and punished with those mischievous persons who put obstructions on the railroads.

But, to speak practically and as a citizen, unlike those who call themselves no-government men, I ask for, not at once no government, but *at once* a better government. Let every man make known what kind of government would command his respect, and that will be one step toward obtaining it.

After all, the practical reason why, when the power is once in the hands of the people, a majority are permitted, and for a long period continue, to rule is not because they are most likely to be in the right, nor because this seems fairest to the minority, but because they are physically the strongest. But a government in which the majority rule in all cases cannot be based on justice, even as far as men understand it. Can there not be a government in which majorities do not virtually decide right and wrong, but conscience? — in which majorities decide only those questions to which the rule of expediency is applicable? Must the citizen ever for a moment, or in the least degree, resign his conscience to the legislator? Why has every man a conscience, then? I think that we should be men first, and subjects afterward. It is not desirable to cultivate a respect for the law, so much as for the right. The only obligation which I have a right to assume is to do at any time what I think right. It is truly enough said, that a corporation has no conscience; but a corporation of conscientious men is a corporation *with* a conscience. Law never made men a whit more just; and, by means of their respect for it, even the well-disposed are daily made the agents of injustice. A common and natural result of an undue respect for law is, that you may see a file of soldiers, colonel, captain, corporal, privates, powder-monkeys, and all, marching in admirable order over hill and dale to the wars, against their wills, ay, against their common sense and consciences, which makes it very steep marching indeed, and produces a palpitation of the heart. They have no doubt that it is a damnable business in which they are concerned; they are all peaceably inclined. Now, what are they? Men at all? or small movable forts and magazines, at the service of some unscrupulous man in power? Visit the Navy-Yard, and behold a marine, such a

man as an American government can make, or
such as it can make a man with its black arts,
— a mere shadow and reminiscence of humanity,
a man laid out alive and standing, and already,
as one may say, buried under arms with funeral
accompaniments, though it may be, —

> " Not a drum was heard, not a funeral note,
>   As his corse to the rampart we hurried ;
> Not a soldier discharged his farewell shot
>   O'er the grave where our hero we buried."

The mass of men serve the state thus, not as
men mainly, but as machines, with their bodies.
They are the standing army, and the militia,
jailers, constables, posse comitatus, etc. In most
cases there is no free exercise whatever of the
judgment or of the moral sense; but they put
themselves on a level with wood and earth and
stones; and wooden men can perhaps be man-
ufactured that will serve the purpose as well.
Such command no more respect than men of
straw or a lump of dirt. They have the same
sort of worth only as horses and dogs. Yet
such as these even are commonly esteemed good
citizens. Others — as most legislators, politicians, lawyers, ministers, and office-holders —
serve the state chiefly with their heads; and, as
they rarely make any moral distinctions, they are
as likely to serve the Devil, without *intending*
it, as God. A very few, as heroes, patriots,

martyrs, reformers in the great sense, and *men*, serve the state with their consciences also, and so necessarily resist it for the most part; and they are commonly treated as enemies by it. A wise man will only be useful as a man, and will not submit to be "clay," and "stop a hole to keep the wind away," but leave that office to his dust at least: —

> " I am too high-born to be propertied,
>   To be a secondary at control,
>   Or useful serving-man and instrument
>   To any sovereign state throughout the world."

He who gives himself entirely to his fellow-men appears to them useless and selfish; but he who gives himself partially to them is pronounced a benefactor and philanthropist.

How does it become a man to behave toward this American government to-day? I answer, that he cannot without disgrace be associated with it. I cannot for an instant recognize that political organization as *my* government which is the *slave's* government also.

All men recognize the right of revolution; that is, the right to refuse allegiance to, and to resist, the government, when its tyranny or its inefficiency are great and unendurable. But almost all say that such is not the case now. But such was the case, they think, in the Revolution of '75. If one were to tell me that this was a bad government because it taxed certain foreign commodities brought to its ports, it is most probable that I should not make an ado about it, for I can do without them. All machines have their friction; and possibly this does enough good to counterbalance the evil. At any rate, it is a great evil to make a stir about it. But when the friction comes to have its machine, and oppression and robbery are organized, I say, let us not have such a machine any longer. In other words, when a sixth of the population of a nation which has undertaken to be the refuge of liberty are slaves, and a whole country is unjustly overrun and conquered by a foreign army, and subjected to military law, I think that it is not too soon for honest men to rebel and revolutionize. What makes this duty the more urgent is the fact that the country so overrun is not our own, but ours is the invading army.

Paley, a common authority with many on moral questions, in his chapter on the "Duty of Submission to Civil Government," resolves all civil obligation into expediency; and he proceeds to say, "that so long as the interest of the whole society requires it, that is, so long as the established government cannot be resisted or changed without public inconveniency, it is the will of God that the established government be obeyed, and no longer. . . . This principle being admitted, the justice of every particular case of resistance is reduced to a computation of the quantity of the danger and grievance on the one side, and of the probability and expense of redressing it on the other." Of this, he says, every man shall judge for himself. But Paley appears never to have contemplated those cases to which the rule of expediency does not apply, in which a people, as well as an individual, must do justice, cost what it may. If I have unjustly wrested a plank from a drowning man, I must restore it to him though I drown myself. This, according to Paley, would be inconvenient. But he that would save his life, in such a case, shall lose it. This people must cease to hold slaves, and to make war on Mexico, though it cost them their existence as a people.

In their practice, nations agree with Paley; but does any one think that Massachusetts does exactly what is right at the present crisis?

" A drab of state, a cloth-o'-silver slut,
   To have her train borne up, and her soul trail in the dirt."

Practically speaking, the opponents to a reform in Massachusetts are not a hundred thousand politicians at the South, but a hundred thousand merchants and farmers here, who are more interested in commerce and agriculture

than they are in humanity, and are not prepared
to do justice to the slave and to Mexico, *cost
what it may.* I quarrel not with far-off foes,
but with those who, near at home, coöperate
with, and do the bidding of, those far away,
and without whom the latter would be harmless. We are accustomed to say, that the mass
of men are unprepared; but improvement is
slow, because the few are not materially wiser
or better than the many. It is not so important that many should be as good as you, as that
there be some absolute goodness somewhere;
for that will leaven the whole lump. There are
thousands who are *in opinion* opposed to slavery
and to the war, who yet in effect do nothing to
put an end to them; who, esteeming themselves
children of Washington and Franklin, sit down
with their hands in their pockets, and say that
they know not what to do, and do nothing; who
even postpone the question of freedom to the
question of free-trade, and quietly read the
prices-current along with the latest advices from
Mexico, after dinner, and, it may be, fall asleep
over them both. What is the price-current of
an honest man and patriot to-day? They hesitate, and they regret, and sometimes they petition; but they do nothing in earnest and with
effect. They will wait, well disposed, for others to remedy the evil, that they may no longer

have it to regret. At most, they give only a cheap vote, and a feeble countenance and God-speed, to the right, as it goes by them. There are nine hundred and ninety-nine patrons of virtue to one virtuous man. But it is easier to deal with the real possessor of a thing than with the temporary guardian of it.

All voting is a sort of gaming, like checkers or backgammon, with a slight moral tinge to it, a playing with right and wrong, with moral questions; and betting naturally accompanies it. The character of the voters is not staked. I cast my vote, perchance, as I think right; but I am not vitally concerned that that right should prevail. I am willing to leave it to the majority. Its obligation, therefore, never exceeds that of expediency. Even voting *for the right* is *doing* nothing for it. It is only expressing to men feebly your desire that it should prevail. A wise man will not leave the right to the mercy of chance, nor wish it to prevail through the power of the majority. There is but little virtue in the action of masses of men. When the majority shall at length vote for the abolition of slavery, it will be because they are indifferent to slavery, or because there is but little slavery left to be abolished by their vote. *They* will then be the only slaves. Only *his* vote can hasten the abolition of slavery who asserts his own freedom by his vote.

I hear of a convention to be held at Baltimore, or elsewhere, for the selection of a candidate for the Presidency, made up chiefly of editors, and men who are politicians by profession; but I think, what is it to any independent, intelligent, and respectable man what decision they may come to? Shall we not have the advantage of his wisdom and honesty, nevertheless? Can we not count upon some independent votes? Are there not many individuals in the country who do not attend conventions? But no: I find that the respectable man, so called, has immediately drifted from his position, and despairs of his country, when his country has more reason to despair of him. He forthwith adopts one of the candidates thus selected as the only *available* one, thus proving that he is himself *available* for any purposes of the demagogue. His vote is of no more worth than that of any unprincipled foreigner or hireling native, who may have been bought. O for a man who is a *man*, and, as my neighbor says, has a bone in his back which you cannot pass your hand through! Our statistics are at fault: the population has been returned too large. How many *men* are there to a square thousand miles in this country? Hardly one. Does not America offer any inducement for men to settle here? The American has dwindled into an

Odd Fellow, — one who may be known by the development of his organ of gregariousness, and a manifest lack of intellect and cheerful self-reliance; whose first and chief concern, on coming into the world, is to see that the Alms-houses are in good repair; and, before yet he has lawfully donned the virile garb, to collect a fund for the support of the widows and orphans that may be; who, in short, ventures to live only by the aid of the Mutual Insurance company, which has promised to bury him decently.

It is not a man's duty, as a matter of course, to devote himself to the eradication of any, even the most enormous wrong; he may still properly have other concerns to engage him; but it is his duty, at least, to wash his hands of it, and, if he gives it no thought longer, not to give it practically his support. If I devote myself to other pursuits and contemplations, I must first see, at least, that I do not pursue them sitting upon another man's shoulders. I must get off him first, that he may pursue his contemplations too. See what gross inconsistency is tolerated. I have heard some of my townsmen say, "I should like to have them order me out to help put down an insurrection of the slaves, or to march to Mexico; — see if I would go;" and yet these very men have each, directly by their allegiance, and so indirectly, at least, by their money, furnished a substitute. The soldier is applauded who refuses to serve in an unjust war by those who do not refuse to sustain the unjust government which makes the war; is applauded by those whose own act and authority he disregards and sets at naught; as if the state were penitent to that degree that it hired one to scourge it while it sinned, but not to that degree that it left off sinning for a moment. Thus, under the name of Order and Civil Government, we are all made at last to pay homage to and support our own meanness. After the first blush of sin comes its indifference; and from immoral it becomes, as it were, *un*moral, and not quite unnecessary to that life which we have made.

The broadest and most prevalent error requires the most disinterested virtue to sustain it. The slight reproach to which the virtue of patriotism is commonly liable, the noble are most likely to incur. Those who, while they disapprove of the character and measures of a government, yield to it their allegiance and support are undoubtedly its most conscientious supporters, and so frequently the most serious obstacles to reform. Some are petitioning the state to dissolve the Union, to disregard the requisitions of the President. Why do they not dissolve it themselves, — the union between themselves and the state, — and refuse to pay their quota into its treasury? Do not they stand in the same relation to the state that the state does to the Union? And have not the same reasons prevented the state from resisting the Union which have prevented them from resisting the state?

How can a man be satisfied to entertain an opinion merely, and enjoy *it?* Is there any enjoyment in it, if his opinion is that he is aggrieved? If you are cheated out of a single dollar by your neighbor, you do not rest satisfied with knowing that you are cheated, or with saying that you are cheated, or even with petitioning him to pay you your due; but you take effectual steps at once to obtain the full amount, and see that you are never cheated again. Action from principle, the perception and the performance of right, changes things and relations; it is essentially revolutionary, and does not consist wholly with anything which was. It not only divides states and churches, it divides families; ay, it divides the *individual*, separating the diabolical in him from the divine.

Unjust laws exist: shall we be content to obey them, or shall we endeavor to amend them, and obey them until we have succeeded, or shall we transgress them at once? Men generally, under such a government as this, think that they ought to wait until they have persuaded the majority to alter them. They think that, if they should resist, the remedy would be worse than the evil. But it is the fault of the government itself that the remedy *is* worse than the evil. *It* makes it worse. Why is it not more apt to anticipate and provide for reform? Why does it not cherish its wise minority? Why does it cry and resist before it is hurt? Why does it not encourage its citizens to be on the alert to point out its faults, and *do* better than it would have them? Why does it always crucify Christ, and excommunicate Copernicus and Luther, and pronounce Washington and Franklin rebels?

One would think, that a deliberate and practical denial of its authority was the only offense never contemplated by government; else, why has it not assigned its definite, its suitable and proportionate penalty? If a man who has no property refuses but once to earn nine shillings for the state, he is put in prison for a period unlimited by any law that I know, and determined only by the discretion of those who placed him there; but if he should steal ninety times nine shillings from the state, he is soon permitted to go at large again.

If the injustice is part of the necessary friction of the machine of government, let it go, let it go: perchance it will wear smooth, — certainly the machine will wear out. If the injustice has a spring, or a pulley, or a rope, or a crank, exclusively for itself, then perhaps you may consider whether the remedy will not be worse than the evil; but if it is of such a nature that it requires you to be the agent of injustice to another, then, I say, break the law. Let your life be a counter friction to stop the machine. What I have to do is to see, at any rate, that I do not lend myself to the wrong which I condemn.

As for adopting the ways which the state has provided for remedying the evil, I know not of such ways. They take too much time, and a man's life will be gone. I have other affairs to attend to. I came into this world, not chiefly to make this a good place to live in, but to live in it, be it good or bad. A man has not everything to do, but something; and because he cannot do *everything*, it is not necessary that he should do *something* wrong. It is not my business to be petitioning the Governor or the Legislature any more than it is theirs to petition me; and if they should not hear my petition, what should I do then? But in this case the state has provided no way: its very Constitution is the evil. This may seem to be harsh and stubborn and unconciliatory; but it is to treat with the utmost kindness and consideration the only spirit that can appreciate or deserves it. So is all change for the better, like birth and death, which convulse the body.

I do not hesitate to say, that those who call themselves Abolitionists should at once effectually withdraw their support, both in person and property, from the government of Massachusetts, and not wait till they constitute a majority of one, before they suffer the right to prevail through them. I think that it is enough if they have God on their side, without waiting for that other one. Moreover, any man more right than his neighbors constitutes a majority of one already.

I meet this American government, or its representative, the state government, directly, and face to face, once a year — no more — in the person of its tax-gatherer; this is the only mode in which a man situated as I am necessarily meets it; and it then says distinctly, Recognize me; and the simplest, the most effectual, and, in the present posture of affairs, the indispensablest mode of treating with it on this head, of expressing your little satisfaction with and love for it, is to deny it then. My civil neighbor, the tax-gatherer, is the very man I have to deal with, — for it is, after all, with men and not with parchment that I quarrel, — and he has voluntarily chosen to be an agent of the government. How shall he ever know well what he is and does as an officer of the government, or as a man, until he is obliged to consider whether he shall treat me, his neighbor, for whom he has respect, as a neighbor and well-disposed man, or as a maniac and disturber of the peace, and see if he can get over this obstruction to his neighborliness without a ruder and more impetuous thought or speech corresponding with his action. I know this well, that if one thousand, if one hundred, if ten men whom I could name, — if ten *honest* men only, — ay, if *one* HONEST man, in this State of Massachusetts, *ceasing to hold slaves*, were actually to withdraw from this copartnership, and be locked up in the county jail therefor, it would be the abolition of slavery in America. For it matters not how small the beginning may seem to be: what is once well done is done forever. But we love better to talk about it: that we say is our mission. Reform keeps many scores of newspapers in its service, but not one man. If my esteemed neighbor, the State's ambassador, who will devote his days to the settlement of the question of human rights in the Council Chamber, instead of being threatened with the prisons of Carolina, were to sit down the prisoner of Massachusetts, that State which is so anxious to foist the sin of slavery upon her sister, — though at present she can discover only an act of inhospitality to be the ground of a quarrel with her, — the Legislature would not wholly waive the subject the following winter.

Under a government which imprisons any unjustly, the true place for a just man is also a prison. The proper place to-day, the only place which Massachusetts has provided for her freer and less desponding spirits, is in her prisons, to be put out and locked out of the State by her own act, as they have already put themselves out by their principles. It is there that the fugitive slave, and the Mexican prisoner on parole, and the Indian come to plead the wrongs of his race should find them; on that separate, but more free and honorable ground, where the State places those who are not *with* her, but *against* her, — the only house in a slave State in which a free man can abide with honor. If any think that their influence would be lost there, and their voices no longer afflict the ear of the State, that they would not be as an enemy within its walls, they do not know by how much truth is stronger than error, nor how much more eloquently and effectively he can combat injustice who has experienced a little in his own person. Cast your whole vote, not a strip of paper merely, but your whole influence. A minority is powerless while it conforms to the majority; it is not even a minority then; but it is irresistible when it clogs by its whole weight. If the alternative is to keep all just men in prison, or give up war and slavery, the State will not hesitate which to choose. If a thousand men were not to pay their tax-bills this year, that would not be a violent and bloody measure, as it would be to pay them, and enable the State to commit violence and shed innocent blood. This is, in fact, the definition of a peaceable revolution, if any such is possible. If the tax-gatherer, or any other public officer, asks me, as one has done, "But what shall I do?" my answer is, "If you really wish to do anything, resign your office." When the subject has refused allegiance, and the officer has resigned his office, then the revolution is accomplished. But even suppose blood should flow. Is there not a sort of blood shed when the conscience is wounded? Through this wound a man's real manhood and immortality flow out, and he bleeds to an everlasting death. I see this blood flowing now.

I have contemplated the imprisonment of the offender, rather than the seizure of his goods, — though both will serve the same purpose, — because they who assert the purest right, and consequently are most dangerous to a corrupt

State, commonly have not spent much time in accumulating property. To such the State renders comparatively small service, and a slight tax is wont to appear exorbitant, particularly if they are obliged to earn it by special labor with their hands. If there were one who lived wholly without the use of money, the State itself would hesitate to demand it of him. But the rich man — not to make any invidious comparison — is always sold to the institution which makes him rich. Absolutely speaking, the more money, the less virtue; for money comes between a man and his objects, and obtains them for him; and it was certainly no great virtue to obtain it. It puts to rest many questions which he would otherwise be taxed to answer; while the only new question which it puts is the hard but superfluous one, how to spend it. Thus his moral ground is taken from under his feet. The opportunities of living are diminished in proportion as what are called the "means" are increased. The best thing a man can do for his culture when he is rich is to endeavor to carry out those schemes which he entertained when he was poor. Christ answered the Herodians according to their condition. "Show me the tribute-money," said he; — and one took a penny out of his pocket; — if you use money which has the image of Cæsar on it, and which he has made current and valuable, that is, *if you are men of the State,* and gladly enjoy the advantages of Cæsar's government, then pay him back some of his own when he demands it. "Render therefore to Cæsar that which is Cæsar's, and to God those things which are God's," — leaving them no wiser than before as to which was which; for they did not wish to know.

When I converse with the freest of my neighbors, I perceive that, whatever they may say about the magnitude and seriousness of the question, and their regard for the public tranquillity, the long and the short of the matter is, that they cannot spare the protection of the existing government, and they dread the consequences to their property and families of disobedience to it. For my own part, I should not like to think that I ever rely on the protection of the State. But, if I deny the authority of the State when it presents its tax-bill, it will soon take and waste all my property, and so harass me and my children without end. This is hard. This makes it impossible for a man to live honestly, and at the same time comfortably, in outward respects. It will not be worth the while to accumulate property; that would be sure to go again. You must hire or squat somewhere, and raise but a small crop, and eat that soon. You must live within yourself, and depend upon yourself always tucked up and ready for a start, and not have many affairs. A man may grow rich in Turkey even, if he will be in all respects a good subject of the Turkish government. Confucius said: "If a state is governed by the principles of reason, poverty and misery are subjects of shame; if a state is not governed by the principles of reason, riches and honors are the subjects of shame." No: until I want the protection of Massachusetts to be extended to me in some distant Southern port, where my liberty is endangered, or until I am bent solely on building up an estate at home by peaceful enterprise, I can afford to refuse allegiance to Massachusetts, and her right to my property and life. It costs me less in every sense to incur the penalty of disobedience to the State than it would to obey. I should feel as if I were worth less in that case.

Some years ago, the State met me in behalf of the Church, and commanded me to pay a certain sum toward the support of a clergyman whose preaching my father attended, but never I myself. "Pay," it said, "or be locked up in the jail." I declined to pay. But, unfortunately, another man saw fit to pay it. I did not see why the schoolmaster should be taxed to support the priest, and not the priest the school-master; for I was not the State's schoolmaster, but I supported myself by voluntary subscription. I did not see why the lyceum should not present its tax-bill, and have the State to back its demand, as well as the Church. However, at the request of the selectmen, I condescended to make some such statement as this in writing:— "Know all men by these presents, that I, Henry Thoreau, do not wish to be regarded as a member of any incorporated society which I have not joined." This I gave to the town clerk; and he has it. The State, having thus learned that I did not wish to be regarded as a member of that church, has never made a like demand on me since; though it said that it must adhere to its original presumption that time. If I had known how to name them, I should then have signed off in detail from all the societies which I never signed on to; but I did not know where to find a complete list.

I have paid no poll-tax for six years. I was put into a jail once on this account, for one night; and, as I stood considering the walls of solid stone, two or three feet thick, the door of wood and iron, a foot thick, and the iron grating which strained the light, I could not help being struck with the foolishness of that insti-

tution which treated me as if I were mere flesh
and blood and bones, to be locked up. I wondered that it should have concluded at length
that this was the best use it could put me to,
and had never thought to avail itself of my services in some way. I saw that, if there was a
wall of stone between me and my townsmen,
there was a still more difficult one to climb or
break through before they could get to be as
free as I was. I did not for a moment feel confined, and the walls seemed a great waste of
stone and mortar. I felt as if I alone of all my
townsmen had paid my tax. They plainly did
not know how to treat me, but behaved like
persons who are underbred. In every threat
and in every compliment there was a blunder;
for they thought that my chief desire was to
stand the other side of that stone wall. I could
not but smile to see how industriously they
locked the door on my meditations, which followed them out again without let or hindrance,
and *they* were really all that was dangerous.
As they could not reach me, they had resolved
to punish my body; just as boys, if they cannot
come at some person against whom they have a
spite, will abuse his dog. I saw that the State
was half-witted, that it was timid as a lone
woman with her silver spoons, and that it
did not know its friends from its foes, and I

lost all my remaining respect for it, and pitied it.

Thus the State never intentionally confronts a man's sense, intellectual or moral, but only his body, his senses. It is not armed with superior wit or honesty, but with superior physical strength. I was not born to be forced. I will breathe after my own fashion. Let us see who is the strongest. What force has a multitude? They only can force me who obey a higher law than I. They force me to become like themselves. I do not hear of *men* being *forced* to live this way or that by masses of men. What sort of life were that to live? When I meet a government which says to me, "Your money or your life," why should I be in haste to give it my money? It may be in a great strait, and not know what to do: I cannot help that. It must help itself; do as I do. It is not worth the while to snivel about it. I am not responsible for the successful working of the machinery of society. I am not the son of the engineer. I perceive that, when an acorn and a chestnut fall side by side, the one does not remain inert to make way for the other, but both obey their own laws, and spring and grow and flourish as best they can, till one, perchance, overshadows and destroys the other. If a plant cannot live according to its nature, it dies; and so a man.

The night in prison was novel and interesting enough. The prisoners in their shirt-sleeves were enjoying a chat and the evening air in the doorway, when I entered. But the jailer said, "Come, boys, it is time to lock up;" and so they dispersed, and I heard the sound of their steps returning into the hollow apartments. My room-mate was introduced to me by the jailer as "a first-rate fellow and a clever man." When the door was locked, he showed me where to hang my hat, and how he managed matters there. The rooms were whitewashed once a month; and this one, at least, was the whitest, most simply furnished, and probably the neatest apartment in the town. He naturally wanted to know where I came from, and what brought me there; and, when I had told him, I asked him in my turn how he came there, presuming him to be an honest man, of course; and, as the world goes, I believe he was. "Why," said he, "they accuse me of burning a barn; but I never did it." As near as I could discover, he had probably gone to bed in a barn when drunk, and smoked his pipe there; and so a barn was burnt. He had the reputation of being a clever man, had been there some three months waiting for his trial to come on, and would have to wait as much longer; but he was quite domesticated and contented, since he got his board for nothing, and thought that he was well treated.

He occupied one window, and I the other; and I saw that if one stayed there long, his principal business would be to look out the window. I had soon read all the tracts that were left there, and examined where former prisoners had broken out, and where a grate had been sawed off, and heard the history of the various occupants of that room; for I found that even here there was a history and a gossip which never circulated beyond the walls of the jail. Probably this is the only house in the town where verses are composed which are afterward printed in a circular form, but not published. I was shown quite a long list of verses which were composed by some young men who had been detected in an attempt to escape, who avenged themselves by singing them.

I pumped my fellow-prisoner as dry as I could, for fear I should never see him again; but at length he showed me which was my bed, and left me to blow out the lamp.

It was like traveling into a far country, such as I had never expected to behold, to lie there for one night. It seemed to me that I never had heard the town-clock strike before, nor the evening sounds of the village; for we slept with the windows open, which were inside the grat-

ing. It was to see my native village in the
light of the Middle Ages, and our Concord was
turned into a Rhine stream, and visions of
knights and castles passed before me. They
were the voices of old burghers that I heard in
the streets. I was an involuntary spectator and
auditor of whatever was done and said in the
kitchen of the adjacent village-inn, — a wholly
new and rare experience to me. It was a
closer view of my native town. I was fairly
inside of it. I never had seen its institutions
before. This is one of its peculiar institutions;
for it is a shire town. I began to comprehend
what its inhabitants were about.

In the morning, our breakfasts were put
through the hole in the door, in small oblong-
square tin pans, made to fit, and holding a pint
of chocolate, with brown bread, and an iron
spoon. When they called for the vessels again,
I was green enough to return what bread I had
left; but my comrade seized it, and said that I
should lay that up for lunch or dinner. Soon
after he was let out to work at haying in a
neighboring field, whither he went every day,
and would not be back till noon; so he bade me
good-day, saying that he doubted if he should
see me again.

When I came out of prison, — for some one
interfered, and paid that tax, — I did not per-

ceive that great changes had taken place on the common, such as he observed who went in a youth and emerged a tottering and gray-headed man; and yet a change had to my eyes come over the scene, — the town, and State, and country, — greater than any that mere time could effect. I saw yet more distinctly the State in which I lived. I saw to what extent the people among whom I lived could be trusted as good neighbors and friends; that their friendship was for summer weather only; that they did not greatly propose to do right; that they were a distinct race from me by their prejudices and superstitions, as the Chinamen and Malays are; that in their sacrifices to humanity they ran no risks, not even to their property; that after all they were not so noble but they treated the thief as he had treated them, and hoped, by a certain outward observance and a few prayers, and by walking in a particular straight though useless path from time to time, to save their souls. This may be to judge my neighbors harshly; for I believe that many of them are not aware that they have such an institution as the jail in their village.

It was formerly the custom in our village, when a poor debtor came out of jail, for his acquaintances to salute him, looking through their fingers, which were crossed to represent the grating of a jail window, "How do ye do?" My neighbors did not thus salute me, but first looked at me, and then at one another, as if I had returned from a long journey. I was put into jail as I was going to the shoemaker's to get a shoe which was mended. When I was let out the next morning, I proceeded to finish my errand, and, having put on my mended shoe, joined a huckleberry party, who were impatient to put themselves under my conduct; and in half an hour, — for the horse was soon tackled, — was in the midst of a huckleberry field, on one of our highest hills, two miles off, and then the State was nowhere to be seen.

This is the whole history of "My Prisons."

I have never declined paying the highway tax, because I am as desirous of being a good neighbor as I am of being a bad subject; and as for supporting schools, I am doing my part to educate my fellow-countrymen now. It is for no particular item in the tax-bill that I refuse to pay it. I simply wish to refuse allegiance to the State, to withdraw and stand aloof from it effectually. I do not care to trace the course of my dollar, if I could, till it buys a man or a musket to shoot one with, — the dollar is innocent, — but I am concerned to trace the effects of my allegiance. In fact, I quietly declare war with the State, after my fashion, though I will still make what use and get what advantage of her I can, as is usual in such cases.

If others pay the tax which is demanded of me, from a sympathy with the State, they do but what they have already done in their own case, or rather they abet injustice to a greater extent than the State requires. If they pay the tax from a mistaken interest in the individual taxed, to save his property, or prevent his going to jail, it is because they have not considered wisely how far they let their private feelings interfere with the public good.

This, then, is my position at present. But one cannot be too much on his guard in such a case, lest his action be biased by obstinacy or an undue regard for the opinions of men. Let him see that he does only what belongs to himself and to the hour.

I think sometimes, Why, this people mean well, they are only ignorant; they would do better if they knew how: why give your neighbors this pain to treat you as they are not inclined to? But I think again, This is no reason why I should do as they do, or permit others to suffer much greater pain of a different kind. Again, I sometimes say to myself, When many millions of men, without heat, without ill will, without personal feeling of any kind, demand of you a few shillings only, without the possibility, such is their constitution, of retracting or altering their present demand, and without the possibility, on your side, of appeal to any other millions, why expose yourself to this overwhelming brute force? You do not resist cold and hunger, the winds and the waves, thus obstinately; you quietly submit to a thousand similar necessities. You do not put your head into the fire. But just in proportion as I regard this as not wholly a brute force, but partly a human force, and consider that I have relations to those millions as to so many millions of men, and not of mere brute or inanimate things, I see that appeal is possible, first and instantaneously, from them to the Maker of them, and, secondly, from them to themselves. But if I put my head deliberately into the fire, there is no appeal to fire or to the Maker of fire, and I have only myself to blame. If I could convince myself that I have any right to be satisfied with men as they are, and to treat them accordingly, and not according, in some respects, to my requisitions and expectations of what they and I ought to be, then, like a good Mussulman and fatalist, I should endeavor to be satisfied with things as they are, and say it is the will of God. And, above all, there is this difference between resisting this and a purely brute or natural force, that I can resist this with some effect; but I cannot expect, like Orpheus, to change the nature of the rocks and trees and beasts.

I do not wish to quarrel with any man or nation. I do not wish to split hairs, to make fine distinctions, or set myself up as better than my neighbors. I seek rather, I may say, even an excuse for conforming to the laws of the land. I am but too ready to conform to them. Indeed, I have reason to suspect myself on this head; and each year, as the tax-gatherer comes round, I find myself disposed to review the acts and position of the general and State governments, and the spirit of the people, to discover a pretext for conformity.

> "We must affect our country as our parents,
>   And if at any time we alienate
>   Our love or industry from doing it honor,
>   We must respect effects and teach the soul
>   Matter of conscience and religion,
>   And not desire of rule or benefit."

I believe that the State will soon be able to take all my work of this sort out of my hands, and then I shall be no better a patriot than my fellow-countrymen. Seen from a lower point of view, the Constitution, with all its faults, is very good; the law and the courts are very respectable; even this State and this American government are, in many respects, very admirable, and rare things, to be thankful for, such as a great many have described them; but seen from a point of view a little higher, they are what I have described them; seen from a higher still, and the highest, who shall say what they are, or that they are worth looking at or thinking of at all?

However, the government does not concern me much, and I shall bestow the fewest possible thoughts on it. It is not many moments that I live under a government, even in this world. If a man is thought-free, fancy-free, imagination-free, that which *is not* never for a long time appearing *to be* to him, unwise rulers or reformers cannot fatally interrupt him.

I know that most men think differently from myself; but those whose lives are by profession devoted to the study of these or kindred subjects content me as little as any. Statesmen and legislators, standing so completely within the institution, never distinctly and nakedly behold it. They speak of moving society, but have no resting-place without it. They may be men of a certain experience and discrimination, and have no doubt invented ingenious and even useful systems, for which we sincerely thank them; but all their wit and usefulness lie within certain not very wide limits. They are wont to forget that the world is not governed by policy

and expediency. Webster never goes behind
government, and so cannot speak with authority
about it. His words are wisdom to those legislators who contemplate no essential reform in
the existing government; but for thinkers, and
those who legislate for all time, he never once
glances at the subject. I know of those whose
serene and wise speculations on this theme
would soon reveal the limits of his mind's range
and hospitality. Yet, compared with the cheap
professions of most reformers, and the still
cheaper wisdom and eloquence of politicians in
general, his are almost the only sensible and
valuable words, and we thank Heaven for him.
Comparatively, he is always strong, original,
and, above all, practical. Still, his quality is
not wisdom, but prudence. The lawyer's truth
is not Truth, but consistency or a consistent
expediency. Truth is always in harmony with
herself, and is not concerned chiefly to reveal
the justice that may consist with wrong-doing.
He well deserves to be called, as he has been
called, the Defender of the Constitution.
There are really no blows to be given by him
but defensive ones. He is not a leader, but
a follower. His leaders are the men of '87.
"I have never made an effort," he says, "and
never propose to make an effort; I have never
countenanced an effort, and never mean to

countenance an effort, to disturb the arrangement as originally made, by which the various States came into the Union." Still thinking of the sanction which the Constitution gives to slavery, he says, "Because it was a part of the original compact, — let it stand." Notwithstanding his special acuteness and ability, he is unable to take a fact out of its merely political relations, and behold it as it lies absolutely to be disposed of by the intellect, — what, for instance, it behooves a man to do here in America to-day with regard to slavery, — but ventures, or is driven, to make some such desperate answer as the following, while professing to speak absolutely, and as a private man, — from which what new and singular code of social duties might be inferred? "The manner," says he, "in which the governments of those States where slavery exists are to regulate it is for their own consideration, under their responsibility to their constituents, to the general laws of propriety, humanity, and justice, and to God. Associations formed elsewhere, springing from a feeling of humanity, or any other cause, have nothing whatever to do with it. They have never received any encouragement from me, and they never will." [1]

[1] These extracts have been inserted since the lecture was read.

They who know of no purer sources of truth, who have traced up its stream no higher, stand, and wisely stand, by the Bible and the Constitution, and drink at it there with reverence and humility; but they who behold where it comes trickling into this lake or that pool, gird up their loins once more, and continue their pilgrimage toward its fountain-head.

No man with a genius for legislation has appeared in America. They are rare in the history of the world. There are orators, politicians, and eloquent men, by the thousand; but the speaker has not yet opened his mouth to speak who is capable of settling the much-vexed questions of the day. We love eloquence for its own sake, and not for any truth which it may utter, or any heroism it may inspire. Our legislators have not yet learned the comparative value of free-trade and of freedom, of union, and of rectitude, to a nation. They have no genius or talent for comparatively humble questions of taxation and finance, commerce and manufactures and agriculture. If we were left solely to the wordy wit of legislators in Congress for our guidance, uncorrected by the seasonable experience and the effectual complaints of the people, America would not long retain her rank among the nations. For eighteen hundred years, though perchance I have no right to say it, the New Testament has been written; yet where is the legislator who has wisdom and practical talent enough to avail himself of the light which it sheds on the science of legislation?

The authority of government, even such as I am willing to submit to, — for I will cheerfully obey those who know and can do better than I, and in many things even those who neither know nor can do so well, — is still an impure one: to be strictly just, it must have the sanction and consent of the governed. It can have no pure right over my person and property but what I concede to it. The progress from an absolute to a limited monarchy, from a limited monarchy to a democracy, is a progress toward a true respect for the individual. Even the Chinese philosopher was wise enough to regard the individual as the basis of the empire. Is a democracy, such as we know it, the last improvement possible in government? Is it not possible to take a step further towards recognizing and organizing the rights of man? There will never be a really free and enlightened State until the State comes to recognize the individual as a higher and independent power, from which all its own power and authority are derived, and treats him accordingly. I please myself with imagining a State at last which can afford to be just to all men, and to treat the individual with respect as a neighbor; which even would not think it inconsistent with its own repose if a few were to live aloof from it, not meddling with it, nor embraced by it, who fulfilled all the duties of neighbors and fellow-men. A State which bore this kind of fruit, and suffered it to drop off as fast as it ripened, would prepare the way for a still more perfect and glorious State, which also I have imagined, but not yet anywhere seen.

SLAVERY IN MASSACHUSETTS

I LATELY attended a meeting of the citizens of Concord, expecting, as one among many, to speak on the subject of slavery in Massachusetts; but I was surprised and disappointed to find that what had called my townsmen together was the destiny of Nebraska, and not of Massachusetts, and that what I had to say would be entirely out of order. I had thought that the house was on fire, and not the prairie; but though several of the citizens of Massachusetts are now in prison for attempting to rescue a slave from her own clutches, not one of the speakers at that meeting expressed regret for it, not one even referred to it. It was only the disposition of some wild lands a thousand miles off which appeared to concern them. The inhabitants of Concord are not prepared to stand by one of their own bridges, but talk only of taking up a position on the highlands beyond the Yellowstone River. Our Buttricks and Davises and Hosmers are retreating thither, and I fear that they will leave no Lexington Common between them and the enemy. There is not one slave in Nebraska; there are perhaps a million slaves in Massachusetts.

They who have been bred in the school of politics fail now and always to face the facts. Their measures are half measures and make-shifts merely. They put off the day of settlement indefinitely, and meanwhile the debt accumulates. Though the Fugitive Slave Law had not been the subject of discussion on that occasion, it was at length faintly resolved by my townsmen, at an adjourned meeting, as I learn, that the compromise compact of 1820 having been repudiated by one of the parties, "Therefore, . . . the Fugitive Slave Law of 1850 must be repealed." But this is not the reason why an iniquitous law should be repealed. The fact which the politician faces is merely that there is less honor among thieves than was supposed, and not the fact that they are thieves.

As I had no opportunity to express my thoughts at that meeting, will you allow me to do so here?

Again it happens that the Boston Court-House is full of armed men, holding prisoner and trying a MAN, to find out if he is not really a SLAVE. Does any one think that justice or God awaits Mr. Loring's decision? For him to sit there deciding still, when this question is already decided from eternity to eternity, and the unlettered slave himself and the multitude around have long since heard and assented to the decision, is simply to make himself ridiculous. We may be tempted to ask from whom he received his commission, and who he is that received it; what novel statutes he obeys, and what precedents are to him of authority. Such an arbiter's very existence is an impertinence. We do not ask him to make up his mind, but to make up his pack.

I listen to hear the voice of a Governor, Commander-in-Chief of the forces of Massachusetts. I hear only the creaking of crickets and the hum of insects which now fill the summer air. The Governor's exploit is to review the troops on muster days. I have seen him on horseback, with his hat off, listening to a chaplain's prayer. It chances that that is all I have ever seen of a Governor. I think that I could manage to get along without one. If he is not of the least use to prevent my being kidnapped, pray of what important use is he likely to be to me? When freedom is most endangered, he dwells in the deepest obscurity. A distinguished clergyman told me that he chose the profession of a clergyman because it afforded the most leisure for literary pursuits. I would recommend to him the profession of a Governor.

Three years ago, also, when the Sims tragedy was acted, I said to myself, There is such an officer, if not such a man, as the Governor of Massachusetts, — what has he been about the last fortnight? Has he had as much as he could do to keep on the fence during this moral earthquake? It seemed to me that no keener satire could have been aimed at, no more cutting insult have been offered to that man, than just what happened, — the absence of all inquiry after him in that crisis. The worst and the most I chance to know of him is that he did not improve that opportunity to make himself known, and worthily known. He could at least have *resigned* himself into fame. It appeared to be forgotten that there was such a man or such an office. Yet no doubt he was endeavoring to fill the gubernatorial chair all the while. He was no Governor of mine. He did not govern me.

But at last, in the present case, the Governor was heard from. After he and the United States government had perfectly succeeded in robbing a poor innocent black man of his liberty for life, and, as far as they could, of his Creator's likeness in his breast, he made a speech to his accomplices, at a congratulatory supper!

I have read a recent law of this State, mak-

ing it penal for any officer of the "Commonwealth" to "detain or aid in the . . . de-
tention," anywhere within its limits, "of any
person, for the reason that he is claimed as a
fugitive slave." Also, it was a matter of noto-
riety that a writ of replevin to take the fugitive
out of the custody of the United States Marshal could not be served for want of sufficient
force to aid the officer.

I had thought that the Governor was, in some
sense, the executive officer of the State; that it
was his business, as a Governor, to see that the
laws of the State were executed; while, as a
man, he took care that he did not, by so doing,
break the laws of humanity; but when there is
any special important use for him, he is useless,
or worse than useless, and permits the laws of
the State to go unexecuted. Perhaps I do not
know what are the duties of a Governor; but if
to be a Governor requires to subject one's self
to so much ignominy without remedy, if it is to
put a restraint upon my manhood, I shall take
care never to be Governor of Massachusetts. I
have not read far in the statutes of this Commonwealth. It is not profitable reading. They
do not always say what is true; and they do not
always mean what they say. What I am concerned to know is, that that man's influence and
authority were on the side of the slaveholder,

and not of the slave, — of the guilty, and not of
the innocent, — of injustice, and not of justice.
I never saw him of whom I speak; indeed, I
did not know that he was Governor until this
event occurred. I heard of him and Anthony
Burns at the same time, and thus, undoubtedly,
most will hear of him. So far am I from being
governed by him. I do not mean that it was
anything to his discredit that I had not heard
of him, only that I heard what I did. The
worst I shall say of him is, that he proved no
better than the majority of his constituents
would be likely to prove. In my opinion, he
was not equal to the occasion.

The whole military force of the State is at
the service of a Mr. Suttle, a slaveholder from
Virginia, to enable him to catch a man whom
he calls his property; but not a soldier is
offered to save a citizen of Massachusetts from
being kidnapped! Is this what all these soldiers, all this *training*, have been for these
seventy - nine years past? Have they been
trained merely to rob Mexico and carry back
fugitive slaves to their masters?

These very nights I heard the sound of a
drum in our streets. There were men *training*
still; and for what? I could with an effort
pardon the cockerels of Concord for crowing
still, for they, perchance, had not been beaten

that morning; but I could not excuse this rub-a-dub of the "trainers." The slave was carried back by exactly such as these; *i. e.*, by the soldier, of whom the best you can say in this connection is that he is a fool made conspicuous by a painted coat.

Three years ago, also, just a week after the authorities of Boston assembled to carry back a perfectly innocent man, and one whom they knew to be innocent, into slavery, the inhabitants of Concord caused the bells to be rung and the cannons to be fired, to celebrate their liberty, — and the courage and love of liberty of their ancestors who fought at the bridge. As if *those* three millions had fought for the right to be free themselves, but to hold in slavery three million others. Nowadays, men wear a fool's-cap, and call it a liberty-cap. I do not know but there are some who, if they were tied to a whipping-post, and could but get one hand free, would use it to ring the bells and fire the cannons to celebrate *their* liberty. So some of my townsmen took the liberty to ring and fire. That was the extent of their freedom; and when the sound of the bells died away, their liberty died away also; when the powder was all expended, their liberty went off with the smoke.

The joke could be no broader if the inmates

of the prisons were to subscribe for all the powder to be used in such salutes, and hire the jailers to do the firing and ringing for them, while they enjoyed it through the grating.

This is what I thought about my neighbors.

Every humane and intelligent inhabitant of Concord, when he or she heard those bells and those cannons, thought not with pride of the events of the 19th of April, 1775, but with shame of the events of the 12th of April, 1851. But now we have half buried that old shame under a new one.

Massachusetts sat waiting Mr. Loring's decision, as if it could in any way affect her own criminality. Her crime, the most conspicuous and fatal crime of all, was permitting him to be the umpire in such a case. It was really the trial of Massachusetts. Every moment that she hesitated to set this man free, every moment that she now hesitates to atone for her crime, she is convicted. The Commissioner on her case is God; not Edward G. God, but simple God.

I wish my countrymen to consider, that whatever the human law may be, neither an individual nor a nation can ever commit the least act of injustice against the obscurest individual without having to pay the penalty for it. A government which deliberately enacts injustice, and persists in it, will at length even become the laughing-stock of the world.

Much has been said about American slavery, but I think that we do not even yet realize what slavery is. If I were seriously to propose to Congress to make mankind into sausages, I have no doubt that most of the members would smile at my proposition, and if any believed me to be in earnest, they would think that I proposed something much worse than Congress had ever done. But if any of them will tell me that to make a man into a sausage would be much worse, — would be any worse, — than to make him into a slave, — than it was to enact the Fugitive Slave Law, — I will accuse him of foolishness, of intellectual incapacity, of making a distinction without a difference. The one is just as sensible a proposition as the other.

I hear a good deal said about trampling this law under foot. Why, one need not go out of his way to do that. This law rises not to the level of the head or the reason; its natural habitat is in the dirt. It was born and bred, and has its life, only in the dust and mire, on a level with the feet; and he who walks with freedom, and does not with Hindoo mercy avoid treading on every venomous reptile, will inevitably tread on it, and so trample it under foot,

— and Webster, its maker, with it, like the dirt-bug and its ball.

Recent events will be valuable as a criticism on the administration of justice in our midst, or, rather, as showing what are the true resources of justice in any community. It has come to this, that the friends of liberty, the friends of the slave, have shuddered when they have understood that his fate was left to the legal tribunals of the country to be decided. Free men have no faith that justice will be awarded in such a case. The judge may decide this way or that; it is a kind of accident, at best. It is evident that he is not a competent authority in so important a case. It is no time, then, to be judging according to his precedents, but to establish a precedent for the future. I would much rather trust to the sentiment of the people. In their vote you would get something of some value, at least, however small; but in the other case, only the trammeled judgment of an individual, of no significance, be it which way it might.

It is to some extent fatal to the courts, when the people are compelled to go behind them. I do not wish to believe that the courts were made for fair weather, and for very civil cases merely; but think of leaving it to any court in the land to decide whether more than three millions of people, in this case a sixth part of a nation, have a right to be freemen or not! But it has been left to the courts of *justice*, so called, — to the Supreme Court of the land, — and, as you all know, recognizing no authority but the Constitution, it has decided that the three millions are and shall continue to be slaves. Such judges as these are merely the inspectors of a pick-lock and murderer's tools, to tell him whether they are in working order or not, and there they think that their responsibility ends. There was a prior case on the docket, which they, as judges appointed by God, had no right to skip; which having been justly settled, they would have been saved from this humiliation. It was the case of the murderer himself.

The law will never make men free; it is men who have got to make the law free. They are the lovers of law and order who observe the law when the government breaks it.

Among human beings, the judge whose words seal the fate of a man furthest into eternity is not he who merely pronounces the verdict of the law, but he, whoever he may be, who, from a love of truth, and unprejudiced by any custom or enactment of men, utters a true opinion or *sentence* concerning him. He it is that *sentences* him. Whoever can discern truth has received his commission from a higher source than the chiefest justice in the world who can discern only law. He finds himself constituted judge of the judge. Strange that it should be necessary to state such simple truths!

I am more and more convinced that, with reference to any public question, it is more important to know what the country thinks of it than what the city thinks. The city does not *think* much. On any moral question, I would rather have the opinion of Boxboro' than of Boston and New York put together. When the former speaks, I feel as if somebody *had* spoken, as if *humanity* was yet, and a reasonable being had asserted its rights, — as if some unprejudiced men among the country's hills had at length turned their attention to the subject, and by a few sensible words redeemed the reputation of the race. When, in some obscure country town, the farmers come together to a special town-meeting, to express their opinion on some subject which is vexing the land, that, I think, is the true Congress, and the most respectable one that is ever assembled in the United States.

It is evident that there are, in this Commonwealth at least, two parties, becoming more and more distinct, — the party of the city, and the party of the country. I know that the country is mean enough, but I am glad to believe that

there is a slight difference in her favor. But
as yet she has few, if any organs, through
which to express herself. The editorials which
she reads, like the news, come from the sea-
board. Let us, the inhabitants of the country,
cultivate self-respect. Let us not send to the
city for aught more essential than our broad-
cloths and groceries; or, if we read the opinions of the city, let us entertain opinions of our
own.

Among measures to be adopted, I would suggest to make as earnest and vigorous an assault
on the press as has already been made, and with
effect, on the church. The church has much
improved within a few years; but the press is,
almost without exception, corrupt. I believe
that in this country the press exerts a greater
and a more pernicious influence than the church
did in its worst period. We are not a religious
people, but we are a nation of politicians. We
do not care for the Bible, but we do care for
the newspaper. At any meeting of politicians,
— like that at Concord the other evening, for
instance, — how impertinent it would be to
quote from the Bible! how pertinent to quote
from a newspaper or from the Constitution!
The newspaper is a Bible which we read every
morning and every afternoon, standing and sitting, riding and walking. It is a Bible which

every man carries in his pocket, which lies on
every table and counter, and which the mail,
and thousands of missionaries, are continually
dispersing.   It is, in short, the only book
which America has printed, and which America
reads. So wide is its influence. The editor
is a preacher whom you voluntarily support.
Your tax is commonly one cent daily, and it
costs nothing for pew hire. But how many of
these preachers preach the truth? I repeat the
testimony of many an intelligent foreigner, as
well as my own convictions, when I say, that
probably no country was ever ruled by so mean
a class of tyrants as, with a few noble exceptions, are the editors of the periodical press in
this country.   And as they live and rule only
by their servility, and appealing to the worse,
and not the better, nature of man, the people
who read them are in the condition of the dog
that returns to his vomit.

The *Liberator* and the *Commonwealth* were
the only papers in Boston, as far as I know,
which made themselves heard in condemnation
of the cowardice and meanness of the authorities of that city, as exhibited in '51.   The
other journals, almost without exception, by
their manner of referring to and speaking of
the Fugitive Slave Law, and the carrying back
of the slave Sims, insulted the common sense

of the country, at least. And, for the most part, they did this, one would say, because they thought so to secure the approbation of their patrons, not being aware that a sounder sentiment prevailed to any extent in the heart of the Commonwealth. I am told that some of them have improved of late; but they are still eminently time-serving. Such is the character they have won.

But, thank fortune, this preacher can be even more easily reached by the weapons of the reformer than could the recreant priest. The free men of New England have only to refrain from purchasing and reading these sheets, have only to withhold their cents, to kill a score of them at once. One whom I respect told me that he purchased Mitchell's *Citizen* in the cars, and then threw it out the window. But would not his contempt have been more fatally expressed if he had not bought it?

Are they Americans? are they New Englanders? are they inhabitants of Lexington and Concord and Framingham, who read and support the Boston *Post*, *Mail*, *Journal*, *Advertiser*, *Courier*, and *Times?* Are these the Flags of our Union? I am not a newspaper reader, and may omit to name the worst.

Could slavery suggest a more complete servility than some of these journals exhibit? Is

there any dust which their conduct does not
lick, and make fouler still with its slime? I do
not know whether the Boston *Herald* is still in
existence, but I remember to have seen it about
the streets when Sims was carried off. Did it
not act its part well, — serve its master faithfully! How could it have gone lower on its
belly? How can a man stoop lower than he is
low? do more than put his extremities in the
place of the head he has? than make his head
his lower extremity? When I have taken up
this paper with my cuffs turned up, I have
heard the gurgling of the sewer through every
column. I have felt that I was handling a
paper picked out of the public gutters, a leaf
from the gospel of the gambling-house, the
groggery, and the brothel, harmonizing with the
gospel of the Merchants' Exchange.

The majority of the men of the North, and
of the South and East and West, are not men
of principle. If they vote, they do not send
men to Congress on errands of humanity; but
while their brothers and sisters are being
scourged and hung for loving liberty, while — I
might here insert all that slavery implies and is
— it is the mismanagement of wood and iron
and stone and gold which concerns them. Do
what you will, O Government, with my wife and
children, my mother and brother, my father

and sister, I will obey your commands to the letter. It will indeed grieve me if you hurt them, if you deliver them to overseers to be hunted by hounds or to be whipped to death; but, nevertheless, I will peaceably pursue my chosen calling on this fair earth, until perchance, one day, when I have put on mourning for them dead, I shall have persuaded you to relent. Such is the attitude, such are the words of Massachusetts.

Rather than do thus, I need not say what match I would touch, what system endeavor to blow up; but as I love my life, I would side with the light, and let the dark earth roll from under me, calling my mother and my brother to follow.

I would remind my countrymen that they are to be men first, and Americans only at a late and convenient hour. No matter how valuable law may be to protect your property, even to keep soul and body together, if it do not keep you and humanity together.

I am sorry to say that I doubt if there is a judge in Massachusetts who is prepared to resign his office, and get his living innocently, whenever it is required of him to pass sentence under a law which is merely contrary to the law of God. I am compelled to see that they put themselves, or rather are by character, in this respect, exactly on a level with the marine who discharges his musket in any direction he is ordered to. They are just as much tools, and as little men. Certainly, they are not the more to be respected, because their master enslaves their understandings and consciences, instead of their bodies.

The judges and lawyers, — simply as such, I mean, — and all men of expediency, try this case by a very low and incompetent standard. They consider, not whether the Fugitive Slave Law is right, but whether it is what they call *constitutional*. Is virtue constitutional, or vice? Is equity constitutional, or iniquity? In important moral and vital questions, like this, it is just as impertinent to ask whether a law is constitutional or not, as to ask whether it is profitable or not. They persist in being the servants of the worst of men, and not the servants of humanity. The question is, not whether you or your grandfather, seventy years ago, did not enter into an agreement to serve the Devil, and that service is not accordingly now due; but whether you will not now, for once and at last, serve God, — in spite of your own past recreancy, or that of your ancestor, — by obeying that eternal and only just CONSTI-TUTION, which He, and not any Jefferson or Adams, has written in your being.

The amount of it is, if the majority vote the Devil to be God, the minority will live and behave accordingly, — and obey the successful candidate, trusting that, some time or other, by some Speaker's casting-vote, perhaps, they may reinstate God. This is the highest principle I can get out or invent for my neighbors. These men act as if they believed that they could safely slide down a hill a little way, — or a good way, — and would surely come to a place, by and by, where they could begin to slide up again. This is expediency, or choosing that course which offers the slightest obstacles to the feet, that is, a downhill one. But there is no such thing as accomplishing a righteous reform by the use of "expediency." There is no such thing as sliding up hill. In morals the only sliders are backsliders.

Thus we steadily worship Mammon, both school and state and church, and on the seventh day curse God with a tintamar from one end of the Union to the other.

Will mankind never learn that policy is not morality, — that it never secures any moral right, but considers merely what is expedient? chooses the available candidate, — who is invariably the Devil, — and what right have his constituents to be surprised, because the Devil does not behave like an angel of light? What is wanted is men, not of policy, but of probity, — who recognize a higher law than the Constitution, or the decision of the majority. The fate of the country does not depend on how you vote at the polls, — the worst man is as strong as the best at that game; it does not depend on what kind of paper you drop into the ballot-box once a year, but on what kind of man you drop from your chamber into the street every morning.

What should concern Massachusetts is not the Nebraska Bill, nor the Fugitive Slave Bill, but her own slaveholding and servility. Let the State dissolve her union with the slave-holder. She may wriggle and hesitate, and ask leave to read the Constitution once more; but she can find no respectable law or precedent which sanctions the continuance of such a union for an instant.

Let each inhabitant of the State dissolve his union with her, as long as she delays to do her duty.

The events of the past month teach me to distrust Fame. I see that she does not finely discriminate, but coarsely hurrahs. She considers not the simple heroism of an action, but only as it is connected with its apparent consequences. She praises till she is hoarse the easy exploit of the Boston tea party, but will be comparatively silent about the braver and more disinterestedly heroic attack on the Boston Court-House, simply because it was unsuccessful!

Covered with disgrace, the State has sat down coolly to try for their lives and liberties the men who attempted to do its duty for it. And this is called *justice!* They who have shown that they can behave particularly well may perchance be put under bonds for *their good behavior*. They whom truth requires at present to plead guilty are, of all the inhabitants of the State, preëminently innocent. While the Governor, and the Mayor, and countless officers of the Commonwealth are at large, the champions of liberty are imprisoned.

Only they are guiltless who commit the crime of contempt of such a court. It behooves every man to see that his influence is on the side of justice, and let the courts make their own characters. My sympathies in this case are wholly with the accused, and wholly against their accusers and judges. Justice is sweet and musical; but injustice is harsh and discordant. The judge still sits grinding at his organ, but it yields no music, and we hear only the sound of the handle. He believes that all the music resides in the handle, and the crowd toss him their coppers the same as before.

Do you suppose that that Massachusetts

which is now doing these things, — which hesitates to crown these men, some of whose lawyers, and even judges, perchance, may be driven to take refuge in some poor quibble, that they may not wholly outrage their instinctive sense of justice, — do you suppose that she is anything but base and servile? that she is the champion of liberty?

Show me a free state, and a court truly of justice, and I will fight for them, if need be; but show me Massachusetts, and I refuse her my allegiance, and express contempt for her courts.

The effect of a good government is to make life more valuable, — of a bad one, to make it less valuable. We can afford that railroad and all merely material stock should lose some of its value, for that only compels us to live more simply and economically; but suppose that the value of life itself should be diminished! How can we make a less demand on man and nature, how live more economically in respect to virtue and all noble qualities, than we do? I have lived for the last month — and I think that every man in Massachusetts capable of the sentiment of patriotism must have had a similar experience — with the sense of having suffered a vast and indefinite loss. I did not know at first what ailed me. At last it occurred to me that what I had lost was a country. I had never respected the government near to which I lived, but I had foolishly thought that I might manage to live here, minding my private affairs, and forget it. For my part, my old and worthiest pursuits have lost I cannot say how much of their attraction, and I feel that my investment in life here is worth many per cent. less since Massachusetts last deliberately sent back an innocent man, Anthony Burns, to slavery. I dwelt before, perhaps, in the illusion that my life passed somewhere only *between* heaven and hell, but now I cannot persuade myself that I do not dwell *wholly within* hell. The site of that political organization called Massachusetts is to me morally covered with volcanic scoriæ and cinders, such as Milton describes in the infernal regions. If there is any hell more unprincipled than our rulers, and we, the ruled, I feel curious to see it. Life itself being worth less, all things with it, which minister to it, are worth less. Suppose you have a small library, with pictures to adorn the walls, — a garden laid out around, — and contemplate scientific and literary pursuits, and discover all at once that your villa, with all its contents, is located in hell, and that the justice of the peace has a cloven foot and a forked tail, — do not these things suddenly lose their value in your eyes?

I feel that, to some extent, the State has fatally interfered with my lawful business. It has not only interrupted me in my passage through Court Street on errands of trade, but it has interrupted me and every man on his onward and upward path, on which he had trusted soon to leave Court Street far behind. What right had it to remind me of Court Street? I have found that hollow which even I had relied on for solid.

I am surprised to see men going about their business as if nothing had happened. I say to myself, "Unfortunates! they have not heard the news." I am surprised that the man whom I just met on horseback should be so earnest to overtake his newly bought cows running away, — since all property is insecure, and if they do not run away again, they may be taken away from him when he gets them. Fool! does he not know that his seed-corn is worth less this year, — that all beneficent harvests fail as you approach the empire of hell? No prudent man will build a stone house under these circumstances, or engage in any peaceful enterprise which it requires a long time to accomplish. Art is as long as ever, but life is more interrupted and less available for a man's proper pursuits. It is not an era of repose. We have used up all our inherited freedom. If we would save our lives, we must fight for them.

I walk toward one of our ponds; but what signifies the beauty of nature when men are base? We walk to lakes to see our serenity reflected in them; when we are not serene, we go not to them. Who can be serene in a country where both the rulers and the ruled are without principle? The remembrance of my country spoils my walk. My thoughts are murder to the State, and involuntarily go plotting against her.

But it chanced the other day that I scented a white water-lily, and a season I had waited for had arrived. It is the emblem of purity. It bursts up so pure and fair to the eye, and so sweet to the scent, as if to show us what purity and sweetness reside in, and can be extracted from, the slime and muck of earth. I think I have plucked the first one that has opened for a mile. What confirmation of our hopes is in the fragrance of this flower! I shall not so soon despair of the world for it, notwithstanding slavery, and the cowardice and want of principle of Northern men. It suggests what kind of laws have prevailed longest and widest, and still prevail, and that the time may come when man's deeds will smell as sweet. Such is the odor which the plant emits. If Nature can compound this fragrance still annually, I shall believe her still young and full of vigor, her integrity and genius unimpaired, and that there is virtue even in man, too, who is fitted to perceive and love it. It reminds me that Nature has been partner to no Missouri Compromise. I scent no compromise in the fragrance of the water-lily. It is not a *Nymphæa* DOUGLASSII. In it, the sweet, and pure, and innocent are wholly sundered from the obscene and baleful. I do not scent in this the time-serving irresolution of a Massachusetts Governor, nor of a Boston Mayor. So behave that the odor of your actions may enhance the general sweetness of the atmosphere, that when we behold or scent a flower, we may not be reminded how inconsistent your deeds are with it; for all odor is but one form of advertisement of a moral quality, and if fair actions had not been performed, the lily would not smell sweet. The foul slime stands for the sloth and vice of man, the decay of humanity; the fragrant flower that springs from it, for the purity and courage which are immortal.

Slavery and servility have produced no sweet-scented flower annually, to charm the senses of men, for they have no real life: they are merely a decaying and a death, offensive to all healthy nostrils. We do not complain that they *live*, but that they do not *get buried*. Let the living bury them; even they are good for manure.

A PLEA FOR CAPTAIN JOHN BROWN

I TRUST that you will pardon me for being
here. I do not wish to force my thoughts upon
you, but I feel forced myself. Little as I know
of Captain Brown, I would fain do my part to
correct the tone and the statements of the newspapers, and of my countrymen generally, respecting his character and actions. It costs us
nothing to be just. We can at least express our
sympathy with, and admiration of, him and his
companions, and that is what I now propose to do.

First, as to his history. I will endeavor to
omit, as much as possible, what you have already read. I need not describe his person to
you, for probably most of you have seen and
will not soon forget him. I am told that his
grandfather, John Brown, was an officer in the
Revolution; that he himself was born in Connecticut about the beginning of this century,
but early went with his father to Ohio. I heard
him say that his father was a contractor who
furnished beef to the army there, in the war of
1812; that he accompanied him to the camp,
and assisted him in that employment, seeing

a good deal of military life, — more, perhaps, than if he had been a soldier; for he was often present at the councils of the officers. Especially, he learned by experience how armies are supplied and maintained in the field, — a work which, he observed, requires at least as much experience and skill as to lead them in battle. He said that few persons had any conception of the cost, even the pecuniary cost, of firing a single bullet in war. He saw enough, at any rate, to disgust him with a military life; indeed, to excite in him a great abhorrence of it; so much so, that though he was tempted by the offer of some petty office in the army, when he was about eighteen, he not only declined that, but he also refused to train when warned, and was fined for it. He then resolved that he would never have anything to do with any war, unless it were a war for liberty.

When the troubles in Kansas began, he sent several of his sons thither to strengthen the party of the Free State men, fitting them out with such weapons as he had; telling them that if the troubles should increase, and there should be need of him, he would follow, to assist them with his hand and counsel. This, as you all know, he soon after did; and it was through his agency, far more than any other's, that Kansas was made free.

For a part of his life he was a surveyor, and at one time he was engaged in wool-growing, and he went to Europe as an agent about that business. There, as everywhere, he had his eyes about him, and made many original observations. He said, for instance, that he saw why the soil of England was so rich, and that of Germany (I think it was) so poor, and he thought of writing to some of the crowned heads about it. It was because in England the peasantry live on the soil which they cultivate, but in Germany they are gathered into villages at night. It is a pity that he did not make a book of his observations.

I should say that he was an old-fashioned man in his respect for the Constitution, and his faith in the permanence of this Union. Slavery he deemed to be wholly opposed to these, and he was its determined foe.

He was by descent and birth a New England farmer, a man of great common sense, deliberate and practical as that class is, and tenfold more so. He was like the best of those who stood at Concord Bridge once, on Lexington Common, and on Bunker Hill, only he was firmer and higher principled than any that I have chanced to hear of as there. It was no abolition lecturer that converted him. Ethan Allen and Stark, with whom he may in some respects be compared, were rangers in a lower and less important field. They could bravely face their country's foes, but he had the courage to face his country herself when she was in the wrong. A Western writer says, to account for his escape from so many perils, that he was concealed under a "rural exterior;" as if, in that prairie land, a hero should, by good rights, wear a citizen's dress only.

He did not go to the college called Harvard, good old Alma Mater as she is. He was not fed on the pap that is there furnished. As he phrased it, "I know no more of grammar than one of your calves." But he went to the great university of the West, where he sedulously pursued the study of Liberty, for which he had early betrayed a fondness, and having taken many degrees, he finally commenced the public practice of Humanity in Kansas, as you all know. Such were *his humanities*, and not any study of grammar. He would have left a Greek accent slanting the wrong way, and righted up a falling man.

He was one of that class of whom we hear a great deal, but, for the most part, see nothing at all, — the Puritans. It would be in vain to kill him. He died lately in the time of Cromwell, but he reappeared here. Why should he not? Some of the Puritan stock are said to

have come over and settled in New England.
They were a class that did something else than .
celebrate their forefathers' day, and eat parched
corn in remembrance of that time. They were
neither Democrats nor Republicans, but men of
simple habits, straightforward, prayerful; not
thinking much of rulers who did not fear God,
not making many compromises, nor seeking
after available candidates.

"In his camp," as one has recently written,
and as I have myself heard him state, "he permitted no profanity; no man of loose morals
was suffered to remain there, unless, indeed, as
a prisoner of war. 'I would rather,' said he,
'have the small-pox, yellow fever, and cholera,
all together in my camp, than a man without
principle. . . . It is a mistake, sir, that our
people make, when they think that bullies are
the best fighters, or that they are the fit men
to oppose these Southerners. Give me men
of good principles, — God-fearing men, — men
who respect themselves, and with a dozen of
them I will oppose any hundred such men as
these Buford ruffians.'" He said that if one
offered himself to be a soldier under him, who
was forward to tell what he could or would do
if he could only get sight of the enemy, he had
but little confidence in him.

He was never able to find more than a score

or so of recruits whom he would accept, and only about a dozen, among them his sons, in whom he had perfect faith. When he was here, some years ago, he showed to a few a little manuscript book, — his "orderly book" I think he called it, — containing the names of his company in Kansas, and the rules by which they bound themselves; and he stated that several of them had already sealed the contract with their blood. When some one remarked that, with the addition of a chaplain, it would have been a perfect Cromwellian troop, he observed that he would have been glad to add a chaplain to the list, if he could have found one who could fill that office worthily. It is easy enough to find one for the United States army. I believe that he had prayers in his camp morning and evening, nevertheless.

He was a man of Spartan habits, and at sixty was scrupulous about his diet at your table, excusing himself by saying that he must eat sparingly and fare hard, as became a soldier, or one who was fitting himself for difficult enterprises, a life of exposure.

A man of rare common sense and directness of speech, as of action; a transcendentalist above all, a man of ideas and principles, — that was what distinguished him. Not yielding to a whim or transient impulse, but carrying out the purpose of a life. I noticed that he did not overstate anything, but spoke within bounds. I remember, particularly, how, in his speech here, he referred to what his family had suffered in Kansas, without ever giving the least vent to his pent-up fire. It was a volcano with an ordinary chimney-flue. Also referring to the deeds of certain Border Ruffians, he said, rapidly paring away his speech, like an experienced soldier, keeping a reserve of force and meaning, "They had a perfect right to be hung." He was not in the least a rhetorician, was not talking to Buncombe or his constituents anywhere, had no need to invent anything but to tell the simple truth, and communicate his own resolution; therefore he appeared incomparably strong, and eloquence in Congress and elsewhere seemed to me at a discount. It was like the speeches of Cromwell compared with those of an ordinary king.

As for his tact and prudence, I will merely say, that at a time when scarcely a man from the Free States was able to reach Kansas by any direct route, at least without having his arms taken from him, he, carrying what imperfect guns and other weapons he could collect, openly and slowly drove an ox-cart through Missouri, apparently in the capacity of a surveyor, with his surveying compass exposed in it, and so passed unsuspected, and had ample opportunity to learn the designs of the enemy. For some time after his arrival he still followed the same profession. When, for instance, he saw a knot of the ruffians on the prairie, discussing, of course, the single topic which then occupied their minds, he would, perhaps, take his compass and one of his sons, and proceed to run an imaginary line right through the very spot on which that conclave had assembled, and when he came up to them, he would naturally pause and have some talk with them, learning their news, and, at last, all their plans perfectly; and having thus completed his real survey he would resume his imaginary one, and run on his line till he was out of sight.

When I expressed surprise that he could live in Kansas at all, with a price set upon his head, and so large a number, including the authorities, exasperated against him, he accounted for it by saying, "It is perfectly well understood that I will not be taken." Much of the time for some years he has had to skulk in swamps, suffering from poverty and from sickness, which was the consequence of exposure, befriended only by Indians and a few whites. But though it might be known that he was lurking in a particular swamp, his foes commonly did not care to go in after him. He could even come out into a town where there were more Border Ruffians than Free State men, and transact some business, without delaying long, and yet not be molested; for, said he, "no little handful of men were willing to undertake it, and a large body could not be got together in season."

As for his recent failure, we do not know the facts about it. It was evidently far from being a wild and desperate attempt. His enemy, Mr. Vallandigham, is compelled to say that "it was among the best planned and executed conspiracies that ever failed."

Not to mention his other successes, was it a failure, or did it show a want of good management, to deliver from bondage a dozen human beings, and walk off with them by broad daylight, for weeks if not months, at a leisurely pace, through one State after another, for half the length of the North, conspicuous to all parties, with a price set upon his head, going into a court-room on his way and telling what he had done, thus convincing Missouri that it was not profitable to try to hold slaves in his neighborhood? — and this, not because the government menials were lenient, but because they were afraid of him.

Yet he did not attribute his success, foolishly, to "his star," or to any magic. He said, truly, that the reason why such greatly superior numbers quailed before him was, as one of his prisoners confessed, because they *lacked a cause,* — a kind of armor which he and his party never lacked. When the time came, few men were found willing to lay down their lives in defense of what they knew to be wrong; they did not like that this should be their last act in this world.

But to make haste to *his* last act, and its effects.

The newspapers seem to ignore, or perhaps are really ignorant, of the fact that there are at least as many as two or three individuals to a town throughout the North who think much as the present speaker does about him and his enterprise. I do not hesitate to say that they are an important and growing party. We aspire to be something more than stupid and timid chattels, pretending to read history and our Bibles, but desecrating every house and every day we breathe in. Perhaps anxious politicians may prove that only seventeen white men and five negroes were concerned in the late enterprise; but their very anxiety to prove this might suggest to themselves that all is not told. Why do they still dodge the truth? They are so anxious because of a dim consciousness of the fact, which they do not distinctly face, that at least a million of the free inhabitants of the

United States would have rejoiced if it had succeeded. They at most only criticise the tactics. Though we wear no crape, the thought of that man's position and probable fate is spoiling many a man's day here at the North for other thinking. If any one who has seen him here can pursue successfully any other train of thought, I do not know what he is made of. If there is any such who gets his usual allowance of sleep, I will warrant him to fatten easily under any circumstances which do not touch his body or purse. I put a piece of paper and a pencil under my pillow, and when I could not sleep I wrote in the dark.

On the whole, my respect for my fellow-men, except as one may outweigh a million, is not being increased these days. I have noticed the cold-blooded way in which newspaper writers and men generally speak of this event, as if an ordinary malefactor, though one of unusual "pluck," — as the Governor of Virginia is reported to have said, using the language of the cock-pit, "the gamest man he ever saw," — had been · caught, and were about to be hung. He was not dreaming of his foes when the governor thought he looked so brave. It turns what sweetness I have to gall, to hear, or hear of, the remarks of some of my neighbors. When we heard at first that he was dead, one of my townsmen observed that "he died as the fool dieth;" which, pardon me, for an instant suggested a likeness in him dying to my neighbor living. Others, craven-hearted, said disparagingly, that "he threw his life away," because he resisted the government. Which way have they thrown *their* lives, pray? — such as would praise a man for attacking singly an ordinary band of thieves or murderers. I hear another ask, Yankee-like, "What will he gain by it?" as if he expected to fill his pockets by this enterprise. Such a one has no idea of gain but in this worldly sense. If it does not lead to a "surprise" party, if he does not get a new pair of boots, or a vote of thanks, it must be a failure. "But he won't gain anything by it." Well, no, I don't suppose he could get four-and-sixpence a day for being hung, take the year round; but then he stands a chance to save a considerable part of his soul, — and *such* a soul! — when *you* do not. No doubt you can get more in your market for a quart of milk than for a quart of blood, but that is not the market that heroes carry their blood to.

Such do not know that like the seed is the fruit, and that, in the moral world, when good seed is planted, good fruit is inevitable, and does not depend on our watering and cultivating; that when you plant, or bury, a hero in his field, a crop of heroes is sure to spring up. This is a seed of such force and vitality, that it does not ask our leave to germinate.

The momentary charge at Balaklava, in obedience to a blundering command, proving what a perfect machine the soldier is, has, properly enough, been celebrated by a poet laureate; but the steady, and for the most part successful, charge of this man, for some years, against the legions of Slavery, in obedience to an infinitely higher command, is as much more memorable than that as an intelligent and conscientious man is superior to a machine. Do you think that that will go unsung?

"Served him right," — "A dangerous man," — "He is undoubtedly insane." So they proceed to live their sane, and wise, and altogether admirable lives, reading their Plutarch a little, but chiefly pausing at that feat of Putnam, who was let down into a wolf's den; and in this wise they nourish themselves for brave and patriotic deeds some time or other. The Tract Society could afford to print that story of Putnam. You might open the district schools with the reading of it, for there is nothing about Slavery or the Church in it; unless it occurs to the reader that some pastors are *wolves* in sheep's clothing. "The American Board of Commissioners for Foreign Missions," even, might dare to protest against *that* wolf. I have heard of boards, and of American boards, but it chances that I never heard of this particular lumber till lately. And yet I hear of Northern men, and women, and children, by families, buying a "life-membership" in such societies as these. A life-membership in the grave! You can get buried cheaper than that.

Our foes are in our midst and all about us. There is hardly a house but is divided against itself, for our foe is the all but universal wooden-ness of both head and heart, the want of vitality in man, which is the effect of our vice; and hence are begotten fear, superstition, bigotry, persecution, and slavery of all kinds. We are mere figure-heads upon a hulk, with livers in the place of hearts. The curse is the worship of idols, which at length changes the worshiper into a stone image himself; and the New Englander is just as much an idolater as the Hindoo. This man was an exception, for he did not set up even a political graven image between him and his God.

A church that can never have done with excommunicating Christ while it exists! Away with your broad and flat churches, and your narrow and tall churches! Take a step forward, and invent a new style of out-houses. Invent a salt that will save you, and defend our nostrils.

The modern Christian is a man who has consented to say all the prayers in the liturgy, provided you will let him go straight to bed and sleep quietly afterward. All his prayers begin with "Now I lay me down to sleep," and he is forever looking forward to the time when he shall go to his "*long* rest." He has consented to perform certain old-established charities, too, after a fashion, but he does not wish to hear of any new-fangled ones; he doesn't wish to have any supplementary articles added to the contract, to fit it to the present time. He shows the whites of his eyes on the Sabbath, and the blacks all the rest of the week. The evil is not merely a stagnation of blood, but a stagnation of spirit. Many, no doubt, are well disposed, but sluggish by constitution and by habit, and they cannot conceive of a man who is actuated by higher motives than they are. Accordingly they pronounce this man insane, for they know that *they* could never act as he does, as long as they are themselves.

We dream of foreign countries, of other times and races of men, placing them at a distance in history or space; but let some significant event like the present occur in our midst, and we discover, often, this distance and this strangeness between us and our nearest neighbors. *They* are our Austrias, and Chinas, and

South Sea Islands. Our crowded society becomes well spaced all at once, clean and handsome to the eye, — a city of magnificent distances. We discover why it was that we never got beyond compliments and surfaces with them before; we become aware of as many versts between us and them as here are between a wandering Tartar and a Chinese town. The thoughtful man becomes a hermit in the thoroughfares of the market - place. Impassable seas suddenly find their level between us, or dumb steppes stretch themselves out there. It is the difference of constitution, of intelligence, and faith, and not streams and mountains, that make the true and impassable boundaries between individuals and between states. None but the like-minded can come plenipotentiary to our court.

I read all the newspapers I could get within a week after this event, and I do not remember in them a single expression of sympathy for these men. I have since seen one noble statement, in a Boston paper, not editorial. Some voluminous sheets decided not to print the full report of Brown's words to the exclusion of other matter. It was as if a publisher should reject the manuscript of the New Testament, and print Wilson's last speech. The same journal which contained this pregnant news was chiefly filled, in parallel columns, with the reports of the political conventions that were being held. But the descent to them was too steep. They should have been spared this contrast, — been printed in an extra, at least. To turn from the voices and deeds of earnest men to the *cackling* of political conventions! Office-seekers and speech-makers, who do not so much as lay an honest egg, but wear their breasts bare upon an egg of chalk! Their great game is the game of straws, or rather that universal aboriginal game of the platter, at which the Indians cried *hub, bub!* Exclude the reports of religious and political conventions, and publish the words of a living man.

But I object not so much to what they have omitted as to what they have inserted. Even the *Liberator* called it "a misguided, wild, and apparently insane — effort." As for the herd of newspapers and magazines, I do not chance to know an editor in the country who will deliberately print anything which he knows will ultimately and permanently reduce the number of his subscribers. They do not believe that it would be expedient. How then can they print truth? If we do not say pleasant things, they argue, nobody will attend to us. And so they do like some traveling auctioneers, who sing an obscene song, in order to draw a crowd around them. Republican editors, obliged to get their sentences ready for the morning edition, and accustomed to look at everything by the twilight of politics, express no admiration, nor true sorrow even, but call these men "deluded fanatics," — "mistaken men," — "insane," or "crazed." It suggests what a *sane* set of editors we are blessed with, *not* "mistaken men;" who know very well on which side their bread is buttered, at least.

A man does a brave and humane deed, and at once, on all sides, we hear people and parties declaring, "I did n't do it, nor countenance *him* to do it, in any conceivable way. It can't be fairly inferred from my past career." I, for one, am not interested to hear you define your position. I don't know that I ever was or ever shall be. I think it is mere egotism, or impertinent at this time. Ye need n't take so much pains to wash your skirts of him. No intelligent man will ever be convinced that he was any creature of yours. He went and came, as he himself informs us, "under the auspices of John Brown and nobody else." The Republican party does not perceive how many his *failure* will make to vote more correctly than they would have them. They have counted the votes of Pennsylvania & Co., but they have not correctly counted Captain Brown's vote. He

has taken the wind out of their sails, — the little wind they had, — and they may as well lie
to and repair.

What though he did not belong to your
clique! Though you may not approve of his
method or his principles, recognize his magnanimity. Would you not like to claim kindred-
ship with him in that, though in no other thing
he is like, or likely, to you? Do you think
that you would lose your reputation so? What
you lost at the spile, you would gain at the
bung.

If they do not mean all this, then they do
not speak the truth, and say what they mean.
They are simply at their old tricks still.

"It was always conceded to him," *says one
who calls him crazy*, "that he was a conscientious man, very modest in his demeanor, apparently inoffensive, until the subject of Slavery
was introduced, when he would exhibit a feeling of indignation unparalleled."

The slave-ship is on her way, crowded with
its dying victims; new cargoes are being added
in mid-ocean; a small crew of slaveholders,
countenanced by a large body of passengers, is
smothering four millions under the hatches, and
yet the politician asserts that the only proper
way by which deliverance is to be obtained
is by "the quiet diffusion of the sentiments of

humanity," without any "outbreak." As if the sentiments of humanity were ever found unaccompanied by its deeds, and you could disperse them, all finished to order, the pure article, as easily as water with a watering-pot, and so lay the dust. What is that that I hear cast overboard? The bodies of the dead that have found deliverance. That is the way we are "diffusing" humanity, and its sentiments with it.

Prominent and influential editors, accustomed to deal with politicians, men of an infinitely lower grade, say, in their ignorance, that he acted "on the principle of revenge." They do not know the man. They must enlarge themselves to conceive of him. I have no doubt that the time will come when they will begin to see him as he was. They have got to conceive of a man of faith and of religious principle, and not a politician or an Indian; of a man who did not wait till he was personally interfered with or thwarted in some harmless business before he gave his life to the cause of the oppressed.

If Walker may be considered the representative of the South, I wish I could say that Brown was the representative of the North. He was a superior man. He did not value his bodily life in comparison with ideal things. He did not recognize unjust human laws, but resisted them as he was bid. For once we are lifted out of the trivialness and dust of politics into the region of truth and manhood. No man in America has ever stood up so persistently and effectively for the dignity of human nature, knowing himself for a man, and the equal of any and all governments. In that sense he was the most American of us all. He needed no babbling lawyer, making false issues, to defend him. He was more than a match for all the judges that American voters, or office-holders of whatever grade, can create. He could not have been tried by a jury of his peers, because his peers did not exist. When a man stands up serenely against the condemnation and vengeance of mankind, rising above them literally *by a whole body,* — even though he were of late the vilest murderer, who has settled that matter with himself, — the spectacle is a sublime one, — did n't ye know it, ye *Liberators,* ye *Tribunes,* ye *Republicans?* — and we become criminal in comparison. Do yourselves the honor to recognize him. He needs none of your respect.

As for the Democratic journals, they are not human enough to affect me at all. I do not feel indignation at anything they may say.

I am aware that I anticipate a little, — that he was still, at the last accounts, alive in the hands of his foes; but that being the case, I have all along found myself thinking and speaking of him as physically dead.

I do not believe in erecting statues to those who still live in our hearts, whose bones have not yet crumbled in the earth around us, but I would rather see the statue of Captain Brown in the Massachusetts State - House yard than that of any other man whom I know. I rejoice that I live in this age, that I am his contemporary.

What a contrast, when we turn to that political party which is so anxiously shuffling him and his plot out of its way, and looking around for some available slaveholder, perhaps, to be its candidate, at least for one who will execute the Fugitive Slave Law, and all those other unjust laws which he took up arms to annul!

Insane! A father and six sons, and one son-in-law, and several more men besides, — as many at least as twelve disciples, — all struck with insanity at once; while the same tyrant holds with a firmer gripe than ever his four millions of slaves, and a thousand sane editors, his abettors, are saving their country and their bacon! Just as insane were his efforts in Kansas. Ask the tyrant who is his most dangerous foe, the sane man or the insane? Do the thousands who know him best, who have rejoiced at his deeds in Kansas, and have afforded him material aid there, think him insane? Such a use of this word is a mere trope with most who persist in using it, and I have no doubt that many of the rest have already in silence retracted their words.

Read his admirable answers to Mason and others. How they are dwarfed and defeated by the contrast! On the one side, half-brutish, half-timid questioning; on the other, truth, clear as lightning, crashing into their obscene temples. They are made to stand with Pilate, and Gessler, and the Inquisition. How ineffectual their speech and action! and what a void their silence! They are but helpless tools in this great work. It was no human power that gathered them about this preacher.

What have Massachusetts and the North sent a few *sane* representatives to Congress for, of late years? — to declare with effect what kind of sentiments? All their speeches put together and boiled down — and probably they themselves will confess it — do not match for manly directness and force, and for simple truth, the few casual remarks of crazy John Brown on the floor of the Harper's Ferry engine-house, — that man whom you are about to hang, to send to the other world, though not to represent *you* there. No, he was not our representative in any sense. He was too fair a specimen of a man to represent the like of us. Who, then, *were* his constituents? If you read his words understandingly you will find out. In his case there is no idle eloquence, no made, nor maiden speech, no compliments to the oppressor. Truth is his inspirer, and earnestness the polisher of his sentences. He could afford to lose his Sharps rifles, while he retained his faculty of speech, — a Sharps rifle of infinitely surer and longer range.

And the New York *Herald* reports the conversation *verbatim!* It does not know of what undying words it is made the vehicle.

I have no respect for the penetration of any man who can read the report of that conversation and still call the principal in it insane. It has the ring of a saner sanity than an ordinary discipline and habits of life, than an ordinary organization, secure. Take any sentence of it, — "Any questions that I can honorably answer, I will; not otherwise. So far as I am myself concerned, I have told everything truthfully. I value my word, sir." The few who talk about his vindictive spirit, while they really admire his heroism, have no test by which to detect a noble man, no amalgam to combine with his pure gold. They mix their own dross with it.

It is a relief to turn from these slanders to

the testimony of his more truthful, but fright-
ened jailers and hangmen. Governor Wise
speaks far more justly and appreciatingly of
him than any Northern editor, or politician, or
public personage, that I chance to have heard
from. I know that you can afford to hear him
again on this subject. He says: "They are
themselves mistaken who take him to be a madman. . . . He is cool, collected, and indomita-
ble, and it is but just to him to say that he was
humane to his prisoners. . . . And he inspired
me with great trust in his integrity as a man of
truth. He is a fanatic, vain and garrulous "
(I leave that part to Mr. Wise), "but firm,
truthful, and intelligent. His men, too, who
survive, are like him. . . . Colonel Washington says that he was the coolest and firmest man
he ever saw in defying danger and death. With
one son dead by his side, and another shot
through, he felt the pulse of his dying son with
one hand, and held his rifle with the other, and
commanded his men with the utmost composure,
encouraging them to be firm, and to sell their
lives as dear as they could. Of the three white
prisoners, Brown, Stevens, and Coppoc, it was
hard to say which was most firm."

Almost the first Northern men whom the
slaveholder has learned to respect!

The testimony of Mr. Vallandigham, though

less valuable, is of the same purport, that "it is vain to underrate either the man or his conspiracy. . . . He is the farthest possible removed from the ordinary ruffian, fanatic, or madman."

"All is quiet at Harper's Ferry," say the journals. What is the character of that calm which follows when the law and the slaveholder prevail? I regard this event as a touchstone designed to bring out, with glaring distinctness, the character of this government. We needed to be thus assisted to see it by the light of history. It needed to see itself. When a government puts forth its strength on the side of injustice, as ours to maintain slavery and kill the liberators of the slave, it reveals itself a merely brute force, or worse, a demoniacal force. It is the head of the Plug-Uglies. It is more manifest than ever that tyranny rules. I see this government to be effectually allied with France and Austria in oppressing mankind. There sits a tyrant holding fettered four millions of slaves; here comes their heroic liberator. This most hypocritical and diabolical government looks up from its seat on the gasping four millions, and inquires with an assumption of innocence: "What do you assault me for? Am I not an honest man? Cease agitation on this subject, or I will make a slave of you, too, or else hang you."

We talk about a *representative* government; but what a monster of a government is that where the noblest faculties of the mind, and the *whole* heart, are not *represented*. A semi-human tiger or ox, stalking over the earth, with its heart taken out and the top of its brain shot away. Heroes have fought well on their stumps when their legs were shot off, but I never heard of any good done by such a government as that.

The only government that I recognize — and it matters not how few are at the head of it, or how small its army — is that power that establishes justice in the land, never that which establishes injustice. What shall we think of a government to which all the truly brave and just men in the land are enemies, standing between it and those whom it oppresses? A government that pretends to be Christian and crucifies a million Christs every day!

Treason! Where does such treason take its rise? I cannot help thinking of you as you deserve, ye governments. Can you dry up the fountains of thought? High treason, when it is resistance to tyranny here below, has its origin in, and is first committed by, the power that makes and forever recreates man. When you have caught and hung all these human rebels, you have accomplished nothing but your own guilt, for you have not struck at the fountain-head. You presume to contend with a foe against whom West Point cadets and rifled cannon *point* not. Can all the art of the cannon-founder tempt matter to turn against its maker? Is the form in which the founder thinks he casts it more essential than the constitution of it and of himself?

The United States have a coffle of four millions of slaves. They are determined to keep them in this condition; and Massachusetts is one of the confederated overseers to prevent their escape. Such are not all the inhabitants of Massachusetts, but such are they who rule and are obeyed here. It was Massachusetts, as well as Virginia, that put down this insurrection at Harper's Ferry. She sent the marines there, and she will have *to pay the penalty of her sin.*

Suppose that there is a society in this State that out of its own purse and magnanimity saves all the fugitive slaves that run to us, and protects our colored fellow-citizens, and leaves the other work to the government, so called. Is not that government fast losing its occupation, and becoming contemptible to mankind? If private men are obliged to perform the offices of government, to protect the weak and dispense justice, then the government becomes only a hired man, or clerk, to perform menial or indifferent services. Of course, that is but the shadow of a government whose existence necessitates a Vigilant Committee. What should we think of the Oriental Cadi even, behind whom worked in secret a Vigilant Committee? But such is the character of our Northern States generally; each has its Vigilant Committee. And, to a certain extent, these crazy governments recognize and accept this relation. They say, virtually, "We'll be glad to work for you on these terms, only don't make a noise about it." And thus the government, its salary being insured, withdraws into the back shop, taking the Constitution with it, and bestows most of its labor on repairing that. When I hear it at work sometimes, as I go by, it reminds me, at best, of those farmers who in winter contrive to turn a penny by following the coopering business. And what kind of spirit is their barrel made to hold? They speculate in stocks, and bore holes in mountains, but they are not competent to lay out even a decent highway. The only *free* road, the Underground Railroad, is owned and managed by the Vigilant Committee. *They* have tunneled under the whole breadth of the land. Such a government is losing its power and respectability as surely as water runs out of a leaky vessel, and is held by one that can contain it.

I hear many condemn these men because they were so few. When were the good and the brave ever in a majority? Would you have had him wait till that time came? — till you and I came over to him? The very fact that he had no rabble or troop of hirelings about him would alone distinguish him from ordinary heroes. His company was small indeed, because few could be found worthy to pass muster. Each one who there laid down his life for the poor and oppressed was a picked man, culled out of many thousands, if not millions; apparently a man of principle, of rare courage, and devoted humanity; ready to sacrifice his life at any moment for the benefit of his fellow-man. It may be doubted if there were as many more their equals in these respects in all the country, — I speak of his followers only, — for their leader, no doubt, scoured the land far and wide, seeking to swell his troop. These alone were ready to step between the oppressor and the oppressed. Surely they were the very best men you could select to be hung. That was the greatest compliment which this country could pay them. They were ripe for her gallows. She has tried a long time, she has hung a good many, but never found the right one before.

When I think of him, and his six sons, and his son - in - law, not to enumerate the others, enlisted for this fight, proceeding coolly, reverently, humanely to work, for months if not years, sleeping and waking upon it, summering and wintering the thought, without expecting any reward but a good conscience, while almost all America stood ranked on the other side, — I say again that it affects me as a sublime spectacle. If he had had any journal advocating "*his cause*," any organ, as the phrase is, monotonously and wearisomely playing the same old tune, and then passing round the hat, it would have been fatal to his efficiency. If he had acted in any way so as to be let alone by the government, he might have been suspected. It was the fact that the tyrant must give place to him, or he to the tyrant, that distinguished him from all the reformers of the day that I know.

It was his peculiar doctrine that a man has a perfect right to interfere by force with the slaveholder, in order to rescue the slave. I agree with him. They who are continually shocked by slavery have some right to be shocked by the violent death of the slaveholder, but no others. Such will be more shocked by his life than by his death. I shall not be forward to think him mistaken in his method who quickest succeeds to liberate the slave. I speak for the slave when I say that I prefer the philanthropy of Captain Brown to that philanthropy which neither shoots me nor liberates me. At any rate, I do not think it is quite sane for one to spend his whole life in talking or writing about this matter, unless he is continuously inspired, and I have not done so. A man may have other affairs to attend to. I do not wish to kill nor to be killed, but I can foresee circumstances in which both these things would be by me unavoidable. We preserve the so-called peace of our community by deeds of petty violence every day. Look at the policeman's billy and handcuffs! Look at the jail! Look at the gallows! Look at the chaplain of the regiment! We are hoping only to live safely on the outskirts of *this* provisional army. So we defend ourselves and our hen-roosts, and maintain slavery. I know that the mass of my countrymen think that the only righteous use that can be made of Sharps rifles and revolvers is to fight duels with them, when we are insulted by other nations, or to hunt Indians, or shoot fugitive slaves with them, or the like. I think that for once the Sharps rifles and the revolvers were employed in a righteous cause. The tools were in the hands of one who could use them.

The same indignation that is said to have cleared the temple once will clear it again. The question is not about the weapon, but the spirit in which you use it. No man has appeared in America, as yet, who loved his fellow-man so well, and treated him so tenderly. He lived for him. He took up his life and he laid it down for him. What sort of violence is that which is encouraged, not by soldiers, but by peaceable citizens, not so much by laymen as by ministers of the Gospel, not so much by the fighting sects as by the Quakers, and not so much by Quaker men as by Quaker women?

This event advertises me that there is such a fact as death, — the possibility of a man's dying. It seems as if no man had ever died in America before; for in order to die you must first have lived. I don't believe in the hearses, and palls, and funerals that they have had. There was no death in the case, because there had been no life; they merely rotted or sloughed off, pretty much as they had rotted or sloughed along. No temple's veil was rent, only a hole dug somewhere. Let the dead bury their dead. The best of them fairly ran down like a clock. Franklin, — Washington, — they were let off without dying; they were merely missing one day. I hear a good many pretend that they are going to die; or that they have died, for aught that I know. Nonsense! I'll defy them to do it. They have n't got life enough in them. They 'll deliquesce like fungi, and keep a hundred eulogists mopping the spot where they left off. Only half a dozen or so have died since the world began. Do you think that you are going to die, sir? No! there's no hope of you. You have n't got your lesson yet. You 've got to stay after school. We make a needless ado about capital punishment, — taking lives, when there is no life to take. *Memento mori!* We don't understand that sublime sentence which some worthy got sculptured on his gravestone once. We 've interpreted it in a groveling and sniveling sense; we 've wholly forgotten how to die.

But be sure you do die nevertheless. Do your work, and finish it. If you know how to begin, you will know when to end.

These men, in teaching us how to die, have at the same time taught us how to live. If this man's acts and words do not create a revival, it will be the severest possible satire on the acts and words that do. It is the best news that America has ever heard. It has already quickened the feeble pulse of the North, and infused more and more generous blood into her veins and heart than any number of years of what is called commercial and political prosperity could. How many a man who was lately contemplating suicide has now something to live for!

One writer says that Brown's peculiar monomania made him to be "dreaded by the Missourians as a supernatural being." Sure enough, a hero in the midst of us cowards is always so dreaded. He is just that thing. He shows himself superior to nature. He has a spark of divinity in him.

> " Unless above himself he can
> Erect himself, how poor a thing is man ! "

Newspaper editors argue also that it is a proof of his *insanity* that he thought he was appointed to do this work which he did, — that he did not suspect himself for a moment! They talk as if it were impossible that a man could be " divinely appointed " in these days to do any work whatever; as if vows and religion were out of date as connected with any man's daily work; as if the agent to abolish slavery could only be somebody appointed by the President, or by some political party. They talk as if a man's death were a failure, and his continued life, be it of whatever character, were a success.

When I reflect to what a cause this man devoted himself, and how religiously, and then reflect to what cause his judges and all who condemn him so angrily and fluently devote themselves, I see that they are as far apart as the heavens and earth are asunder.

The amount of it is, our "*leading men*" are a harmless kind of folk, and they know *well enough* that *they* were not divinely appointed, but elected by the votes of their party.

Who is it whose safety requires that Captain Brown be hung? Is it indispensable to any Northern man? Is there no resource but to cast this man also to the Minotaur? If you do not wish it, say so distinctly. While these things are being done, beauty stands veiled and music is a screeching lie. Think of him, — of his rare qualities! — such a man as it takes ages to make, and ages to understand; no mock hero, nor the representative of any party. A man such as the sun may not rise upon again in this benighted land. To whose making went the costliest material, the finest adamant; sent to be the redeemer of those in captivity; and the only use to which you can put him is to hang him at the end of a rope! You who pretend to care for Christ crucified, consider what you are about to do to him who offered himself to be the saviour of four millions of men.

Any man knows when he is justified, and all the wits in the world cannot enlighten him on that point. The murderer always knows that he is justly punished; but when a government takes the life of a man without the consent of his conscience, it is an audacious government, and is taking a step towards its own dissolution. Is it not possible that an individual may be

right and a government wrong? Are laws to
be enforced simply because they were made? or
declared by any number of men to be good, if
they are *not* good? Is there any necessity for
a man's being a tool to perform a deed of which
his better nature disapproves? Is it the intention of law-makers that *good* men shall be hung
ever? Are judges to interpret the law according to the letter, and not the spirit? What
right have *you* to enter into a compact with
yourself that you *will* do thus or so, against the
light within you? Is it for *you* to *make up*
your mind, — to form any resolution whatever,
— and not accept the convictions that are
forced upon you, and which ever pass your understanding? I do not believe in lawyers, in
that mode of attacking or defending a man,
because you descend to meet the judge on his
own ground, and, in cases of the highest importance, it is of no consequence whether a man
breaks a human law or not. Let lawyers decide
trivial cases. Business men may arrange that
among themselves. If they were the interpre-
ters of the everlasting laws which rightfully
bind man, that would be another thing. A
counterfeiting law-factory, standing half in a
slave land and half in a free! What kind of
laws for free men can you expect from that?

I am here to plead his cause with you. I

plead not for his life, but for his character, — his immortal life; and so it becomes your cause wholly, and is not his in the least. Some eighteen hundred years ago Christ was crucified; this morning, perchance, Captain Brown was hung. These are the two ends of a chain which is not without its links. He is not Old Brown any longer; he is an angel of light.

I see now that it was necessary that the bravest and humanest man in all the country should be hung. Perhaps he saw it himself. I *almost fear* that I may yet hear of his deliverance, doubting if a prolonged life, if *any* life, can do as much good as his death.

"Misguided!" "Garrulous!" "Insane!" "Vindictive!" So ye write in your easy-chairs, and thus he wounded responds from the floor of the Armory, clear as a cloudless sky, true as the voice of nature is: "No man sent me here; it was my own prompting and that of my Maker. I acknowledge no master in human form."

And in what a sweet and noble strain he proceeds, addressing his captors, who stand over him: "I think, my friends, you are guilty of a great wrong against God and humanity, and it would be perfectly right for any one to interfere with you so far as to free those you willfully and wickedly hold in bondage."

And, referring to his movement: "It is, in my opinion, the greatest service a man can render to God."

"I pity the poor in bondage that have none to help them; that is why I am here; not to gratify any personal animosity, revenge, or vindictive spirit. It is my sympathy with the oppressed and the wrongéd, that are as good as you, and as precious in the sight of God."

You don't know your testament when you see it.

"I want you to understand that I respect the rights of the poorest and weakest of colored people, oppressed by the slave power, just as much as I do those of the most wealthy and powerful."

"I wish to say, furthermore, that you had better, all you people at the South, prepare yourselves for a settlement of that question, that must come up for settlement sooner than you are prepared for it. The sooner you are prepared the better. You may dispose of me very easily. I am nearly disposed of now; but this question is still to be settled, — this negro question, I mean; the end of that is not yet."

I foresee the time when the painter will paint that scene, no longer going to Rome for a subject; the poet will sing it; the historian record it; and, with the Landing of the Pilgrims and the Declaration of Independence, it will be the ornament of some future national gallery, when at least the present form of slavery shall be no more here. We shall then be at liberty to weep for Captain Brown. Then, and not till then, we will take our revenge.

THE LAST DAYS OF JOHN BROWN

John Brown's career for the last six weeks of his life was meteor-like, flashing through the darkness in which we live. I know of nothing so miraculous in our history.

If any person, in a lecture or conversation at that time, cited any ancient example of heroism, such as Cato or Tell or Winkelried, passing over the recent deeds and words of Brown, it was felt by any intelligent audience of Northern men to be tame and inexcusably far-fetched.

For my own part, I commonly attend more to nature than to man, but any affecting human event may blind our eyes to natural objects. I was so absorbed in him as to be surprised whenever I detected the routine of the natural world surviving still, or met persons going about their affairs indifferent. It appeared strange to me that the "little dipper" should be still diving quietly in the river, as of yore; and it suggested that this bird might continue to dive here when Concord should be no more.

I felt that he, a prisoner in the midst of his enemies and under sentence of death, if consulted as to his next step or resource, could answer more wisely than all his countrymen beside. He best understood his position; he contemplated it most calmly. Comparatively, all other men, North and South, were beside themselves. Our thoughts could not revert to any greater or wiser or better man with whom to contrast him, for he, then and there, was above them all. The man this country was about to hang appeared the greatest and best in it.

Years were not required for a revolution of public opinion; days, nay hours, produced marked changes in this case. Fifty who were ready to say, on going into our meeting in honor of him in Concord, that he ought to be hung, would not say it when they came out. They heard his words read; they saw the earnest faces of the congregation; and perhaps they joined at last in singing the hymn in his praise.

The order of instructors was reversed. I heard that one preacher, who at first was shocked and stood aloof, felt obliged at last, after he was hung, to make him the subject of a sermon, in which, to some extent, he eulogized the man, but said that his act was a failure. An influential class-teacher thought it necessary, after the services, to tell his grown-up pupils that at first he thought as the preacher

did then, but now he thought that John Brown
was right. But it was understood that his pupils were as much ahead of the teacher as he
was ahead of the priest; and I know for a cer-
tainty that very little boys at home had already
asked their parents, in a tone of surprise, why
God did not interfere to save him. In each
case, the constituted teachers were only half
conscious that they were not *leading*, but being
dragged, with some loss of time and power.

The more conscientious preachers, the Bible
men, they who talk about principle, and doing
to others as you would that they should do unto
you, — how could they fail to recognize him, by
far the greatest preacher of them all, with the
Bible in his life and in his acts, the embodi-
ment of principle, who actually carried out the
golden rule? All whose moral sense had been
aroused, who had a calling from on high to
preach, sided with him. What confessions he
extracted from the cold and conservative! It
is remarkable, but on the whole it is well, that
it did not prove the occasion for a new sect of
Brownites being formed in our midst.

They, whether within the Church or out of
it, who adhere to the spirit and let go the letter, and are accordingly called infidel, were as
usual foremost to recognize him. Men have
been hung in the South before for attempting

to rescue slaves, and the North was not much stirred by it. Whence, then, this wonderful difference? We were not so sure of *their* devotion to principle. We made a subtle distinction, forgot human laws, and did homage to an idea. The North, I mean the *living* North, was suddenly all transcendental. It went behind the human law, it went behind the apparent failure, and recognized eternal justice and glory. Commonly, men live according to a formula, and are satisfied if the order of law is observed, but in this instance they, to some extent, returned to original perceptions, and there was a slight revival of old religion. They saw that what was called order was confusion, what was called justice, injustice, and that the best was deemed the worst. This attitude suggested a more intelligent and generous spirit than that which actuated our forefathers, and the possibility, in the course of ages, of a revolution in behalf of another and an oppressed people.

Most Northern men, and a few Southern ones, were wonderfully stirred by Brown's behavior and words. They saw and felt that they were heroic and noble, and that there had been nothing quite equal to them in their kind in this country, or in the recent history of the world. But the minority were unmoved by them. They were only surprised and provoked

by the attitude of their neighbors. They saw
that Brown was brave, and that he believed
that he had done right, but they did not detect
any further peculiarity in him. Not being accustomed to make fine distinctions, or to appreciate magnanimity, they read his letters and
speeches as if they read them not. They were
not aware when they approached a heroic statement, — they did not know when they *burned*.
They did not feel that he spoke with authority,
and hence they only remembered that the *law*
must be executed. They remembered the old
formula, but did not hear the new revelation.
The man who does not recognize in Brown's
words a wisdom and nobleness, and therefore
an authority, superior to our laws, is a modern
Democrat. This is the test by which to discover him. He is not willfully but constitution-
ally blind on this side, and he is consistent
with himself. Such has been his past life; no
doubt of it. In like manner he has read history
and his Bible, and he accepts, or seems to accept, the last only as an established formula,
and not because he has been convicted by it.
You will not find kindred sentiments in his
commonplace book, if he has one.

When a noble deed is done, who is likely to
appreciate it? They who are noble themselves.
I was not surprised that certain of my neigh-

bors spoke of John Brown as an ordinary felon, for who are they? They have either much flesh, or much office, or much coarseness of some kind. They are not ethereal natures in any sense. The dark qualities predominate in them. Several of them are decidedly pachy-dermatous. I say it in sorrow, not in anger. How can a man behold the light who has no answering inward light? They are true to their *right*, but when they look this way they *see* nothing, they are blind. For the children of the light to contend with them is as if there should be a contest between eagles and owls. Show me a man who feels bitterly toward John Brown, and let me hear what noble verse he can repeat. He 'll be as dumb as if his lips were stone.

It is not every man who can be a Christian, even in a very moderate sense, whatever education you give him. It is a matter of constitution and temperament, after all. He may have to be born again many times. I have known many a man who pretended to be a Christian, in whom it was ridiculous, for he had no genius for it. It is not every man who can be a free-man, even.

Editors persevered for a good while in saying that Brown was crazy; but at last they said only that it was "a crazy scheme," and the only

evidence brought to prove it was that it cost
him his life. I have no doubt that if he had
gone with five thousand men, liberated a thousand slaves, killed a hundred or two slaveholders, and had as many more killed on his own
side, but not lost his own life, these same editors would have called it by a more respectable
name. Yet he has been far more successful
than that. He has liberated many thousands
of slaves, both North and South. They seem
to have known nothing about living or dying
for a principle. They all called him crazy then;
who calls him crazy now?

All through the excitement occasioned by his
remarkable attempt and subsequent behavior
the Massachusetts Legislature, not taking any
steps for the defense of her citizens who were
likely to be carried to Virginia as witnesses
and exposed to the violence of a slaveholding
mob, was wholly absorbed in a liquor-agency
question, and indulging in poor jokes on the
word "extension." Bad spirits occupied their
thoughts. I am sure that no statesman up to
the occasion could have attended to that question at all at that time, — a very vulgar question to attend to at any time!

When I looked into a liturgy of the Church
of England, printed near the end of the last
century, in order to find a service applicable to

the case of Brown, I found that the only martyr recognized and provided for by it was King Charles the First, an eminent scamp. Of all the inhabitants of England and of the world, he was the only one, according to this authority, whom that church had made a martyr and saint of; and for more than a century it had celebrated his martyrdom, so called, by an annual service. What a satire on the Church is that!

Look not to legislatures and churches for your guidance, nor to any soulless *incorporated* bodies, but to *inspirited* or inspired ones.

What avail all your scholarly accomplishments and learning, compared with wisdom and manhood? To omit his other behavior, see what a work this comparatively unread and unlettered man wrote within six weeks. Where is our professor of *belles-lettres*, or of logic and rhetoric, who can write so well? He wrote in prison, not a History of the World, like Raleigh, but an American book which I think will live longer than that. I do not know of such words, uttered under such circumstances, and so copiously withal, in Roman or English or any history. What a variety of themes he touched on in that short space! There are words in that letter to his wife, respecting the education of his daughters, which deserve to be framed and hung over every mantelpiece in

the land. Compare this earnest wisdom with
that of Poor Richard.

The death of Irving, which at any other
time would have attracted universal attention,
having occurred while these things were tran-
spiring, went almost unobserved. I shall have
to read of it in the biography of authors.

Literary gentlemen, editors, and critics think
that they know how to write, because they
have studied grammar and rhetoric; but they
are egregiously mistaken. The *art* of composition is as simple as the discharge of a bullet
from a rifle, and its masterpieces imply an infinitely greater force behind them. This unlettered man's speaking and writing are standard
English. Some words and phrases deemed vul-
garisms and Americanisms before, he has made
standard American; such as "*It will pay.*" It
suggests that the one great rule of composition
— and if I were a professor of rhetoric I should
insist on this — is, to *speak the truth*. This
first, this second, this third; pebbles in your
mouth or not. This demands earnestness and
manhood chiefly.

We seem to have forgotten that the expression, a *liberal* education, originally meant
among the Romans one worthy of *free* men;
while the learning of trades and professions by
which to get your livelihood merely was consid-

ered worthy of *slaves* only. But taking a hint from the word, I would go a step further, and say that it is not the man of wealth and leisure simply, though devoted to art, or science, or literature, who, in a true sense, is *liberally* educated, but only the earnest and *free* man. In a slaveholding country like this, there can be no such thing as a *liberal* education tolerated by the State; and those scholars of Austria and France who, however learned they may be, are contented under their tyrannies have received only a *servile* education.

Nothing could his enemies do but it redounded to his infinite advantage, — that is, to the advantage of his cause. They did not hang him at once, but reserved him to preach to them. And then there was another great blunder. They did not hang his four followers with him; that scene was still postponed; and so his victory was prolonged and completed. No theatrical manager could have arranged things so wisely to give effect to his behavior and words. And who, think you, *was* the manager? *Who* placed the slave-woman and her child, whom he stooped to kiss for a symbol, between his prison and the gallows?

We soon saw, as he saw, that he was not to be pardoned or rescued by men. That would have been to disarm him, to restore to him a

material weapon, a Sharps rifle, when he had
taken up the sword of the spirit, — the sword
with which he has really won his greatest and
most memorable victories. Now he has not
laid aside the sword of the spirit, for he is pure
spirit himself, and his sword is pure spirit also.

> " He nothing common did or mean
>   Upon that memorable scene,
>   Nor called the gods with vulgar spite,
>   To vindicate his helpless right ;
>   But bowed his comely head
>   Down as upon a bed."

What a transit was that of his horizontal
body alone, but just cut down from the gallows-
tree! We read that at such a time it passed
through Philadelphia, and by Saturday night
had reached New York. Thus like a meteor
it shot through the Union from the Southern
regions toward the North! No such freight had
the cars borne since they carried him South-
ward alive.

On the day of his translation, I heard, to be
sure, that he was *hung*, but I did not know
what that meant; I felt no sorrow on that account; but not for a day or two did I even *hear*
that he was *dead*, and not after any number of
days shall I believe it. Of all the men who
were said to be my contemporaries, it seemed
to me that John Brown was the only one who

had not died. I never hear of a man named Brown now, — and I hear of them pretty often, — I never hear of any particularly brave and earnest man, but my first thought is of John Brown, and what relation he may be to him. I meet him at every turn. He is more alive than ever he was. He has earned immortality. He is not confined to North Elba nor to Kansas. He is no longer working in secret. He works in public, and in the clearest light that shines on this land.

AFTER THE DEATH OF JOHN BROWN

[At the services held in Concord, Massachusetts, December 2, 1859, in commemoration of John Brown, executed that day, Mr. Thoreau said:] So universal and widely related is any transcendent moral greatness, and so nearly identical with greatness everywhere and in every age, — as a pyramid contracts the nearer you approach its apex, — that, when I now look over my commonplace book of poetry, I find that the best of it is oftenest applicable, in part or wholly, to the case of Captain Brown. Only what is true, and strong, and solemnly earnest will recommend itself to our mood at this time. Almost any noble verse may be read, either as his elegy or eulogy, or be made the text of an oration on him. Indeed, such are now discovered to be the parts of a universal liturgy, applicable to those rare cases of heroes and martyrs for which the ritual of no church has provided. This is the formula established on high, — their burial service, — to which every great genius has contributed its stanza or line. As Marvell wrote: —

"When the sword glitters o'er the judge's head,
And fear has coward churchmen silenced,
Then is the poet's time; 't is then he draws,
And single fights forsaken virtue's cause;
He, when the wheel of empire whirleth back,
And though the world's disjointed axle crack,
Sings still of ancient rights and better times,
Seeks suffering good, arraigns successful crimes."

The sense of grand poetry, read by the light of this event, is brought out distinctly like an invisible writing held to the fire: —

"All heads must come
To the cold tomb, —
Only the actions of the just
Smell sweet and blossom in the dust."

We have heard that the Boston lady who recently visited our hero in prison found him wearing still the clothes, all cut and torn by sabres and by bayonet thrusts, in which he had been taken prisoner; and thus he had gone to his trial; and without a hat. She spent her time in prison mending those clothes, and, for a memento, brought home a pin covered with blood.

What are the clothes that endure?

"The garments lasting evermore
Are works of mercy to the poor;
And neither tetter, time, nor moth
Shall fray that silk or fret this cloth."

The well-known verses called "The Soul's Errand," supposed, by some, to have been written by Sir Walter Raleigh when he was expecting to be executed the following day, are at least worthy of such an origin, and are equally applicable to the present case. [Mr. Thoreau then read these verses, as well as a number of poetical passages selected by another citizen of Concord, and closed with the following translation from Tacitus made by himself.]

You, Agricola, are fortunate, not only because your life was glorious, but because your death was timely. As they tell us who heard your last words, unchanged and willing you accepted your fate; as if, as far as in your power, you would make the emperor appear innocent. But, besides the bitterness of having lost a parent, it adds to our grief, that it was not permitted us to minister to your health, . . . to gaze on your countenance, and receive your last embrace; surely, we might have caught some words and commands which we could have treasured in the inmost part of our souls. This is our pain, this our wound. . . . You were buried with the fewer tears, and in your last earthly light your eyes looked around for something which they did not see.

If there is any abode for the spirits of the pious, if, as wise men suppose, great souls are not extinguished with the body, may you rest placidly, and call your family from weak regrets and womanly laments to the contemplation of your virtues, which must not be lamented, either silently or aloud. Let us honor you by our admiration rather than by short-lived praises, and, if nature aid us, by our emulation of you. That is true honor, that the piety of whoever is most akin to you. This also I would teach your family, so to venerate your memory as to call to mind all your actions and words, and embrace your character and the form of your soul rather than of your body; not because I think that statues which are made of marble or brass are to be condemned, but as the features of men, so images of the features are frail and perishable. The form of the soul is eternal; and this we can retain and express, not by a foreign material and art, but by our own lives. Whatever of Agricola we have loved, whatever we have admired, remains, and will remain, in the minds of men and the records of history, through the eternity of ages. For oblivion will overtake many of the ancients, as if they were inglorious and ignoble: Agricola, described and transmitted to posterity, will survive.

LIFE WITHOUT PRINCIPLE

AT a lyceum, not long since, I felt that the lecturer had chosen a theme too foreign to himself, and so failed to interest me as much as he might have done. He described things not in or near to his heart, but toward his extremities and superficies. There was, in this sense, no truly central or centralizing thought in the lecture. I would have had him deal with his privatest experience, as the poet does. The greatest compliment that was ever paid me was when one asked me what *I thought*, and attended to my answer. I am surprised, as well as delighted, when this happens, it is such a rare use he would make of me, as if he were acquainted with the tool. Commonly, if men want anything of me, it is only to know how many acres I make of their land, — since I am a surveyor, — or, at most, what trivial news I have burdened myself with. They never will go to law for my meat; they prefer the shell. A man once came a considerable distance to ask me to lecture on Slavery; but on conversing with him, I found that he and his clique expected seven eighths of the lecture to be theirs, and only one eighth mine; so I declined. I take it for granted, when I am invited to lecture anywhere, — for I have had a little experience in that business, — that there is a desire to hear what *I think* on some subject, though I may be the greatest fool in the country, — and not that I should say pleasant things merely, or such as the audience will assent to; and I resolve, accordingly, that I will give them a strong dose of myself. They have sent for me, and engaged to pay for me, and I am determined that they shall have me, though I bore them beyond all precedent.

So now I would say something similar to you, my readers. Since *you* are my readers, and I have not been much of a traveler, I will not talk about people a thousand miles off, but come as near home as I can. As the time is short, I will leave out all the flattery, and retain all the criticism.

Let us consider the way in which we spend our lives.

This world is a place of business. What an infinite bustle! I am awaked almost every night by the panting of the locomotive. It interrupts my dreams. There is no sabbath. It would be glorious to see mankind at leisure for once. It is nothing but work, work, work. I cannot easily buy a blank-book to write thoughts in; they are commonly ruled for dollars and cents. An Irishman, seeing me making a minute in the fields, took it for granted that I was calculating my wages. If a man was tossed out of a window when an infant, and so made a cripple for life, or scared out of his wits by the Indians, it is regretted chiefly because he was thus incapacitated for — business! I think that there is nothing, not even crime, more opposed to poetry, to philosophy, ay, to life itself, than this incessant business.

There is a coarse and boisterous money-making fellow in the outskirts of our town, who is going to build a bank-wall under the hill along the edge of his meadow. The powers have put this into his head to keep him out of mischief, and he wishes me to spend three weeks digging there with him. The result will be that he will perhaps get some more money to hoard, and leave for his heirs to spend foolishly. If I do this, most will commend me as an industrious and hard-working man; but if I choose to devote myself to certain labors which yield more real profit, though but little money, they may be inclined to look on me as an idler. Nevertheless, as I do not need the police of meaningless labor to regulate me, and do not see anything absolutely praiseworthy in this fellow's undertaking any more than in many

an enterprise of our own or foreign governments, however amusing it may be to him or
them, I prefer to finish my education at a different school.

If a man walk in the woods for love of them
half of each day, he is in danger of being regarded as a loafer; but if he spends his whole
day as a speculator, shearing off those woods
and making earth bald before her time, he is
esteemed an industrious and enterprising citizen.   As if a town had no interest in its forests
but to cut them down!

Most men would feel insulted if it were proposed to employ them in throwing stones over a
wall, and then in throwing them back, merely
that they might earn their wages.   But many
are no more worthily employed now.   For instance: just after sunrise, one summer morning,
I noticed one of my neighbors walking beside
his team, which was slowly drawing a heavy
hewn stone swung under the axle, surrounded
by an atmosphere of industry, — his day's work
begun, — his brow commenced to sweat, — a reproach to all sluggards and idlers, — pausing
abreast the shoulders of his oxen, and half turning round with a flourish of his merciful whip,
while they gained their length on him.   And I
thought, Such is the labor which the American
Congress exists to protect, — honest, manly toil,

—honest as the day is long, — that makes his bread taste sweet, and keeps society sweet, — which all men respect and have consecrated; one of the sacred band, doing the needful but irksome drudgery. Indeed, I felt a slight reproach, because I observed this from a window, and was not abroad and stirring about a similar business. The day went by, and at evening I passed the yard of another neighbor, who keeps many servants, and spends much money foolishly, while he adds nothing to the common stock, and there I saw the stone of the morning lying beside a whimsical structure intended to adorn this Lord Timothy Dexter's premises, and the dignity forthwith departed from the teamster's labor, in my eyes. In my opinion, the sun was made to light worthier toil than this. I may add that his employer has since run off, in debt to a good part of the town, and, after passing through Chancery, has settled somewhere else, there to become once more a patron of the arts.

The ways by which you may get money almost without exception lead downward. To have done anything by which you earned money *merely* is to have been truly idle or worse. If the laborer gets no more than the wages which his employer pays him, he is cheated, he cheats himself. If you would get money as a writer or lecturer, you must be popular, which is to go down perpendicularly. Those services which the community will most readily pay for, it is most disagreeable to render. You are paid for being something less than a man. The State does not commonly reward a genius any more wisely. Even the poet-laureate would rather not have to celebrate the accidents of royalty. He must be bribed with a pipe of wine; and perhaps another poet is called away from his muse to gauge that very pipe. As for my own business, even that kind of surveying which I could do with most satisfaction my employers do not want. They would prefer that I should do my work coarsely and not too well, ay, not well enough. When I observe that there are different ways of surveying, my employer commonly asks which will give him the most land, not which is most correct. I once invented a rule for measuring cord-wood, and tried to introduce it in Boston; but the measurer there told me that the sellers did not wish to have their wood measured correctly, — that he was already too accurate for them, and therefore they commonly got their wood measured in Charlestown before crossing the bridge.

The aim of the laborer should be, not to get his living, to get "a good job," but to perform

well a certain work; and, even in a pecuniary
sense, it would be economy for a town to pay
its laborers so well that they would not feel that
they were working for low ends, as for a livelihood merely, but for scientific, or even moral
ends. Do not hire a man who does your work
for money, but him who does it for love of it.

It is remarkable that there are few men so
well employed, so much to their minds, but that
a little money or fame would commonly buy
them off from their present pursuit. I see ad-
vertisements for *active* young men, as if activity
were the whole of a young man's capital. Yet
I have been surprised when one has with confidence proposed to me, a grown man, to embark
in some enterprise of his, as if I had absolutely
nothing to do, my life having been a complete
failure hitherto. What a doubtful compliment
this to pay me! As if he had met me halfway
across the ocean beating up against the wind,
but bound nowhere, and proposed to me to go
along with him! If I did, what do you think
the underwriters would say? No, no! I am
not without employment at this stage of the
voyage. To tell the truth, I saw an advertisement for able-bodied seamen, when I was a
boy, sauntering in my native port, and as soon
as I came of age I embarked.

The community has no bribe that will tempt

a wise man. You may raise money enough to tunnel a mountain, but you cannot raise money enough to hire a man who is minding *his own* business. An efficient and valuable man does what he can, whether the community pay him for it or not. The inefficient offer their inefficiency to the highest bidder, and are forever expecting to be put into office. One would suppose that they were rarely disappointed.

Perhaps I am more than usually jealous with respect to my freedom. I feel that my connection with and obligation to society are still very slight and transient. Those slight labors which afford me a livelihood, and by which it is allowed that I am to some extent serviceable to my contemporaries, are as yet commonly a pleasure to me, and I am not often reminded that they are a necessity. So far I am successful. But I foresee that if my wants should be much increased, the labor required to supply them would become a drudgery. If I should sell both my forenoons and afternoons to society, as most appear to do, I am sure that for me there would be nothing left worth living for. I trust that I shall never thus sell my birthright for a mess of pottage. I wish to suggest that a man may be very industrious, and yet not spend his time well. There is no more fatal blunderer than he who consumes the greater part of his life getting his living. All great enterprises are self-supporting. The poet, for instance, must sustain his body by his poetry, as a steam planing-mill feeds its boilers with the shavings it makes. You must get your living by loving. But as it is said of the merchants that ninety-seven in a hundred fail, so the life of men generally, tried by this standard, is a failure, and bankruptcy may be surely prophesied.

Merely to come into the world the heir of a fortune is not to be born, but to be still-born, rather. To be supported by the charity of friends, or a government-pension, — provided you continue to breathe, — by whatever fine synonyms you describe these relations, is to go into the almshouse. On Sundays the poor debtor goes to church to take an account of stock, and finds, of course, that his outgoes have been greater than his income. In the Catholic Church, especially, they go into Chancery, make a clean confession, give up all, and think to start again. Thus men will lie on their backs, talking about the fall of man, and never make an effort to get up.

As for the comparative demand which men make on life, it is an important difference between two, that the one is satisfied with a level success, that his marks can all be hit by point-blank shots, but the other, however low and

unsuccessful his life may be, constantly elevates
his aim, though at a very slight angle to the
horizon. I should much rather be the last man,
— though, as the Orientals say, "Greatness
doth not approach him who is forever looking
down; and all those who are looking high are
growing poor."

It is remarkable that there is little or nothing
to be remembered written on the subject of getting a living; how to make getting a living not
merely honest and honorable, but altogether
inviting and glorious; for if *getting* a living is
not so, then living is not. One would think,
from looking at literature, that this question
had never disturbed a solitary individual's mus-
ings. Is it that men are too much disgusted
with their experience to speak of it? The lesson of value which money teaches, which the
Author of the Universe has taken so much pains
to teach us, we are inclined to skip altogether.
As for the means of living, it is wonderful
how indifferent men of all classes are about it,
even reformers, so called, — whether they inherit, or earn, or steal it. I think that Society
has done nothing for us in this respect, or at
least has undone what she has done. Cold and
hunger seem more friendly to my nature than
those methods which men have adopted and
advise to ward them off.

The title *wise* is, for the most part, falsely applied. How can one be a wise man, if he does not know any better how to live than other men? — if he is only more cunning and intellectually subtle? Does Wisdom work in a treadmill? or does she teach how to succeed *by her example?* Is there any such thing as wisdom not applied to life? Is she merely the miller who grinds the finest logic? It is pertinent to ask if Plato got his *living* in a better way or more successfully than his contemporaries, — or did he succumb to the difficulties of life like other men? Did he seem to prevail over some of them merely by indifference, or by assuming grand airs? or find it easier to live, because his aunt remembered him in her will? The ways in which most men get their living, that is, live, are mere make-shifts, and a shirking of the real business of life, — chiefly because they do not know, but partly because they do not mean, any better.

The rush to California, for instance, and the attitude, not merely of merchants, but of philosophers and prophets, so called, in relation to it, reflect the greatest disgrace on mankind. That so many are ready to live by luck, and so get the means of commanding the labor of others less lucky, without contributing any value to society! And that is called enterprise! I know of no more startling development of the immorality of trade, and all the common modes of getting a living. The philosophy and poetry and religion of such a mankind are not worth the dust of a puff-ball. The hog that gets his living by rooting, stirring up the soil so, would be ashamed of such company. If I could command the wealth of all the worlds by lifting my finger, I would not pay *such* a price for it. Even Mahomet knew that God did not make this world in jest. It makes God to be a moneyed gentleman who scatters a handful of pennies in order to see mankind scramble for them. The world's raffle! A subsistence in the domains of Nature a thing to be raffled for! What a comment, what a satire, on our institutions! The conclusion will be, that mankind will hang itself upon a tree. And have all the precepts in all the Bibles taught men only this? and is the last and most admirable invention of the human race only an improved muck-rake? Is this the ground on which Orientals and Occidentals meet? Did God direct us so to get our living, digging where we never planted, — and He would, perchance, reward us with lumps of gold?

God gave the righteous man a certificate entitling him to food and raiment, but the unrighteous man found a facsimile of the same in

God's coffers, and appropriated it, and obtained food and raiment like the former. It is one of the most extensive systems of counterfeiting that the world has seen. I did not know that mankind were suffering for want of gold. I have seen a little of it. I know that it is very malleable, but not so malleable as wit. A grain of gold will gild a great surface, but not so much as a grain of wisdom.

The gold-digger in the ravines of the mountains is as much a gambler as his fellow in the saloons of San Francisco. What difference does it make whether you shake dirt or shake dice? If you win, society is the loser. The gold-digger is the enemy of the honest laborer, whatever checks and compensations there may be. It is not enough to tell me that you worked hard to get your gold. So does the Devil work hard. The way of transgressors may be hard in many respects. The humblest observer who goes to the mines sees and says that gold-digging is of the character of a lottery; the gold thus obtained is not the same thing with the wages of honest toil. But, practically, he forgets what he has seen, for he has seen only the fact, not the principle, and goes into trade there, that is, buys a ticket in what commonly proves another lottery, where the fact is not so obvious.

After reading Howitt's account of the Aus-
tralian gold-diggings one evening, I had in my
mind's eye, all night, the numerous valleys,
with their streams, all cut up with foul pits,
from ten to one hundred feet deep, and half a
dozen feet across, as close as they can be dug,
and partly filled with water, — the locality to
which men furiously rush to probe for their
fortunes, — uncertain where they shall break
ground, — not knowing but the gold is under
their camp itself, — sometimes digging one
hundred and sixty feet before they strike the
vein, or then missing it by a foot, — turned
into demons, and regardless of each others'
rights, in their thirst for riches, — whole valleys, for thirty miles, suddenly honeycombed
by the pits of the miners, so that even hundreds
are drowned in them, — standing in water, and
covered with mud and clay, they work night
and day, dying of exposure and disease. Having read this, and partly forgotten it, I was
thinking, accidentally, of my own unsatisfac-
tory life, doing as others do; and with that
vision of the diggings still before me, I asked
myself why *I* might not be washing some gold
daily, though it were only the finest particles,
— why *I* might not sink a shaft down to the
gold within me, and work that mine. *There* is
a Ballarat, a Bendigo for you, — what though

it were a sulky-gully? At any rate, I might pursue some path, however solitary and narrow and crooked, in which I could walk with love and reverence. Wherever a man separates from the multitude, and goes his own way in this mood, there indeed is a fork in the road, though ordinary travelers may see only a gap in the paling. His solitary path across-lots will turn out the *higher way* of the two.

Men rush to California and Australia as if the true gold were to be found in that direction; but that is to go to the very opposite extreme to where it lies. They go prospecting farther and farther away from the true lead, and are most unfortunate when they think themselves most successful. Is not our *native* soil auriferous? Does not a stream from the golden mountains flow through our native valley? and has not this for more than geologic ages been bringing down the shining particles and forming the nuggets for us? Yet, strange to tell, if a digger steal away, prospecting for this true gold, into the unexplored solitudes around us, there is no danger that any will dog his steps, and endeavor to supplant him. He may claim and undermine the whole valley even, both the cultivated and the uncultivated portions, his whole life long in peace, for no one will ever dispute his claim. They will not mind his cradles or his toms. He is not confined to a claim twelve feet square, as at Ballarat, but may mine anywhere, and wash the whole wide world in his tom.

Howitt says of the man who found the great nugget which weighed twenty-eight pounds, at the Bendigo diggings in Australia: "He soon began to drink; got a horse, and rode all about, generally at full gallop, and, when he met people, called out to inquire if they knew who he was, and then kindly informed them that he was 'the bloody wretch that had found the nugget.' At last he rode full speed against a tree, and nearly knocked his brains out." I think, however, there was no danger of that, for he had already knocked his brains out against the nugget. Howitt adds, "He is a hopelessly ruined man." But he is a type of the class. They are all fast men. Hear some of the names of the places where they dig: "Jackass Flat," — "Sheep's-Head Gully," — "Murderer's Bar," etc. Is there no satire in these names? Let them carry their ill-gotten wealth where they will, I am thinking it will still be "Jackass Flat," if not "Murderer's Bar," where they live.

The last resource of our energy has been the robbing of graveyards on the Isthmus of Darien, an enterprise which appears to be but in its

infancy; for, according to late accounts, an act
has passed its second reading in the legislature
of New Granada, regulating this kind of min-
ing; and a correspondent of the "Tribune"
writes: "In the dry season, when the weather
will permit of the country being properly pros-
pected, no doubt other rich *guacas* [that is,
graveyards] will be found." To emigrants he
says: "Do not come before December; take the
Isthmus route in preference to the Boca del
Toro one; bring no useless baggage, and do
not cumber yourself with a tent; but a good
pair of blankets will be necessary; a pick,
shovel, and axe of good material will be almost
all that is required:" advice which might have
been taken from the "Burker's Guide." And
he concludes with this line in Italics and small
capitals: "*If you are doing well at home*, STAY
THERE," which may fairly be interpreted to
mean, "If you are getting a good living by robbing graveyards at home, stay there."

But why go to California for a text? She
is the child of New England, bred at her own
school and church.

It is remarkable that among all the preachers
there are so few moral teachers. The prophets
are employed in excusing the ways of men.
Most reverend seniors, the *illuminati* of the
age, tell me, with a gracious, reminiscent smile,

betwixt an aspiration and a shudder, not to be too tender about these things, — to lump all that, that is, make a lump of gold of it. The highest advice I have heard on these subjects was groveling. The burden of it was, — It is not worth your while to undertake to reform the world in this particular. Do not ask how your bread is buttered; it will make you sick, if you do, — and the like. A man had better starve at once than lose his innocence in the process of getting his bread. If within the sophisticated man there is not an unsophisticated one, then he is but one of the Devil's angels. As we grow old, we live more coarsely, we relax a little in our disciplines, and, to some extent, cease to obey our finest instincts. But we should be fastidious to the extreme of sanity, disregarding the gibes of those who are more unfortunate than ourselves.

In our science and philosophy, even, there is commonly no true and absolute account of things. The spirit of sect and bigotry has planted its hoof amid the stars. You have only to discuss the problem, whether the stars are inhabited or not, in order to discover it. Why must we daub the heavens as well as the earth? It was an unfortunate discovery that Dr. Kane was a Mason, and that Sir John Franklin was another. But it was a more cruel suggestion

that possibly that was the reason why the former
went in search of the latter. There is not a
popular magazine in this country that would
dare to print a child's thought on important
subjects without comment. It must be submitted to the D. D.'s. I would it were the chicka-
dee-dees.

You come from attending the funeral of mankind to attend to a natural phenomenon. A
little thought is sexton to all the world.

I hardly know an *intellectual* man, even, who
is so broad and truly liberal that you can think
aloud in his society. Most with whom you endeavor to talk soon come to a stand against
some institution in which they appear to hold
stock, — that is, some particular, not universal,
way of viewing things. They will continually
thrust their own low roof, with its narrow sky-
light, between you and the sky, when it is the
unobstructed heavens you would view. Get out
of the way with your cobwebs, wash your windows, I say! In some lyceums they tell me
that they have voted to exclude the subject of
religion. But how do I know what their religion is, and when I am near to or far from it?
I have walked into such an arena and done my
best to make a clean breast of what religion I
have experienced, and the audience never suspected what I was about. The lecture was as

harmless as moonshine to them. Whereas, if I had read to them the biography of the greatest scamps in history, they might have thought that I had written the lives of the deacons of their church. Ordinarily, the inquiry is, Where did you come from? or, Where are you going? That was a more pertinent question which I overheard one of my auditors put to another once, — "What does he lecture for?" It made me quake in my shoes.

To speak impartially, the best men that I know are not serene, a world in themselves. For the most part, they dwell in forms, and flatter and study effect only more finely than the rest. We select granite for the underpinning of our houses and barns; we build fences of stone; but we do not ourselves rest on an underpinning of granitic truth, the lowest primitive rock. Our sills are rotten. What stuff is the man made of who is not coexistent in our thought with the purest and subtilest truth? I often accuse my finest acquaintances of an immense frivolity; for, while there are manners and compliments we do not meet, we do not teach one another the lessons of honesty and sincerity that the brutes do, or of steadiness and solidity that the rocks do. The fault is commonly mutual, however; for we do not habitually demand any more of each other.

That excitement about Kossuth, consider how characteristic, but superficial, it was! — only another kind of politics or dancing. Men were making speeches to him all over the country, but each expressed only the thought, or the want of thought, of the multitude. No man stood on truth. They were merely banded together, as usual one leaning on another, and all together on nothing; as the Hindoos made the world rest on an elephant, the elephant on a tortoise, and the tortoise on a serpent, and had nothing to put under the serpent. For all fruit of that stir we have the Kossuth hat.

Just so hollow and ineffectual, for the most part, is our ordinary conversation. Surface meets surface. When our life ceases to be inward and private, conversation degenerates into mere gossip. We rarely meet a man who can tell us any news which he has not read in a newspaper, or been told by his neighbor; and, for the most part, the only difference between us and our fellow is that he has seen the newspaper, or been out to tea, and we have not. In proportion as our inward life fails, we go more constantly and desperately to the post-office. You may depend on it, that the poor fellow who walks away with the greatest number of letters proud of his extensive correspondence has not heard from himself this long while.

I do not know but it is too much to read one newspaper a week. I have tried it recently, and for so long it seems to me that I have not dwelt in my native region. The sun, the clouds, the snow, the trees say not so much to me. You cannot serve two masters. It requires more than a day's devotion to know and to possess the wealth of a day.

We may well be ashamed to tell what things we have read or heard in our day. I do not know why my news should be so trivial, — considering what one's dreams and expectations are, why the developments should be so paltry. The news we hear, for the most part, is not news to our genius. It is the stalest repetition. You are often tempted to ask why such stress is laid on a particular experience which you have had, — that, after twenty-five years, you should meet Hobbins, Registrar of Deeds, again on the sidewalk. Have you not budged an inch, then? Such is the daily news. Its facts appear to float in the atmosphere, insignificant as the sporules of fungi, and impinge on some neglected *thallus*, or surface of our minds, which affords a basis for them, and hence a parasitic growth. We should wash ourselves clean of such news. Of what consequence, though our planet explode, if there is no character involved in the explosion? In health we have not the least curiosity about such events. We do not live for idle amusement. I would not run round a corner to see the world blow up.

All summer, and far into the autumn, per-chance, you unconsciously went by the newspa-pers and the news, and now you find it was because the morning and the evening were full of news to you. Your walks were full of inci-dents. You attended, not to the affairs of Europe, but to your own affairs in Massachu-setts fields. If you chance to live and move and have your being in that thin stratum in which the events that make the news transpire, — thinner than the paper on which it is printed, — then these things will fill the world for you; but if you soar above or dive below that plane, you cannot remember nor be reminded of them. Really to see the sun rise or go down every day, so to relate ourselves to a universal fact, would preserve us sane forever. Nations! What are nations? Tartars, and Huns, and Chinamen! Like insects, they swarm. The historian strives in vain to make them memorable. It is for want of a man that there are so many men. It is individuals that populate the world. Any man thinking may say with the Spirit of Lodin, —

> "I look down from my height on nations,
>   And they become ashes before me; —

Calm is my dwelling in the clouds;
Pleasant are the great fields of my rest."

Pray, let us live without being drawn by dogs, Esquimaux-fashion, tearing over hill and dale, and biting each other's ears.

Not without a slight shudder at the danger, I often perceive how near I had come to admitting into my mind the details of some trivial affair, — the news of the street; and I am astonished to observe how willing men are to lumber their minds with such rubbish, — to permit idle rumors and incidents of the most insignificant kind to intrude on ground which should be sacred to thought. Shall the mind be a public arena, where the affairs of the street and the gossip of the tea-table chiefly are discussed? Or shall it be a quarter of heaven itself, — an hypæthral temple, consecrated to the service of the gods? I find it so difficult to dispose of the few facts which to me are significant, that I hesitate to burden my attention with those which are insignificant, which only a divine mind could illustrate. Such is, for the most part, the news in newspapers and conversation. It is important to preserve the mind's chastity in this respect. Think of admitting the details of a single case of the criminal court into our thoughts, to stalk profanely through their very *sanctum sanctorum* for an hour, ay,

for many hours! to make a very bar-room of
the mind's inmost apartment, as if for so long
the dust of the street had occupied us, — the
very street itself, with all its travel, its bustle,
and filth, had passed through our thoughts'
shrine! Would it not be an intellectual and
moral suicide? When I have been compelled
to sit spectator and auditor in a court room for
some hours, and have seen my neighbors, who
were not compelled, stealing in from time to
time, and tiptoeing about with washed hands
and faces, it has appeared to my mind's eye,
that, when they took off their hats, their ears
suddenly expanded into vast hoppers for sound,
between which even their narrow heads were
crowded. Like the vanes of windmills, they
caught the broad but shallow stream of sound,
which, after a few titillating gyrations in their
coggy brains, passed out the other side. I wondered if, when they got home, they were as
careful to wash their ears as before their hands
and faces. It has seemed to me, at such a
time, that the auditors and the witnesses, the
jury and the counsel, the judge and the criminal at the bar, — if I may presume him guilty
before he is convicted, — were all equally criminal, and a thunderbolt might be expected to
descend and consume them all together.

By all kinds of traps and signboards, threatening the extreme penalty of the divine law, exclude such trespassers from the only ground which can be sacred to you. It is so hard to forget what it is worse than useless to remember! If I am to be a thoroughfare, I prefer that it be of the mountain-brooks, the Parnassian streams, and not the town-sewers. There is inspiration, that gossip which comes to the ear of the attentive mind from the courts of heaven. There is the profane and stale revelation of the bar-room and the police court. The same ear is fitted to receive both communications. Only the character of the hearer determines to which it shall be open, and to which closed. I believe that the mind can be permanently profaned by the habit of attending to trivial things, so that all our thoughts shall be tinged with triviality. Our very intellect shall be macadamized, as it were, — its foundation broken into fragments for the wheels of travel to roll over; and if you would know what will make the most durable pavement, surpassing rolled stones, spruce blocks, and asphaltum, you have only to look into some of our minds which have been subjected to this treatment so long.

If we have thus desecrated ourselves, — as who has not? — the remedy will be by wariness and devotion to reconsecrate ourselves, and

make once more a fane of the mind. We
should treat our minds, that is, ourselves, as
innocent and ingenuous children, whose guardi-
ans we are, and be careful what objects and
what subjects we thrust on their attention.
Read not the Times. Read the Eternities.
Conventionalities are at length as bad as im-
purities. Even the facts of science may dust
the mind by their dryness, unless they are in a
sense effaced each morning, or rather rendered
fertile by the dews of fresh and living truth.
Knowledge does not come to us by details, but
in flashes of light from heaven. Yes, every
thought that passes through the mind helps to
wear and tear it, and to deepen the ruts, which,
as in the streets of Pompeii, evince how much
it has been used. How many things there are
concerning which we might well deliberate
whether we had better know them, — had better
let their peddling-carts be driven, even at the
slowest trot or walk, over that bridge of glorious span by which we trust to pass at last from
the farthest brink of time to the nearest shore
of eternity! Have we no culture, no refinement, — but skill only to live coarsely and serve
the Devil? — to acquire a little worldly wealth,
or fame, or liberty, and make a false show with
it, as if we were all husk and shell, with no
tender and living kernel to us? Shall our in-

stitutions be like those chestnut - burs which contain abortive nuts, perfect only to prick the fingers?

America is said to be the arena on which the battle of freedom is to be fought; but surely it cannot be freedom in a merely political sense that is meant. Even if we grant that the American has freed himself from a political tyrant, he is still the slave of an economical and moral tyrant. Now that the republic — the *res-publica* — has been settled, it is time to look after the *res-privata*, — the private state, — to see, as the Roman senate charged its consuls, "*ne quid res-*PRIVATA *detrimenti caperet*," that the *private* state receive no detriment.

Do we call this the land of the free? What is it to be free from King George and continue the slaves of King Prejudice? What is it to be born free and not to live free? What is the value of any political freedom, but as a means to moral freedom? Is it a freedom to be slaves, or a freedom to be free, of which we boast? We are a nation of politicians, concerned about the outmost defenses only of freedom. It is our children's children who may perchance be really free. We tax ourselves unjustly. There is a part of us which is not represented. It is taxation without representation. We quarter troops, we quarter fools and cattle of all sorts upon ourselves. We quarter our gross bodies on our poor souls, till the former eat up all the latter's substance.

With respect to a true culture and manhood, we are essentially provincial still, not metropolitan, — mere Jonathans. We are provincial, because we do not find at home our standards; because we do not worship truth, but the reflection of truth; because we are warped and narrowed by an exclusive devotion to trade and commerce and manufactures and agriculture and the like, which are but means, and not the end.

So is the English Parliament provincial. Mere country - bumpkins, they betray themselves, when any more important question arises for them to settle, the Irish question, for instance, — the English question why did I not say? Their natures are subdued to what they work in. Their "good breeding" respects only secondary objects. The finest manners in the world are awkwardness and fatuity when contrasted with a finer intelligence. They appear but as the fashions of past days, — mere courtliness, knee-buckles and small-clothes, out of date. It is the vice, but not the excellence of manners, that they are continually being deserted by the character; they are cast-off clothes or shells, claiming the respect which belonged to the living creature. You are presented with

the shells instead of the meat, and it is no excuse generally, that, in the case of some fishes,
the shells are of more worth than the meat.
The man who thrusts his manners upon me
does as if he were to insist on introducing me
to his cabinet of curiosities, when I wished to
see himself. It was not in this sense that the
poet Decker called Christ "the first true gentleman that ever breathed." I repeat that in this
sense the most splendid court in Christendom is
provincial, having authority to consult about
Transalpine interests only, and not the affairs
of Rome. A prætor or proconsul would suffice
to settle the questions which absorb the attention of the English Parliament and the American Congress.

Government and legislation! these I thought
were respectable professions. We have heard
of heaven-born Numas, Lycurguses, and Solons,
in the history of the world, whose *names* at
least may stand for ideal legislators; but think
of legislating to *regulate* the breeding of slaves,
or the exportation of tobacco! What have divine legislators to do with the exportation or
the importation of tobacco? what humane ones
with the breeding of slaves? Suppose you were
to submit the question to any son of God, —
and has He no children in the nineteenth century? is it a family which is extinct? — in what

condition would you get it again? What shall a State like Virginia say for itself at the last day, in which these have been the principal, the staple productions? What ground is there for patriotism in such a State? I derive my facts from statistical tables which the States themselves have published.

A commerce that whitens every sea in quest of nuts and raisins, and makes slaves of its sailors for this purpose! I saw, the other day, a vessel which had been wrecked, and many lives lost, and her cargo of rags, juniper-berries, and bitter almonds were strewn along the shore. It seemed hardly worth the while to tempt the dangers of the sea between Leghorn and New York for the sake of a cargo of juniper-berries and bitter almonds. America sending to the Old World for her bitters! Is not the sea-brine, is not shipwreck, bitter enough to make the cup of life go down here? Yet such, to a great extent, is our boasted commerce; and there are those who style themselves statesmen and philosophers who are so blind as to think that progress and civilization depend on precisely this kind of interchange and activity, — the activity of flies about a molasses-hogshead. Very well, observes one, if men were oysters. And very well, answer I, if men were mosquitoes.

Lieutenant Herndon, whom our Government sent to explore the Amazon, and, it is said, to extend the area of slavery, observed that there was wanting there "an industrious and active population, who know what the comforts of life are, and who have artificial wants to draw out the great resources of the country." But what are the "artificial wants" to be encouraged? Not the love of luxuries, like the tobacco and slaves of, I believe, his native Virginia, nor the ice and granite and other material wealth of our native New England; nor are "the great resources of a country" that fertility or barrenness of soil which produces these. The chief want, in every State that I have been into, was a high and earnest purpose in its inhabitants. This alone draws out "the great resources" of Nature, and at last taxes her beyond her resources; for man naturally dies out of her. When we want culture more than potatoes, and illumination more than sugar-plums, then the great resources of a world are taxed and drawn out, and the result, or staple production, is, not slaves, nor operatives, but men, — those rare fruits called heroes, saints, poets, philosophers, and redeemers.

In short, as a snow-drift is formed where there is a lull in the wind, so, one would say, where there is a lull of truth, an institution springs up. But the truth blows right on over it, nevertheless, and at length blows it down.

What is called politics is comparatively something so superficial and inhuman, that practically I have never fairly recognized that it concerns me at all. The newspapers, I perceive, devote some of their columns specially to politics or government without charge; and this, one would say, is all that saves it; but as I love literature and to some extent the truth also, I never read those columns at any rate. I do not wish to blunt my sense of right so much. I have not got to answer for having read a single President's Message. A strange age of the world this, when empires, kingdoms, and republics come a-begging to a private man's door, and utter their complaints at his elbow! I cannot take up a newspaper but I find that some wretched government or other, hard pushed, and on its last legs, is interceding with me, the reader, to vote for it, — more importunate than an Italian beggar; and if I have a mind to look at its certificate, made, perchance, by some benevolent merchant's clerk, or the skipper that brought it over, for it cannot speak a word of English itself, I shall probably read of the eruption of some Vesuvius, or the overflowing of some Po, true or forged, which brought it into this condition. I do not hesitate, in such a case, to suggest work, or the almshouse; or why not keep its castle in silence, as I do commonly? The poor President, what with preserving his popularity and doing his duty, is completely bewildered. The newspapers are the ruling power. Any other government is reduced to a few marines at Fort Independence. If a man neglects to read the Daily Times, government will go down on its knees to him, for this is the only treason in these days.

Those things which now most engage the attention of men, as politics and the daily routine, are, it is true, vital functions of human society, but should be unconsciously performed, like the corresponding functions of the physical body. They are *infra*-human, a kind of vegetation. I sometimes awake to a half-consciousness of them going on about me, as a man may become conscious of some of the processes of digestion in a morbid state, and so have the dyspepsia, as it is called. It is as if a thinker submitted himself to be rasped by the great gizzard of creation. Politics is, as it were, the gizzard of society, full of grit and gravel, and the two political parties are its two opposite halves, — sometimes split into quarters, it may be, which grind on each other. Not only individuals, but states, have thus a confirmed dys-

pepsia, which expresses itself, you can imagine
by what sort of eloquence. Thus our life is
not altogether a forgetting, but also, alas! to a
great extent, a remembering, of that which we
should never have been conscious of, certainly
not in our waking hours. Why should we not
meet, not always as dyspeptics, to tell our bad
dreams, but sometimes as *eu*peptics, to congratulate each other on the ever-glorious morning? I do not make an exorbitant demand,
surely.

THE PROMETHEUS BOUND OF
ÆSCHYLUS

PERSONS OF THE DRAMA

KRATOS *and* BIA (Strength and Force).
HEPHAISTUS (Vulcan).
PROMETHEUS.
CHORUS OF OCEAN NYMPHS.
OCEANUS.
IO, *Daughter of Inachus.*
HERMES.

KRATOS *and* BIA, HEPHAISTUS, PROMETHEUS.

Kr. We are come to the far-bounding plain
　　　of earth,
To the Scythian way, to the unapproached soli-
　　　tude.
Hephaistus' orders must have thy attention,
Which the Father has enjoined on thee, this
　　　bold one
To the high-hanging rocks to bind
In indissoluble fetters of adamantine bonds.
For thy flower, the splendor of fire useful in all
　　　arts,
Stealing, he bestowed on mortals; and for such
A crime 't is fit he should give satisfaction to
　　　the gods;

That he may learn the tyranny of Zeus
To love, and cease from his man-loving ways.
    Heph. Kratos and Bia, your charge from
        Zeus
Already has its end, and nothing further in the
        way;
But I cannot endure to bind
A kindred god by force to a bleak precipice, —
Yet absolutèly there's necessity that I have
        courage for these things;
For it is hard the Father's words to banish.
High - plotting son of the right - counseling
        Themis,
Unwilling thee unwilling in brazen fetters hard
        to be loosed
I am about to nail to this inhuman hill,
Where neither voice [you'll hear], nor form of
        any mortal
See, but, scorched by the sun's clear flame,
Will change your color's bloom; and to you glad
The various-robed night will conceal the light,
And sun disperse the morning frost again;
And always the burden of the present ill
Will wear you; for he that will relieve you has
        not yet been born.
Such fruits you've reaped from your man-lov-
        ing ways,
For a god, not shrinking from the wrath of
        gods,

You have bestowed honors on mortals more than
    just,
For which this pleasureless rock you 'll sentinel,
Standing erect, sleepless, not bending a knee;
And many sighs and lamentations to no purpose
Will you utter; for the mind of Zeus is hard to
    be changed;
And he is wholly rugged who may newly rule.

    Kr. Well, why dost thou delay and pity in
    vain?
Why not hate the god most hostile to gods,
Who has betrayed thy prize to mortals?

    Heph. The affinity indeed is appalling, and
    the familiarity.

    Kr. I agree, but to disobey the Father's
    words
How is it possible? Fear you not this more?

    Heph. Ay, you are always without pity, and
    full of confidence.

    Kr. For 't is no remedy to bewail this one;
Cherish not vainly troubles which avail naught.

    Heph. O much hated handicraft!

    Kr. Why hatest it? for in simple truth, for
    these misfortunes
Which are present now Art 's not to blame.

    Heph. Yet I would 't had fallen to another's
    lot.

    Kr. All things were done but to rule the gods,
For none is free but Zeus.

Heph. I knew it, and have naught to say
    against these things.

Kr. Will you not haste then to put the
    bonds about him,

That the Father may not observe you loitering?

Heph. Already at hand the shackles you may
    see.

Kr. Taking them, about his hands with firm
    strength

Strike with the hammer, and nail him to the
    rocks.

Heph. 'T is done, and not in vain this work.

Kr. Strike harder, tighten, nowhere relax,

For he is skillful to find out ways e'en from the
    impracticable.

Heph. Ay, but this arm is fixed inextricably.

Kr. And this now clasp securely, that

He may learn he is a duller schemer than is
    Zeus.

Heph. Except him would none justly blame
    me.

Kr. Now with an adamantine wedge's stub-
    born fang

Through the breasts nail strongly.

Heph. Alas! alas! Prometheus, I groan for
    thy afflictions.

Kr. And do you hesitate? for Zeus' enemies

Do you groan? Beware lest one day you your-
    self will pity.

Heph. You see a spectacle hard for eyes to
    behold.

Kr. I see him meeting his deserts;
But round his sides put straps.

Heph. To do this is necessity, insist not much.

Kr. Surely I will insist and urge beside;
Go downward, and the thighs surround with
    force.

Heph. Already it is done, the work, with no
    long labor.

Kr. Strongly now drive the fetters, through
    and through,
For the critic of the works is difficult.

Heph. Like your form your tongue speaks.

Kr. Be thou softened, but for my stubborn-
    ness
Of temper and harshness reproach me not.

Heph. Let us withdraw, for he has a net
    about his limbs.

Kr. There now insult, and the shares of gods
Plundering on ephemerals bestow; what thee
Can mortals in these ills relieve?
Falsely thee the divinities Prometheus
Call; for you yourself need one *foreseeing*
In what manner you will escape this fortune.

PROMETHEUS, *alone.*

O divine ether, and ye swift-winged winds,
Fountains of rivers, and countless smilings

Of the ocean waves, and earth, mother of all,
And thou all-seeing orb of the sun I call.
Behold me what a god I suffer at the hands of
      gods.
See by what outrages
Tormented the myriad-yeared
Time I shall endure; such the new
Ruler of the blessed has contrived for me,
Unseemly bonds.
Alas! alas! the present and the coming
Woe I groan; where ever of these sufferings
Must an end appear.
But what say I? I know beforehand all,
Exactly what will be, nor to me strange
Will any evil come. The destined fate
As easily as possible it behooves to bear, know-
      ing
Necessity's is a resistless strength.
But neither to be silent nor unsilent about this
Lot is possible for me; for a gift to mortals
Giving, I wretched have been yoked to these
      necessities;
Within a hollow reed by stealth I carry off
      fire's
Stolen source, which seemed the teacher
Of all art to mortals, and a great resource.
For such crimes penalty I pay,
Under the sky, riveted in chains.
Ah! ah! alas! alas!

What echo, what odor has flown to me obscure,
Of god, or mortal, or else mingled, —
Came it to this terminal hill
A witness of my sufferings, or wishing what?
Behold bound me an unhappy god,
The enemy of Zeus, fallen under
The ill will of all the gods, as many as
Enter into the hall of Zeus,
Through too great love of mortals.
Alas! alas! what fluttering do I hear
Of birds near? for the air rustles
With the soft rippling of wings.
Everything to me is fearful which creeps this
     way.

PROMETHEUS *and* CHORUS.

Ch. Fear nothing; for friendly this band
Of wings with swift contention
Drew to this hill, hardly
Persuading the paternal mind.
The swift-carrying breezes sent me;
For the echo of beaten steel pierced the recesses
Of the caves, and struck out from me reserved
     modesty;
And I rushed unsandaled in a winged chariot.
     Pr. Alas! alas! alas! alas!
Offspring of the fruitful Tethys,
And of him rolling around all
The earth with sleepless stream children,

Of Father Ocean; behold, look on me;
By what bonds embraced
On this cliff's topmost rocks
I shall maintain unenvied watch.

 Ch. I see, Prometheus; but to my eyes a fearful
Mist has come surcharged
With tears, looking upon thy body
Shrunk to the rocks
By these mischiefs of adamantine bonds;
Indeed, new helmsmen rule Olympus;
And with new laws Zeus strengthens himself, annulling the old,
And the before great now makes unknown.

 Pr. Would that under earth, and below Hades,
Receptacle of dead, to impassable
Tartarus he had sent me, to bonds indissoluble
Cruelly conducting, that neither god
Nor any other had rejoiced at this.
But now the sport of winds, unhappy one,
A source of pleasure to my foes I suffer.

 Ch. Who so hard-hearted
Of the gods, to whom these things are pleasant?
Who does not sympathize with thy
Misfortunes, excepting Zeus? for he in wrath always

Fixing his stubborn mind,
Afflicts the heavenly race;
Nor will he cease, until his heart is sated;
Or with some palm some one may take the
      power hard to be taken.

  Pr. Surely yet, though in strong
Fetters I am now maltreated,
The ruler of the blessed will have need of me,
To show the new conspiracy by which
He 's robbed of sceptre and of honors,
And not at all me with persuasion's honey-
      tongued
Charms will he appease, nor ever,
Shrinking from his firm threats, will I
Declare this, till from cruel
Bonds he may release, and to do justice
For this outrage be willing.

  Ch. You are bold; and to bitter
Woes do nothing yield,
But too freely speak.
But my mind piercing fear disturbs;
For I 'm concerned about thy fortunes,
Where at length arriving you may see
An end to these afflictions. For manners
Inaccessible, and a heart hard to be dissuaded
      has the son of Kronos.

  Pr. I know, that — Zeus is stern and having
Justice to himself. But after all
Gentle-minded

He will one day be, when thus he 's crushed,
And his stubborn wrath allaying,
Into agreement with me and friendliness
Earnest to me earnest he at length will come.

 Ch. The whole account disclose and tell us
  plainly,
In what crime taking you Zeus
Thus disgracefully and bitterly insults;
Inform us, if you are nowise hurt by the re-
  cital.

 Pr. Painful indeed it is to me to tell these
  things,
And a pain to be silent, and every way unfor-
  tunate.
When first the divinities began their strife,
And discord 'mong themselves arose,
Some wishing to cast Kronos from his seat,
That Zeus might reign, forsooth, others the
  contrary
Striving, that Zeus might never rule the gods;
Then I, the best advising, to persuade
The Titans, sons of Uranus and Chthon,
Unable was; but crafty stratagems
Despising with rude minds,
They thought without trouble to rule by force;
But to me my mother not once only, Themis,
And Gæa, of many names one form,
How the future should be accomplished had
  foretold,

That not by power nor by strength
Would it be necessary, but by craft the victors
    should prevail.
Such I in words expounding,
They deigned not to regard at all.
The best course therefore of those occurring
    then
Appeared to be, taking my mother to me,
Of my own accord to side with Zeus glad to re-
    ceive me;
And by my counsels Tartarus' black-pitted
Depths conceals the ancient Kronos,
With his allies.   In such things by me
The tyrant of the gods having been helped,
With base rewards like these repays me;
For there is somehow in kingship
This disease, not to trust its friends.
What then you ask, for what cause
He afflicts me, this will I now explain.
As soon as on his father's throne
He sat, he straightway to the gods distributes
    honors,
Some to one and to another some, and arranged
The government; but of unhappy mortals ac-
    count
Had none; but blotting out the race
Entire, wished to create another new.
And these things none opposed but I,
But I adventured; I rescued mortals

From going destroyed to Hades.
Therefore indeed with such afflictions am I
    bent,
To suffer grievous, and piteous to behold,
And, holding mortals up to pity, myself am
    not
Thought worthy to obtain it; but without pity
Am I thus corrected, a spectacle inglorious to
    Zeus.

  Ch. Of iron heart and made of stone,
Whoe'er, Prometheus, with thy sufferings
Does not grieve; for I should not have wished
    to see
These things, and having seen them I am
    grieved at heart.

    Pr. Indeed to friends I 'm piteous to behold.
    Ch. Did you in no respect go beyond this?
    Pr. True, mortals I made cease foreseeing
    fate.
    Ch. Having found what remedy for this all?
    Pr. Blind hopes in them I made to dwell.
    Ch. A great advantage this you gave to
    men.
    Pr. Beside these, too, I bestowed on them
    fire.
    Ch. And have mortals flamy fire?
    Pr. From which indeed they will learn many
    arts.
    Ch. Upon such charges then does Zeus

Maltreat you, and nowhere relax from ills?
Is there no term of suffering lying before thee?

   Pr. Nay, none at all, but when to him it
      may seem good.

   Ch. And how will it seem good? What
      hope? See you not that
You have erred? But how you 've erred, for
      me to tell
Not pleasant, and to you a pain. But these
      things
Let us omit, and seek you some release from
      sufferings.

   Pr. Easy, whoever out of trouble holds his
Foot, to admonish and remind those faring
Ill. But all these things I knew;
Willing, willing I erred, I 'll not deny;
Mortals assisting I myself found trouble.
Not indeed with penalties like these thought I
That I should pine on lofty rocks,
Gaining this drear unneighbored hill.
But bewail not my present woes,
But alighting, the fortunes creeping on
Hear ye, that ye may learn all to the end.
Obey me, obey, sympathize
With him now suffering. Thus indeed affliction,
Wandering round, sits now by one, then by an-
    other.

   Ch. Not to unwilling ears do you urge
This, Prometheus.

And now with light foot the swift-rushing
Seat leaving, and the pure ether,
Path of birds, to this peaked
Ground I come; for thy misfortunes
I wish fully to hear.

PROMETHEUS, CHORUS, *and* OCEANUS.

Oc. I come to the end of a long way
Traveling to thee, Prometheus,
By my will without bits directing
This wing-swift bird;
For at thy fortunes know I grieve.
And, I think, affinity thus
Impels me, but apart from birth,
There's not to whom a higher rank
I would assign than thee.
And you will know these things as true, and not
     in vain
To flatter with the tongue is in me. Come,
     therefore,
Show how it is necessary to assist you;
For never will you say, than Ocean
There's a firmer friend to thee.

Pr. Alas! what now?   And you then of my
     sufferings
Come spectator?   How didst thou dare, leaving
The stream which bears thy name, and rock-
     roofed
Caves self-built, to the iron-mother

Earth to go? To behold my fate
Hast come, and to compassionate my ills?
Behold a spectacle, this, the friend of Zeus,
Having with him stablished his tyranny,
With what afflictions by himself I 'm bent.

   Oc. I see, Prometheus, and would admonish
Thee the best, although of varied craft.
Know thyself, and fit thy manners
New; for new also the king among the gods.
For if thus rude and whetted words
Thou wilt hurl out, quickly may Zeus, though
       sitting
Far above, hear thee, so that thy present wrath
Of troubles child's play will seem to be.
But, O wretched one, dismiss the indignation
      which thou hast,
And seek deliverance from these woes.
Like an old man, perhaps, I seem to thee to say
      these things;
Such, however, are the wages
Of the too lofty speaking tongue, Prometheus;
But thou art not yet humble, nor dost yield to
      ills,
And beside the present wish to receive others
      still.
But thou wouldst not, with my counsel,
Against the pricks extend your limbs, seeing
      that
A stern monarch irresponsible reigns.

And now I go, and will endeavor,
If I can, to release thee from these sufferings.
But be thou quiet, nor too rudely speak.
Know'st thou not well, with thy superior wisdom, that
On a vain tongue punishment is inflicted?

 Pr. I congratulate thee that thou art without blame,
Having shared and dared all with me;
And now leave off, and let it not concern thee.
For altogether thou wilt not persuade him, for he 's not easily persuaded,
But take heed yourself lest you be injured by the way.

 Oc. Far better thou art to advise those near
Than thyself; by deed and not by word I judge.
But me hastening by no means mayest thou detain,
For I boast, I boast, this favor will Zeus
Grant me, from these sufferings to release thee.

 Pr. So far I praise thee, and will never cease;
For zeal you nothing lack. But
Strive not; for in vain, naught helping
Me, thou 'lt strive, if aught to strive you wish.
But be thou quiet, holding thyself aloof,
For I would not, though I 'm unfortunate, that on this account
Evils should come to many.

Oc. Surely not, for me too the fortunes of
    thy brother
Atlas grieve, who towards the evening-places
Stands, the pillar of heaven and earth
Upon his shoulders bearing, a load not easy to
    be borne.
And the earth-born inhabitant of the Cilician
Caves seeing, I pitied, the savage monster
With a hundred heads, by force o'ercome,
Typhon impetuous, who stood 'gainst all the
    gods,
With frightful jaws hissing out slaughter;
And from his eyes flashed a gorgonian light,
Utterly to destroy by force the sovereignty of
    Zeus;
But there came to him Zeus' sleepless bolt,
Descending thunder, breathing flame,
Which struck him out from lofty
Boastings. For struck to his very heart,
His strength was scorched and thundered out.
And now a useless and extended carcass
Lies he near a narrow passage of the sea,
Pressed down under the roots of Ætna.
And on the topmost summit seated, Hephaistus
Hammers the ignited mass, whence will burst
    out at length
Rivers of fire, devouring with wild jaws
Fair-fruited Sicily's smooth fields;
Such rage will Typhon make boil over

With hot discharges of insatiable fire-breathing
    tempest,
Though by the bolt of Zeus burnt to a coal.

  Pr. Thou art not inexperienced, nor dost
    want
My counsel; secure thyself as thou know'st
    how;
And I against the present fortune will bear up,
Until the thought of Zeus may cease from
    wrath.

  Oc. Know'st thou not this, Prometheus, that
Words are healers of distempered wrath?

  Pr. If any seasonably soothe the heart,
And swelling passion check not rudely.

  Oc. In the consulting and the daring
What harm seest thou existing? Teach me.

  Pr. Trouble superfluous, and light-minded
    folly.

  Oc. Be this my ail then, since it is
Most profitable, being wise, not to seem wise.

  Pr. This will seem to be my error.

  Oc. Plainly homeward thy words remand
    me.

  Pr. Aye, let not grief for me into hostility
    cast thee.

  Oc. To the new occupant of the all-powerful
    seats?

  Pr. Beware lest ever his heart be angered.

  Oc. Thy fate, Prometheus, is my teacher.

Pr. Go thou, depart; preserve the present
mind.

Oc. To me rushing this word you utter.
For the smooth path of the air sweeps with his
wings
The four-legged bird; and gladly would
In the stalls at home bend a knee.

PROMETHEUS *and* CHORUS.

Ch. I mourn for thee thy ruinous
Fate, Prometheus,
And tear-distilling from my tender
Eyes a stream has wet
My cheeks with flowing springs;
For these, unenvied, Zeus
By his own laws enforcing,
Haughty above the gods
That were displays his sceptre.
And every region now
With groans resounds,
Mourning the illustrious
And ancient honor
Of thee and of thy kindred;
As many mortals as the habitable seat
Of sacred Asia pasture,
With thy lamentable
Woes have sympathy;
And of the Colchian land, virgin
Inhabitants, in fight undaunted,

And Scythia's multitude, who the last
Place of earth, about
Mæotis lake possess,
And Arabia's martial flower,
And who the high-hung citadels
Of Caucasus inhabit near,
A hostile army, raging
With sharp-prowed spears.
Only one other god before, in sufferings
Subdued by injuries
Of adamantine bonds, I 've seen, Titanian
Atlas, who always with superior strength
The huge and heavenly globe
On his back bears;
And with a roar the sea waves
Dashing, groans the deep,
And the dark depth of Hades murmurs under-
      neath
The earth, and fountains of pure-running rivers
Heave a pitying sigh.
    Pr. Think not, indeed, through weakness or
      through pride
That I am silent; for with the consciousness I
      gnaw my heart,
Seeing myself thus basely used.
And yet to these new gods their shares
Who else than I wholly distributed?
But of these things I am silent; for I should
      tell you

What you know; the sufferings of mortals too
You 've heard, how I made intelligent
And possessed of sense them ignorant before.
But I will speak, not bearing any grudge to men,
But showing in what I gave the good intention;
At first, indeed, seeing they saw in vain,
And hearing heard not; but like the forms
Of dreams, for that long time, rashly con-
         founded
All, nor brick-woven dwellings
Knew they, placed in the sun, nor wood-work;
But digging down they dwelt, like puny
Ants, in sunless nooks of caves.
And there was naught to them, neither of win-
         ter sign,
Nor of flower-giving spring, nor fruitful
Summer, that was sure; but without knowledge
Did they all, till I taught them the risings
Of the stars, and goings down, hard to deter-
         mine.
And numbers, chief of inventions,
I found out for them, and the assemblages of
         letters,
And memory, Muse-mother, doer of all things;
And first I joined in pairs wild animals
Obedient to the yoke; and that they might be
Alternate workers with the bodies of men
In the severest toils, I harnessed the rein-loving
         horses

To the car, the ornament of over-wealthy lux-
　　ury.
And none else than I invented the sea-wander-
　　ing
Flaxen-winged vehicles of sailors.
Such inventions I wretched having found out
For men, myself have not the ingenuity by
　　which
From the now present ill I may escape.
　　Ch. You suffer unseemly ill; deranged in
　　mind
You err; and as some bad physician, falling
Sick you are dejected, and cannot find
By what remedies you may be healed.
　　Pr. Hearing the rest from me more will you
　　wonder
What arts and what expedients I planned.
That which was greatest, if any might fall
　　sick,
There was alleviation none, neither to eat,
Nor to anoint, nor drink, but for the want
Of medicines they were reduced to skeletons,
　　till to them
I showed the mingling of mild remedies,
By which all ails they drive away.
And many modes of prophecy I settled,
And distinguished first of dreams what a real
Vision is required to be, and omens hard to be
　　determined

I made known to them; and tokens by the way,
And flight of crooked-taloned birds I accurately
Defined, which lucky are,
And unlucky, and what mode of life
Have each, and to one another what
Hostilities, attachments, and assemblings;
The entrails' smoothness, and what color hav-
    ing
They would be to the divinities acceptable;
Of the gall and liver the various symmetry,
And the limbs concealed in fat; and the
    long
Flank burning, to an art hard to be guessed
I showed the way to mortals; and flammeous
    signs
Explained, before obscure.
Such indeed these; and under ground
Concealed the helps to men,
Brass, iron, silver, gold, who
Would affirm that he discovered before me?
None, I well know, not wishing in vain to
    boast.
But learn all in one word,
All arts to mortals from Prometheus.

    Ch. Assist not mortals now unseasonably,
And neglect yourself unfortunate; for I
Am of good hope that, from these bonds
Released, you will yet have no less power than
    Zeus.

Pr. Never thus has Fate the Accomplisher
Decreed to fulfill these things, but by a myriad
ills
And woes subdued, thus bonds I flee;
For art's far weaker than necessity.

    Ch. Who then is helmsman of necessity?

    Pr. The Fates three-formed, and the remembering Furies.

    Ch. Than these then is Zeus weaker?

    Pr. Ay, he could not escape what has been fated.

    Ch. But what to Zeus is fated, except always to rule?

    Pr. This thou wilt not learn; seek not to know.

    Ch. Surely some awful thing it is which you withhold.

    Pr. Remember other words, for this by no means
Is it time to tell, but to be concealed
As much as possible; for keeping this do I
Escape unseemly bonds and woes.

    Ch. Never may the all-ruling
Zeus put into my mind
Force antagonist to him.
Nor let me cease drawing near
The gods with holy sacrifices
Of slain oxen, by Father Ocean's
Ceaseless passage,

Nor offend with words,
But in me this remain
And ne'er be melted out.
'T is something sweet with bold
Hopes the long life to
Extend, in bright
Cheerfulness the cherishing spirit.
But I shudder, thee beholding
By a myriad sufferings tormented. . . .
For not fearing Zeus,
In thy private mind thou dost regard
Mortals too much, Prometheus.
Come, though a thankless
Favor, friend, say where is any strength,
From ephemerals any help? Saw you not
The powerless inefficiency,
Dream-like, in which the blind . . .
Race of mortals are entangled?
Never counsels of mortals
May transgress the harmony of Zeus.
I learned these things looking on
Thy destructive fate, Prometheus.
For different to me did this strain come,
And that which round thy baths
And couch I hymned,
With the design of marriage, when my father's
        child
With bridal gifts persuading, thou didst lead
Hesione the partner of thy bed.

PROMETHEUS, CHORUS, *and* IO.

Io. What earth, what race, what being shall
    I say is this
I see in bridles of rock
Exposed? By what crime's
Penalty dost thou perish? Show, to what part
Of earth I miserable have wandered.
Ah! ah! alas! alas!
Again some fly doth sting me wretched,
Image of earth-born Argus, cover it earth;
I fear the myriad-eyed herdsman beholding;
For he goes having a treacherous eye,
Whom not e'en dead the earth conceals.
But me, wretched from the Infernals passing,
He pursues, and drives fasting along the sea-
    side
Sand, while low resounds a wax-compacted reed,
Uttering sleep-giving law; alas! alas! O gods!
Where, gods! where lead me far-wandering
    courses?
In what sin, O son of Kronos,
In what sin ever having taken,
To these afflictions hast thou yoked me? alas!
    alas!
With fly-driven fear a wretched
Frenzied one dost thus afflict?
With fire burn, or with earth cover, **or**
To sea monsters give for food, nor

Envy me my prayers, king.
Enough much-wandered wanderings
Have exercised me, nor can I learn where
I shall escape from sufferings.

    Ch. Hear'st thou the address of the cow-
        horned virgin?

    Pr. And how not hear the fly-whirled virgin,
Daughter of Inachus, who Zeus' heart warmed
With love, and now the courses over long,
By Here hated, forcedly performs?

    Io. Whence utterest thou my father's name?
Tell me, miserable, who thou art,
That to me, O suffering one, me born to suffer,
Thus true things dost address?
The god-sent ail thou 'st named,
Which wastes me stinging
With maddening goads, alas! alas!
With foodless and unseemly leaps
Rushing headlong, I came,
By wrathful plots subdued.
Who of the wretched, who, alas! alas! suffers
        like me?
But to me clearly show
What me awaits to suffer,
What not necessary; what remedy of ill,
Teach, if indeed thou know'st; speak out,
Tell the ill-wandering virgin.

    Pr. I 'll clearly tell thee all you wish to
        learn.

Not weaving in enigmas, but in simple speech,
As it is just to open the mouth to friends.
Thou seest the giver of fire to men, Prometheus.

   Io. O thou who didst appear a common help
      to mortals,
Wretched Prometheus, to atone for what do
      you endure this?

   Pr. I have scarce ceased my sufferings
      lamenting.

   Io. Would you not grant this favor to me?

   Pr. Say what you ask; for you 'd learn all
      from me.

   Io. Say who has bound thee to the cliff.

   Pr. The will indeed of Zeus, Hephaistus'
      hand.

   Io. And penalty for what crimes dost thou
      pay?

   Pr. Thus much only can I show thee.

   Io. But beside this, declare what time will be
To me unfortunate the limit of my wandering.

   Pr. Not to learn is better for thee than to
      learn these things.

   Io. Conceal not from me what I am to suf-
      fer.

   Pr. Indeed, I grudge thee not this favor.

   Io. Why, then, dost thou delay to tell the
      whole?

   Pr. There 's no unwillingness, but I hesitate
      to vex thy mind.

Io. Care not for me more than is pleasant to
    me.

Pr. Since you are earnest, it behooves to
    speak; hear then.

Ch. Not yet indeed; but a share of pleasure
    also give to me.

First we 'll learn the malady of this one,
Herself relating her destructive fortunes,
And the remainder of her trials let her learn
    from thee.

Pr. 'T is thy part, Io, to do these a favor,
As well for every other reason, and as they are
    sisters of thy father.

Since to weep and to lament misfortunes,
There where one will get a tear
From those attending, is worthy the delay.

Io. I know not that I need distrust you,
But in plain speech you shall learn
All that you ask for; and yet e'en telling I
    lament
The god-sent tempest, and dissolution
Of my form — whence to me miserable it came.
For always visions in the night, moving about
My virgin chambers, enticed me
With smooth words: "O greatly happy virgin,
Why be a virgin long? is permitted to obtain
The greatest marriage. For Zeus with love's
    dart
Has been warmed by thee, and wishes to unite

In love; but do thou, O child, spurn not the
    couch
Of Zeus, but go out to Lerna's deep
Morass, and stables of thy father's herds,
That the divine eye may cease from desire."
With such dreams every night
Was I unfortunate distressed, till I dared tell
My father of the night-wandering visions.
And he to Pytho and Dodona frequent
Prophets sent, that he might learn what it was
    necessary
He should say or do, to do agreeably to the
    gods.
And they came bringing ambiguous
Oracles, darkly and indistinctly uttered.
But finally a plain report came to Inachus,
Clearly enjoining him and telling
Out of my home and country to expel me,
Discharged to wander to the earth's last bounds;
And if he was not willing, from Zeus would
    come
A fiery thunderbolt, which would annihilate all
    his race.
Induced by such predictions of the Loxian,
Against his will he drove me out,
And shut me from the houses; but Zeus' rein
Compelled him by force to do these things.
Immediately my form and mind were
Changed, and horned, as you behold, stung

By a sharp-mouthed fly, with frantic leaping
Rushed I to Cenchrea's palatable stream,
And Lerna's source; but a herdsman born-of-
   earth
Of violent temper, Argus, accompanied, with
   numerous
Eyes my steps observing.
But unexpectedly a sudden fate
Robbed him of life; and I, fly-stung,
By lash divine am driven from land to land.
You hear what has been done; and if you have
   to say aught,
What 's left of labors, speak; nor pitying me
Comfort with false words; for an ill
The worst of all, I say, are made-up words.
   Ch. Ah! ah! enough, alas!
Ne'er, ne'er did I presume such cruel words
Would reach my ears, nor thus unsightly
And intolerable hurts, sufferings, fears with a
   two-edged
Goad would chill my soul;
Alas! alas! fate! fate!
I shudder, seeing the state of Io.
   Pr. Beforehand sigh'st thou, and art full of
   fears,
Hold till the rest also thou learn'st.
   Ch. Tell, teach; for to the sick 't is sweet
To know the remaining pain beforehand clearly.
   Pr. Your former wish ye got from me

With ease; for first ye asked to learn from
    her
Relating her own trials;
The rest now hear, what sufferings 't is neces-
    sary
This young woman should endure from Here.
But do thou, offspring of Inachus, my words
Cast in thy mind, that thou may'st learn the
    boundaries of the way.
First, indeed, hence towards the rising of the
    sun
Turning thyself, travel uncultivated lands,
And to the Scythian nomads thou wilt come,
    who woven roofs
On high inhabit, on well-wheeled carts,
With far-casting bows equipped;
Whom go not near, but to the sea-resounding
    cliffs
Bending thy feet, pass from the region.
On the left hand the iron-working
Chalybes inhabit, whom thou must needs be-
    ware,
For they are rude and inaccessible to strangers.
And thou wilt come to the Hybristes river, not
    ill named,
Which pass not, for not easy is 't to pass,
Before you get to Caucasus itself, highest
Of mountains, where the stream spurts out its
    tide

From the very temples; and passing over
The star-neighbored summits, 't is necessary to
     go
The southern way, where thou wilt come to the
     man-hating
Army of the Amazons, who Themiscyra one day
Will inhabit, by the Thermedon, where 's
Salmydessia, rough jaw of the sea,
Inhospitable to sailors, step-mother of ships;
They will conduct thee on thy way, and very
     cheerfully.
And to the Cimmerian isthmus thou wilt come,
Just on the narrow portals of a lake, which
     leaving
It behooves thee with stout heart to pass the
     Mœotic straits;
And there will be to mortals ever a great fame
Of thy passage, and Bosphorus from thy name
'T will be called.   And leaving Europe's plain
The continent of Asia thou wilt reach. — Seem-
     eth to thee, forsooth,
The tyrant of the gods in everything to be
Thus violent?   For he a god, with this mortal
Wishing to unite, drove her to these wanderings.
A bitter wooer didst thou find, O virgin,
For thy marriage.   For the words you now
     have heard
Think not yet to be the prelude.

    Io. Ah! me! me! alas! alas!

Pr. Again dost shriek and heave a sigh? What

Wilt thou do when the remaining ills thou learn'st?

Ch. And hast thou any further suffering to tell her?

Pr. Ay, a tempestuous sea of baleful woe.

Io. What profit, then, for me to live, and not in haste

To cast myself from this rough rock,

That rushing down upon the plain I may be released

From every trouble? For better once for all to die,

Than all my days to suffer evilly.

Pr. Unhappily my trials would'st thou hear,

To whom to die has not been fated;

For this would be release from sufferings;

But now there is no end of ills lying

Before me, until Zeus falls from sovereignty.

Io. And is Zeus ever to fall from power?

Pr. Thou would'st be pleased, I think, to see this accident.

Io. How should I not, who suffer ill from Zeus?

Pr. That these things then are so, be thou assured.

Io. By what one will the tyrant's power be robbed?

Pr. Himself, by his own senseless counsels.

Io. In what way show, if there's no harm.

Pr. He will make such a marriage as one day he'll repent.

Io. Of god or mortal? If to be spoken, tell.

Pr. What matters which? For these things are not to be told.

Io. By a wife will he be driven from the throne?

Pr. Ay, she will bring forth a son superior to his father.

Io. Is there no refuge for him from this fate?

Pr. None, surely, till I may be released from bonds.

Io. Who then is to release thee, Zeus unwilling?

Pr. He must be some one of thy descendants.

Io. How sayest thou — that my child will deliver thee from ills?

Pr. Third of thy race after ten other births.

Io. This oracle is not yet easy to be guessed.

Pr. But do not seek to understand thy sufferings.

Io. First proffering gain to me, do not then withhold it.

Pr. I'll grant thee one of two relations.

Io. What two propose, and give to me my choice.

Pr. I give; choose whether thy remaining
     troubles
I shall tell thee clearly, or him that will release
     me.

Ch. Consent to do her the one favor,
Me the other, nor deem us undeserving of thy
     words;
To her indeed tell what remains of wandering,
And to me, who will release; for I desire this.

Pr. Since ye are earnest, I will not resist
To tell the whole, as much as ye ask for.
To thee first, Io, vexatious wandering I will
     tell,
Which engrave on the remembering tablets of
     the mind.
When thou hast passed the flood boundary of
     continents,
Towards the flaming orient sun-traveled . . .
Passing through the tumult of the sea, until
     you reach
The Gorgonian plains of Cisthene, where
The Phorcides dwell, old virgins,
Three, swan-shaped, having a common eye,
One-toothed, whom neither the sun looks on
With his beams, nor nightly moon ever.
And near, their winged sisters three,
Dragon-scaled Gorgons, odious to men,
Whom no mortal beholding will have breath;
Such danger do I tell thee.

But hear another odious sight;
Beware the gryphons, sharp-mouthed
Dogs of Zeus, which bark not, and the one-eyed
      Arimaspian
Host, going on horseback, who dwell about
The golden-flowing flood of Pluto's channel;
These go not near. But to a distant land
Thou 'lt come, a dusky race, who near the
      fountains
Of the sun inhabit, where is the Æthiopian
      river.
Creep down the banks of this, until thou com'st
To a descent, where from Byblinian mounts
The Nile sends down its sacred palatable stream.
This will conduct thee to the triangled land
Nilean, where, Io, 't is decreed
Thou and thy progeny shall form the distant
      colony.
If aught of this is unintelligible to thee, **and**
      hard to be found out,
Repeat thy questions, and learn clearly;
For more leisure than I want is granted me.
   Ch. If to her aught remaining or omitted
Thou hast to tell of her pernicious wandering,
Speak; but if thou hast said all, give us
The favor which we ask, for surely thou remem-
      ber'st.
   Pr. The whole term of her traveling has she
      heard.

But that she may know that not in vain she
      hears me,
I 'll tell what before coming hither she endured,
Giving this as proof of my relations.
The great multitude of words I will omit,
And proceed unto the very limit of thy wander-
      ings.
When then you came to the Molossian ground,
And near the high-ridged Dodona, where
Oracle and seat is of Thesprotian Zeus,
And prodigy incredible, the speaking oaks,
By whom you clearly, and naught enigmati-
      cally,
Were called the illustrious wife of Zeus
About to be, if aught of these things soothes
      thee;
Thence, driven by the fly, you came
The seaside way to the great gulf of Rhea,
From which by courses retrograde you are now
      tempest-tossed.
But for time to come the sea gulf,
Clearly know, will be called Ionian,
Memorial of thy passage to all mortals.
Proofs to thee are these of my intelligence,
That it sees somewhat more than the apparent.
But the rest to you and her in common I will tell,
Having come upon the very track of former
      words.
There is a city Canopus, last of the land,

By Nile's very mouth and bank;
There at length Zeus makes thee sane,
Stroking with gentle hand, and touching only.
And, named from Zeus' begetting,
Thou wilt bear dark Epaphus, who will reap
As much land as broad-flowing Nile doth water;
And fifth from him, a band of fifty children
Again to Argos shall unwilling come,
Of female sex, avoiding kindred marriage
Of their cousins; but they, with minds inflamed,
Hawks by doves not far left behind,
Will come pursuing marriages
Not to be pursued, but heaven will take ven-
   geance on their bodies;
For them Pelasgia shall receive by Mars
Subdued with woman's hand with night-watch-
   ing boldness.
For each wife shall take her husband's life,
Staining a two-edged dagger in his throat.
Such 'gainst my foes may Cypris come. —
But one of the daughters shall love soften
Not to slay her bedfellow, but she will waver
In her mind; and one of two things will prefer,
To hear herself called timid, rather than stained
   with blood;
She shall in Argos bear a royal race. —
Of a long speech is need this clearly to discuss.
From this seed, however, shall be born a
   brave,

Famed for his bow, who will release me
From these sufferings.   Such oracle my ancient
Mother told me, Titanian Themis;
But how and by what means, this needs long
      speech
To tell, and nothing, learning, wilt thou gain.
   Io. Ah me! ah wretched me!
Spasms again and brain-struck
Madness burn me within, and a fly's dart
Stings me — not wrought by fire.
My heart with fear knocks at my breast,
And my eyes whirl round and round,
And from my course I'm borne by madness'
Furious breath, unable to control my tongue;
While confused words dash idly
'Gainst the waves of horrid woe.
   Ch. Wise, wise indeed was he,
Who first in mind
This weighed, and with the tongue expressed,
To marry according to one's degree is best by
      far;
Nor, being a laborer with the hands,
To woo those who are by wealth corrupted,
Nor, those by birth made great.
Never, never me
Fates . . .
May you behold the sharer of Zeus' couch.
Nor may I be brought near to any husband
      among those from heaven,

For I fear, seeing the virginhood of Io,
Not content with man, through marriage vexed
With these distressful wanderings by Here.
But for myself, since an equal marriage is with-
out fear,
I am not concerned lest the love of the almighty
Gods cast its inevitable eye on me.
Without war indeed this war, producing
Troubles; nor do I know what would become of
me;
For I see not how I should escape the subtlety
of Zeus.

Pr. Surely shall Zeus, though haughty now,
Yet be humble, such marriage
He prepares to make, which from sovereignty
And the throne will cast him down obscure;
and Father Kronos'
Curse will then be all fulfilled,
Which falling from the ancient seats he impre-
cated.
And refuge from such ills none of the gods
But I can show him clearly.
I know these things, and in what manner. Now
therefore
Being bold, let him sit trusting to lofty
Sounds, and brandishing with both hands his
fire-breathing weapon,
For naught will these avail him, not
To fall disgracefully intolerable falls;

Such wrestler does he now prepare,
Himself against himself, a prodigy most hard
      to be withstood;
Who, indeed, will invent a better flame than
      lightning,
And a loud sound surpassing thunder;
And shiver the trident, Neptune's weapon,
The marine earth-shaking ail.
Stumbling upon this ill he 'll learn
How different to govern and to serve.

   Ch. Ay, as you hope you vent this against
      Zeus.

   Pr. What will be done, and also what I
      hope, I say.

   Ch. And are we to expect that any will rule
      Zeus?

   Pr. Even than these more grievous ills he 'll
      have.

   Ch. How fear'st thou not, hurling such
      words?

   Pr. What should I fear, to whom to die has
      not been fated?

   Ch. But suffering more grievous still than
      this he may inflict.

   Pr. Then let him do it; all is expected by
      me.

   Ch. Those reverencing Adrastia are wise.

   Pr. Revere, pray, flatter each successive
      ruler.

Me less than nothing Zeus concerns.
Let him do, let him prevail this short time
As he will, for long he will not rule the gods, —
But I see here, indeed, Zeus' runner,
The new tyrant's drudge;
Doubtless he brings some new message.

PROMETHEUS, CHORUS, *and* HERMES.

Her. To thee, the sophist, the bitterly bitter,
The sinner against gods, the giver of honors
To ephemerals, the thief of fire, I speak;
The Father commands thee to tell the marriage
Which you boast, by which he falls from power;
And that too not enigmatically,
But each particular declare; nor cause me
Double journeys, Prometheus; for thou see'st
    that
Zeus is not appeased by such.

Pr. Solemn-mouthed and full of wisdom
Is thy speech, as of the servant of the gods.
Ye newly rule, and think forsooth
To dwell in griefless citadels; have I not seen
Two tyrants fallen from these?
And third I shall behold him ruling now,
Basest and speediest. Do I seem to thee
To fear and shrink from the new gods?
Nay, much and wholly I fall short of this.
The way thou cam'st go through the dust
    again;

For thou wilt learn naught which thou ask'st of
    me.

  Her. Ay, by such insolence before
You brought yourself into these woes.

  Pr. Plainly know, I would not change
My ill fortune for thy servitude,
For better, I think, to serve this rock
Than be the faithful messenger of Father Zeus.
Thus to insult the insulting it is fit.

  Her. Thou seem'st to enjoy thy present
    state.

  Pr. I enjoy? Enjoying thus my enemies
Would I see; and thee 'mong them I count.

  Her. Dost thou blame me for aught of thy
    misfortunes?

  Pr. In plain words, all gods I hate,
As many as well treated wrong me unjustly.

  Her. I hear thee raving, no slight ail.

  Pr. Ay, I should ail, if ail one's foes to
    hate.

  Her. If prosperous, thou couldst not be
    borne.

  Pr. Ah me!

  Her. This word Zeus does not know.

  Pr. But time growing old teaches all things.

  Her. And still thou know'st not yet how to
    be prudent.

  Pr. For I should not converse with thee a
    servant.

Her. Thou seem'st to say naught which the Father wishes.

Pr. And yet his debtor I'd requite the favor.

Her. Thou mock'st me verily as if I were a child.

Pr. And art thou not a child, and simpler still than this,

If thou expectest to learn aught from me?
There is not outrage nor expedient, by which
Zeus will induce me to declare these things,
Before he loose these grievous bonds.
Let there be hurled then flaming fire,
And the white-winged snows, and thunders
Of the earth, let him confound and mingle all.
For none of these will bend me till I tell
By whom 't is necessary he should fall from sovereignty.

Her. Consider now if these things seem helpful.

Pr. Long since these were considered and resolved.

Her. Venture, O vain one, venture, at length,

In view of present sufferings to be wise.

Pr. In vain you vex me, as a wave, exhorting.

Ne'er let it come into thy mind that I, fearing
Zeus' anger, shall become woman-minded,

And beg him, greatly hated,
With womanish upturnings of the hands,
To loose me from these bonds. I am far from
    it.
   Her. Though saying much I seem in vain to
    speak;
For thou art nothing softened nor appeased
By prayers; but champing at the bit like a new-
    yoked
Colt, thou strugglest and contend'st against
    the reins.
But thou art violent with feeble wisdom.
For stubbornness to him who is not wise,
Itself alone, is less than nothing strong.
But consider, if thou art not persuaded by my
    words,
What storm and triple surge of ills
Will come upon thee not to be avoided; for first
    this rugged
Cliff with thunder and lightning flame
The Father 'll rend, and hide
Thy body, and a strong arm will bury thee.
When thou hast spent a long length of time,
Thou wilt come back to light; and Zeus'
Winged dog, a bloodthirsty eagle, ravenously
Shall tear the great rag of thy body,
Creeping an uninvited guest all day,
And banquet on thy liver black by eating.
Of such suffering expect not any end,

Before some god appear
Succeeding to thy labors, and wish to go to ray-
       less
Hades, and the dark depths of Tartarus.
Therefore deliberate; since this is not made
Boasting, but in earnest spoken;
For to speak falsely does not know the mouth
Of Zeus, but every word he does.   So
Look about thee, and consider, nor ever think
Obstinacy better than prudence.

    Ch. To us indeed Hermes appears to say not
         unseasonable things,
For he directs thee, leaving off
Self-will, to seek prudent counsel.
Obey; for it is base to err, for a wise man.

    Pr. To me foreknowing these messages
He has uttered, but for a foe to suffer ill
From foes is naught unseemly.
Therefore 'gainst me let there be hurled
Fire's double-pointed curl, and air
Be provoked with thunder, and a tumult
Of wild winds; and earth from its foundations
Let a wind rock, and its very roots,
And with a rough surge mingle
The sea waves with the passages
Of the heavenly stars, and to black
Tartarus let him quite cast down my
Body, by necessity's strong eddies.
Yet after all he will not kill me.

Her. Such words and counsels you may hear
From the brain-struck.
For what lacks he of being mad?
And if prosperous, what does he cease from
     madness?
Do you, therefore, who sympathize
With this one's suffering,
From these places quick withdraw somewhere,
Lest the harsh bellowing thunder
Stupefy your minds.

    Ch. Say something else, and exhort me
To some purpose; for surely
Thou hast intolerably abused this word.
How direct me to perform a baseness?
I wish to suffer with him whate'er is necessary,
For I have learned to hate betrayers;
Nor is the pest
Which I abominate more than this.

    Her. Remember then what I foretell;
Nor by calamity pursued
Blame fortune, nor e'er say
That Zeus into unforeseen
Ill has cast you; surely not, but yourselves
You yourselves; for knowing,
And not suddenly nor clandestinely,
You'll be entangled through your folly
In an impassable net of woe.

    Pr. Surely indeed, and no more in word,
Earth is shaken;

And a hoarse sound of thunder
Bellows near; and wreaths of lightning
Flash out fiercely blazing, and whirlwinds dust
Whirl up; and leap the blasts
Of all winds, 'gainst one another
Blowing in opposite array;
And air with sea is mingled;
Such impulse against me from Zeus,
Producing fear, doth plainly come.
O revered Mother, O Ether
Revolving common light to all,
You see me, how unjust things I endure!

TRANSLATIONS FROM PINDAR

ELYSIUM.

OLYMPIA II. 109–150.

EQUALLY by night always,
And by day, having the sun, the good
Lead a life without labor, not disturbing the
    earth
With violent hands, nor the sea water,
For a scanty living; but honored
By the gods, who take pleasure in fidelity to
    oaths,
They spend a tearless existence;
While the others suffer unsightly pain.
But as many as endured threefold
Probation, keeping the mind from all
Injustice, go the way of Zeus to Kronos' tower,
Where the ocean breezes blow around
The island of the blessed; and flowers of gold
    shine,
Some on the land from dazzling trees,
And the water nourishes others;
With garlands of these they crown their hands
    and hair,

According to the just decrees of Rhadamanthus,
Whom Father Kronos, the husband of Rhea,
Having the highest throne of all, has ready by
    himself as his assistant judge.
Peleus and Kadmus are regarded among these;
And his mother brought Achilles, when she had
Persuaded the heart of Zeus with prayers,
Who overthrew Hector, Troy's
Unconquered, unshaken column, and gave Cyc-
    nus
To death, and Morning's Æthiop son.

OLYMPIA v. 34–39.

Always around virtues labor and expense strive
    toward a work
Covered with danger; but those succeeding
    seem to be wise even to the citizens.

OLYMPIA vi. 14–17.

Dangerless virtues,
Neither among men, nor in hollow ships,
Are honorable; but many remember if a fair
    deed is done.

ORIGIN OF RHODES.

OLYMPIA vii. 100–129.

Ancient sayings of men relate,
That when Zeus and the Immortals divided
    earth,

Rhodes was not yet apparent in the deep sea;
But in salt depths the island was hid.
And Helios being absent no one claimed for
    him his lot;
So they left him without any region for his
    share,
The pure god.   And Zeus was about to make a
    second drawing of lots
For him warned.   But he did not permit him;
For he said that within the white sea he had
    seen a certain land springing up from
    the bottom,
Capable of feeding many men, and suitable for
    flocks.
And straightway He commanded golden-filleted
    Lachesis
To stretch forth her hands, and not contradict
The great oath of the gods, but with the son of
    Kronos
Assent that, to the bright air being sent by his
    nod,
It should hereafter be his prize.   And his
    words were fully performed,
Meeting with truth.   The island sprang from
    the watery
Sea; and the genial Father of penetrating
    beams,
Ruler of fire-breathing horses, has it.

Olympia viii. 95, 96.

A man doing fit things
Forgets Hades.

HERCULES NAMES THE HILL OF KRONOS.

Olympia x. 59–68.

He named the Hill of Kronos, for before name-
 less,
While Œnomaus ruled, it was moistened with
 much snow;
And at this first rite the Fates stood by,
And Time, who alone proves
Unchanging truth.

OLYMPIA AT EVENING.

Olympia x. 85–92.

With the javelin Phrastor struck the mark;
And Eniceus cast the stone afar,
Whirling his hand, above them all,
And with applause it rushed
Through a great tumult;
And the lovely evening light
Of the fair-faced moon shone on the scene.

FAME.

OLYMPIA x. 109–117.

When, having done fair things, O Agesidamus,
Without the reward of song, a man may come
To Hades' rest, vainly aspiring
He obtains with toil some short delight.
But the sweet-voiced lyre
And the sweet flute bestow some favor;
For Zeus' Pierian daughters
Have wide fame.

TO ASOPICHUS, OF ORCHOMENOS, ON HIS VICTORY IN THE STADIC COURSE.

OLYMPIA xiv.

O ye, who inhabit for your lot the seat of the
      Cephisian
Streams, yielding fair steeds, renowned Graces,
Ruling bright Orchomenos,
Protectors of the ancient race of Minyæ,
Hear, when I pray.
For with you are all pleasant
And sweet things to mortals;
If wise, if fair, if noble,
Any man.   For neither do the gods,
Without the august Graces,
Rule the dance,
Nor feasts; but stewards

Of all works in heaven,
Having placed their seats
By golden-bowed Pythian Apollo,
They reverence the eternal power
Of the Olympian Father.
August Aglaia and song-loving
Euphrosyne, children of the mightiest god,
Hear now, and Thalia loving song,
Beholding this band, in favorable fortune
Lightly dancing; for in Lydian
Manner meditating,
I come celebrating Asopichus,
Since Minya by thy means is victor at the Olym-
   pic games.
Now to Persephone's
Black-walled house go, Echo,
Bearing to his father the famous news;
That seeing Cleodamus thou mayest say,
That in renowned Pisa's vale
His son crowned his young hair
With plumes of illustrious contests.

TO THE LYRE.

PYTHIA I. 8–11.

Thou extinguishest even the spear-like bolt
Of everlasting fire. And the eagle sleeps on
   the sceptre of Zeus,
Drooping his swift wings on either side,
The king of birds.

PYTHIA I. 25–28.

Whatever things Zeus has not loved
Are terrified, hearing
The voice of the Pierians,
On earth and the immeasurable sea.

PYTHIA II. 159–161.

A plain-spoken man brings advantage to every
      government, —
To a monarchy, and when the
Impetuous crowd, and when the wise, rule a city.

As a whole the third Pythian Ode, to Hiero,
on his victory in the single-horse race, is one of
the most memorable. We extract first the account of

ÆSCULAPIUS.

PYTHIA III. 83–110.

As many therefore as came suffering
From spontaneous ulcers, or wounded
In their limbs with glittering steel,
Or with the far-cast stone,
Or by the summer's heat o'ercome in body,
Or by winter, relieving he saved from
Various ills; some cherishing
With soothing strains,
Others having drunk refreshing draughts, or
      applying

Remedies to the limbs, others by cutting off he
    made erect.
But even wisdom is bound by gain,
And gold appearing in the hand persuaded even
    him, with its bright reward,
To bring a man from death
Already overtaken.   But the Kronian, smiting
With both hands, quickly took away
The breath from his breasts;
And the rushing thunderbolt hurled him to
    death.
It is necessary for mortal minds
To seek what is reasonable from the divinities,
Knowing what is before the feet, of what des-
    tiny we are.
Do not, my soul, aspire to the life
Of the Immortals, but exhaust the practicable
    means.

In the conclusion of the ode the poet reminds
the victor, Hiero, that adversity alternates with
prosperity in the life of man, as in the instance
of

PELEUS AND CADMUS.

PYTHIA III. 145–205.

The Immortals distribute to men
With one good two
Evils.   The foolish, therefore,

APOLLO.

PYTHIA v. 87–90.

He bestowed the lyre,
And he gives the muse to whom he wishes,
Bringing peaceful serenity to the breast.

MAN.

PYTHIA viii. 136.

The phantom of a shadow are men.

HYPSEUS' DAUGHTER CYRENE.

PYTHIA ix. 31–44.

He reared the white-armed child Cyrene,
Who loved neither the alternating motion of
    the loom,
Nor the superintendence of feasts,
With the pleasures of companions;
But, with javelins of steel
And the sword contending,
To slay wild beasts;
Affording surely much
And tranquil peace to her father's herds;
Spending little sleep
Upon her eyelids,
As her sweet bedfellow, creeping on at dawn.

THE HEIGHT OF GLORY.

Pythia x. 33–48.

Fortunate and celebrated
By the wise is that man
Who, conquering by his hands or virtue
Of his feet, takes the highest prizes
Through daring and strength,
And living still sees his youthful son
Deservedly obtaining Pythian crowns.
The brazen heaven is not yet accessible to
     him.
But whatever glory we
Of mortal race may reach,
He goes beyond, even to the boundaries
Of navigation.   But neither in ships, nor going
     on foot,
Couldst thou find the wonderful way to the
     contests of the Hyperboreans.

TO ARISTOCLIDES, VICTOR AT THE NEMEAN GAMES.

Nemea iii. 32–37.

If, being beautiful,
And doing things like to his form,
The child of Aristophanes
Went to the height of manliness, no further

Is it easy to go over the untraveled sea,
Beyond the pillars of Hercules.

THE YOUTH OF ACHILLES.

NEMEA III. 69-90.

One with native virtues
Greatly prevails; but he who
Possesses acquired talents, an obscure man,
Aspiring to various things, never with fearless
Foot advances, but tries
A myriad virtues with inefficient mind.
Yellow-haired Achilles, meanwhile, remaining
  in the house of Philyra,
Being a boy played
Great deeds; often brandishing
Iron-pointed javelins in his hands,
Swift as the winds, in fight he wrought death to
  savage lions;
And he slew boars, and brought their bodies
Palpitating to Kronian Centaurus,
As soon as six years old. And all the while
Artemis and bold Athene admired him,
Slaying stags without dogs or treacherous nets;
For he conquered them on foot.

NEMEA IV. 66-70.

Whatever virtues sovereign destiny has given me,
I well know that time, creeping on,
Will fulfill what was fated.

NEMEA v. 1–8.

The kindred of Pytheas, a victor in the Ne-
mean games, had wished to procure an ode from
Pindar for less than three drachmæ, asserting
that they could purchase a statue for that sum.
In the following lines he nobly reproves their
meanness, and asserts the value of his labors,
which, unlike those of the statuary, will bear
the fame of the hero to the ends of the earth.

No image-maker am I, who being still make
    statues
Standing on the same base.   But on every
Merchant-ship and in every boat, sweet song,
Go from Ægina to announce that Lampo's son,
Mighty Pytheas,
Has conquered the pancratian crown at the Ne-
    mean games.

THE DIVINE IN MAN.

NEMEA vi. 1–13.

One the race of men and of gods;
And from one mother
We all breathe.
But quite different power
Divides us, so that the one is nothing,
But the brazen heaven remains always

A secure abode.   Yet in some respect we are
    related,
Either in mighty mind or form, to the Immor-
    tals;
Although not knowing
To what resting-place,
By day or night, Fate has written that we shall
    run.

THE TREATMENT OF AJAX.

NEMEA VIII. 44–51.

In secret votes the Danaans aided Ulysses;
And Ajax, deprived of golden arms, struggled
    with death.
Surely, wounds of another kind they wrought
In the warm flesh of their foes, waging war
With the man-defending spear.

THE VALUE OF FRIENDS.

NEMEA VIII. 68–75.

Virtue increases, being sustained by wise men
    and just,
As when a tree shoots up with gentle dews into
    the liquid air.
There are various uses of friendly men;
But chiefest in labors; and even pleasure
Requires to place some pledge before the eyes.

DEATH OF AMPHIARAUS.

NEMEA IX. 41–66.

Once they led to seven-gated Thebes an army
    of men, not according
To the lucky flight of birds.   Nor did the Kro-
    nian,
Brandishing his lightning, impel to march
From home insane, but to abstain from the way.
But to apparent destruction
The host made haste to go, with brazen arms
And horse equipments, and on the banks
Of Ismenus, defending sweet return,
Their white-flowered bodies fattened fire.
For seven pyres devoured young-limbed
Men.   But to Amphiaraus
Zeus rent the deep-bosomed earth
With his mighty thunderbolt,
And buried him with his horses,
Ere, being struck in the back
By the spear of Periclymenus, his warlike
Spirit was disgraced.
For in dæmonic fears
Flee even the sons of gods.

CASTOR AND POLLUX.

NEMEA x. 153–171.

Pollux, son of Zeus, shared his immortality
with his brother Castor, son of Tyndarus, and

while one was in heaven, the other remained in the infernal regions, and they alternately lived and died every day, or, as some say, every six months. While Castor lies mortally wounded by Idas, Pollux prays to Zeus, either to restore his brother to life, or permit him to die with him, to which the god answers, —

> Nevertheless, I give thee
> Thy choice of these: if, indeed, fleeing
> Death and odious age,
> You wish to dwell on Olympus,
> With Athene and black-speared Mars,
> Thou hast this lot;
> But if thou thinkest to fight
> For thy brother, and share
> All things with him,
> Half the time thou mayest breathe, being be-
> neath the earth,
> And half in the golden halls of heaven.
> The god thus having spoken, he did not
> Entertain a double wish in his mind.
> And he released first the eye, and then the
> voice,
> Of brazen-mitred Castor.

TOIL.

Isthmia i. 65–71.

One reward of labors is sweet to one man, one
    to another, —
To the shepherd, and the plougher, and the
    bird-catcher,
And whom the sea nourishes.
But every one is tasked to ward off
Grievous famine from the stomach.

THE VENALITY OF THE MUSE.

Isthmia ii. 9–18.

Then the Muse was not
Fond of gain, nor a laboring woman;
Nor were the sweet-sounding,
Soothing strains
Of Terpsichore sold,
With silvered front.
But now she directs to observe the saying
Of the Argive, coming very near the truth,
Who cried, "Money, money, man,"
Being bereft of property and friends.

HERCULES' PRAYER CONCERNING AJAX, SON OF TELAMON.

Isthmia vi. 62–73.

"If ever, O Father Zeus, thou hast heard
My supplication with willing mind,

Now I beseech thee, with prophetic
Prayer, grant a bold son from Eribœa
To this man, my fated guest;
Rugged in body
As the hide of this wild beast
Which now surrounds me, which, first of all
My contests, I slew once in Nemea; and let his
      mind agree."
To him thus having spoken, Heaven sent
A great eagle, king of birds,
And sweet joy thrilled him inwardly.

THE FREEDOM OF GREECE.

      First at Artemisium
The children of the Athenians laid the shining
Foundation of freedom,
And at Salamis and Mycale,
And in Platæa, making it firm
As adamant.

FROM STRABO.

APOLLO.

      Having risen he went
Over land and sea,
And stood over the vast summits of mountains,
And threaded the recesses, penetrating to the
      foundations of the groves.

FROM PLUTARCH.

Heaven being willing, even on an osier thou
    mayest sail.
[Thus rhymed by the old translator of Plutarch:
"Were it the will of heaven, an osier bough
Were vessel safe enough the seas to plough."]

FROM SEXTUS EMPIRICUS.

Honors and crowns of the tempest-footed
Horses delight one;
Others live in golden chambers;
And some even are pleased traversing securely
The swelling of the sea in a swift ship.

FROM STOBÆUS.

This I will say to thee:
The lot of fair and pleasant things
It behooves to show in public to all the people;
But if any adverse calamity sent from heaven
    befall
Men, this it becomes to bury in darkness.

    Pindar said of the physiologists, that they
"plucked the unripe fruit of wisdom."

    Pindar said that "hopes were the dreams of
those awake."

FROM CLEMENS OF ALEXANDRIA.

To Heaven it is possible from black
Night to make arise unspotted light,
And with cloud-blackening darkness to obscure
The pure splendor of day.

First, indeed, the Fates brought the wise-coun-
    seling
Uranian Themis, with golden horses,
By the fountains of Ocean to the awful ascent
Of Olympus, along the shining way,
To be the first spouse of Zeus the Deliverer.
And she bore the golden-filleted, fair-wristed
Hours, preservers of good things.

Equally tremble before God
And a man dear to God.

FROM ÆLIUS ARISTIDES.

Pindar used such exaggerations [in praise of
poetry] as to say that even the gods themselves,
when at his marriage Zeus asked if they wanted
anything, "asked him to make certain gods for
them who should celebrate these great works
and all his creation with speech and song."

POEMS

INSPIRATION

If with light head erect I sing,
Though all the Muses lend their force,
From my poor love of anything,
The verse is weak and shallow as its source.

But if with bended neck I grope,
Listening behind me for my wit,
With faith superior to hope,
More anxious to keep back than forward it;

Making my soul accomplice there
Unto the flame my heart hath lit,
Then will the verse forever wear, —
Time cannot bend the line which God has writ.

I hearing get, who had but ears,
And sight, who had but eyes before;
I moments live, who lived but years,
And truth discern, who knew but learning's
        lore.

Now chiefly is my natal hour,
And only now my prime of life;
Of manhood's strength it is the flower,
'T is peace's end, and war's beginning strife.

It comes in summer's broadest noon,
By a gray wall, or some chance place,
Unseasoning time, insulting June,
And vexing day with its presuming face.

I will not doubt the love untold,
Which not my worth nor want hath bought,
Which wooed me young, and wooes me old,
And to this evening hath me brought.

PILGRIMS

"HAVE you not seen,
  In ancient times,
  Pilgrims pass by
  Toward other climes,
  With shining faces,
  Youthful and strong,
  Mounting this hill
  With speech and with song?"

"Ah, my good sir,
  I know not those ways:

Little my knowledge,
Tho' many my days.
When I have slumbered,
I have heard sounds
As of travelers passing
These my grounds.

" 'T was a sweet music
Wafted them by,
I could not tell
If afar off or nigh.
Unless I dreamed it,
This was of yore:
I never told it
To mortal before,
Never remembered
But in my dreams
What to me waking
A miracle seems."

TO A STRAY FOWL

Poor bird! destined to lead thy life
Far in the adventurous west,
And here to be debarred to-night
From thy accustomed nest;
Must thou fall back upon old instinct now,
Well-nigh extinct under man's fickle care?
Did Heaven bestow its quenchless inner light,

So long ago, for thy small want to-night?
Why stand'st upon thy toes to crow so late?
The moon is deaf to thy low feathered fate;
Or dost thou think so to possess the night,
And people the drear dark with thy brave
       sprite?
And now with anxious eye thou look'st about,
While the relentless shade draws on its veil,
For some sure shelter from approaching dews,
And the insidious steps of nightly foes.
I fear imprisonment has dulled thy wit,
Or ingrained servitude extinguished it.
But no; dim memory of the days of yore,
By Brahmapootra and the Jumna's shore,
Where thy proud race flew swiftly o'er the
       heath,
And sought its food the jungle's shade beneath,
Has taught thy wings to seek yon friendly
       trees,
As erst by Indus' banks and far Ganges.

THE BLACK KNIGHT

Be sure your fate
Doth keep apart its state,
Not linked with any band,
Even the nobles of the land;
In tented fields with cloth of gold
No place doth hold

But is more chivalrous than they are,
And sigheth for a nobler war;
A finer strain its trumpet sings,
A brighter gleam its armor flings.
The life that I aspire to live
No man proposeth me;
Only the promise of my heart
Wears its emblazonry.

THE MOON

Time wears her not; she doth his chariot guide;
  Mortality below her orb is placed.
                                        RALEIGH.

THE full-orbed moon with unchanged ray
  Mounts up the eastern sky,
Not doomed to these short nights for aye,
  But shining steadily.

She does not wane, but my fortune,
  Which her rays do not bless;
My wayward path declineth soon,
  But she shines not the less.

And if she faintly glimmers here,
  And palèd is her light,
Yet alway in her proper sphere
  She's mistress of the night.

OMNIPRESENCE

Who equaleth the coward's haste,
And still inspires the faintest heart;
Whose lofty fame is not disgraced,
Though it assume the lowest part.

INSPIRATION

If thou wilt but stand by my ear,
When through the field thy anthem's rung,
When that is done I will not fear
But the same power will abet my tongue.

PRAYER

Great God! I ask thee for no meaner pelf
Than that I may not disappoint myself;
That in my conduct I may soar as high
As I can now discern with this clear eye;
And next in value, which thy kindness lends,
That I may greatly disappoint my friends,
Howe'er they think or hope it that may be,
They may not dream how thou 'st distinguished
      me;
That my weak hand may equal my firm faith,
And my life practice more than my tongue
      saith;

That my low conduct may not show,
Nor my relenting lines,
That I thy purpose did not know,
Or overrated thy designs.

MISSION

I 'VE searched my faculties around,
To learn why life to me was lent:
I will attend the faintest sound,
And then declare to man what God hath meant.

DELAY

No generous action can delay
Or thwart our higher, steadier aims;
But if sincere and true are they,
It will arouse our sight, and nerve our frames.

GENERAL INDEX

176 ; before the wind, 324 ; *also*, 301, 302, 325, 327, 373, 380, 429 ; 9, 216.

Skeleton, 7, 374.

Sketch of Concord Jail, 8, 361.

Skies, the, 1, 473.

Skinner, 7, 340.

Skins, sale of, 2, 432 ; 7, 393.

Skulls, 6, 235.

Skunk, 5, 3, 74, 276 ; description of, 104, 105 ; 6, 155 ; young of the, 196.

Skunk-cabbage, 5, 74, 88, 277 ; 6, 113 ; 7, 187, 189, 398 ; 8, 132, 275, 380.

Sky, ever-changing, 7, 285, 428 ; ready to answer our moods, 8, 39, 192, 256 ; poverty in winter night's, 83 ; color in, 100, 127, 128, 157, 201, 206, 225 ; its blueness at night, 215 ; *also*, 73, 96, 133, 193, 216, 311, 384, 418.

Slave, fugitive, 7, 49.

Slavery, 6, 86, 174 ; Massachusetts and, 10, 138, 139 ; what it is, 179 ; how to deal with, 227, 228.

SLAVERY IN MASSACHUSETTS, 10, 171–196.

Sleepers, railroad, 2, 146.

Sleepy Hollow, 5, 140.

Slippery elm, 6, 52.

Small things, 7, 83.

Smellie, William, 6, 202.

Smilax herbacea (carrion flower), 6, 123, 242.

Smith, Ansell, clearing and settlement of, 3, 167–177.

Smith, Capt. John, quoted, 1, 114 ; 4, 216, 309 ; map of New England by, 276.

Smith's (A.) Hill, 7, 404.

Smith's (C.) Hill, 7, 24, 25.

Smith's River, 1, 108.

Smoke, from chimneys, 7, 59, 79, 272, 315 ; 8, 100 ; from a chimney, 153, 154 ; *also*, 343 ; winter morning, 9, 201 ; seen from a hill-top, 212 ; the smell of, 460.

Smoothness of ocean, 4, 148.

Snail, white (Helix albolabris), 5, 304.

Snake, under water in torpid state, 2, 67 ; the, 9, 152.

Snake, green, 7, 87.

Snake, striped, 5, 305 ; 6, 92 ; 7, 22, 87.

Snake, water, 6, 1.

Snake-head, 1, 22.

Snake sloughs, 6, 133.

Snapdragon, 6, 101, 199.

Snapdragon, Canada, 6, 36 ; 7, 113.

Snapdragon catchfly, 6, 5.

Snare, 7, 325.

Snipe, 5, 281, 307, 323 ; 7, 157, 159.

Snipe-shooting grounds, 9, 60.

Snow, 5, 22, 49, 87, 126, 179, 210, 295, 312, 317 ; holes in, made by leaves, 290 ; drifts on Mt. Washington, 6, 291, 293, 301 ; the first, 7, 113, 230, 318, 398 ; 158, 231 ; on distant mountains, 243 ; 317, 346 ; on trees, 323 ; in pellets, 324 ; silent and sudden change made by, 341 ; days lengthened by the light reflected from, 346, 443 ; falling in the distance, 359 ; in pitch-pine woods, 443 ; simple beauty of, 451 ; on trees, 8, 26, 44, 116 ; a revealer, 39, 79, 89, 100 ; depth of, 62, 101 ; descent of, 149 ; composition of, 166 ; surface of, 188 ; Cotton Mather's description of, 328 ; in Fitchburg, 330 ; *also*, 54, 79, 140, 168, 181, 207, 209, 260, 261, 300, 321, 323, 327, 408, 419 ; 9, 221, 222 ; not recognized in Hebrew Scriptures, 223.

Snow, the Great, 2, 186 ; 201 ; dating from the, 394 ; walking in the, 410.

Snow arch, 6, 293, 301.

Snowberry, Creeping, used as tea, 3, 281.

Snowbird, slate-colored (Fringilla hiemalis), 7, 17, 157, 328, 366, 383 ; 8, 13, 48, 54, 361 ; 9, 134.

Snow-bow seen in the East, 8, 127.

Snow-buntings, 5, 20, 41, 50 ; 7, 227, 347, 409, 423 ; quotations from authorities on, 8, 55 ; description of, 307 ; *also*, 89, 220.

Snow-cave, 8, 210.

Snow-drifts, 8, 22, 39, 54 ; equilibrium between currents of air marked by, 88 ; *also*, 101, 117, 146, 152, 261, 425.

Snow-flakes, 8, 62, 119, 125, 137, 149, 166.

Snow-flea, 7, 161, 183, 394, 409, 440 ; 8, 117, 179, 237 ; the creature of the thaw, 297 ; *also*, 312, 369.

Snow-shoes, the Indian's, and the saints' slippers, 8, 91.

Snow-stars, 8, 120.

Snowstorm, silent and sudden change wrought by, 7, 341 ; a distant, 359 ; 8, 151, 225.

Snow's Hollow, 4, 70.

Snuff, water horehound substituted for, 8, 16.

Soapwort gentian, the, 1, 22.